WINE
WITH
FOOD

To Jill + Ed,
With great appreciation + admiration,

ERIC ASIMOV
FLORENCE FABRICANT

WINE
WITH
FOOD

To Jill and Ed,
With Great appreciation and delicious wishes—
Florence Fabricant

PAIRING NOTES AND RECIPES FROM

The New York Times

RIZZOLI
NEW YORK

New York · Paris · London · Milan

For Jack and Peter,
may they always be blessed with pleasures at the table
—ERIC ASIMOV

For Richard,
ever the willing taster and critic
—FLORENCE FABRICANT

CONTENTS

INTRODUCTION
BY ERIC ASIMOV

WE'RE PRIVILEGED TO LIVE IN THE GREATEST TIME IN HISTORY TO DRINK WINE. We now have access to a wider diversity of wines than ever before, made in more styles, from grapes unheard of twenty years ago, grown in places never before associated with good wine. The sheer volume of choices will thrill the intrepid wine explorer. The more hesitant may find themselves paralyzed by the torrent of unfamiliar labels and names.

This book is intended to encourage exploration by making the case that with wine, it's really hard to make a mistake. You will undoubtedly find some wines you like better than others. You will find other wines that you can't abide, despite what the experts say. You will not always agree with Florence Fabricant and me. Why, we don't always agree with each other.

That's how we all learn, by drinking and thinking. Consuming wine without reflection is fine, so long as your intention is simply to enjoy the moment without building your knowledge. Reading books or taking classes without drinking is about as useful as trying to learn the piano without an instrument. The accumulation of practical experience—that is, opening bottles and drinking wine—along with a modest effort to record your reactions to the wines is the surest way to develop a sense of ease and comfort in this ever-expanding world.

By this way of thinking, you do not risk making wrong choices. You are simply adding to your body of experiences. Of course, nobody wants to open a bottle that does not satisfy. But even unappealing bottles teach us something about our own tastes. The long-term benefits of experience far outweigh the transitory disappointments.

I would make the same argument about pairing wine and food, a fairly simple and pleasant procedure that has been made to seem arcane and complicated by well-meaning guidebooks and treatises. Just as experience in the kitchen leads good home cooks to overcome an initially slavish obedience to recipes, the repeated exercise of picking a wine for dinner will help conquer self-doubt and develop an instinctive sense of what works.

You will see that each type of wine discussed in this book is accompanied by one or more recipes. But the last thing that either Florence or I want to convey is that you must be bound by these suggested pairings. Nothing could be further from the truth. A description of a good wine represents a snapshot, freezing one moment in a bottle's evolution, and a proposed pairing reflects only one point on the spectrum of possibilities. Some ideas may be precisely to your taste, and some not. Suggesting wine pairings should never inhibit an impulse to explore.

The only danger is the fear of making a mistake. Seriously bad choices are rare. I once wrote a column about drinking red wine with oysters, an unorthodox approach that at the time seemed to be fashionable in Paris. In the conventional wisdom, nobody in his right mind would pair reds with raw oysters, not with so many pleasurable tried-and-true white choices like Muscadet, Chablis, and Sancerre. But I tried a selection of red wines. None were horrendous. A few were quite pleasurable. Would I reach for a Chinon, for example, over a Muscadet? Not by choice. But it wouldn't be a disaster if I did. I know people who swear that nothing goes with steak better than an aged auslese riesling. Really? I haven't tried it yet, though if I did, I would keep a good red in reserve. But I am open to the possibility. The point is this: Pairing is an exploration. Even less felicitous matches have something to teach. The only time it is truly important to match food and wine with painstaking care is with a rare, delicate, and expensive bottle, when it would be a shame to miss out on the wine's nuances and complexities. In those cases, simple, classic pairings are often best.

It is easy to see why the notion of food-and-wine pairing makes people crazy. For one thing, simple but overly broad rules of thumb—whites with fish, reds with meat—have devolved into how-to tomes full of complicated charts, classifications, and materials to memorize. Sometimes, the discussion of complex wine characteristics like body, tannins, pH, and so on is juxtaposed against basic information (it's pronounced PEE-noh GREE-joe), suggesting perhaps that novices can easily grasp and benefit from byzantine pairing guidelines.

I'm sorry, but the truth is that experience is the only surefire method for feeling more at ease with wine and food. To learn how to ski, you must set off down the mountain and not be afraid to fall. And falls happen, even with the experts.

Sommeliers and chefs handle pairings differently than the rest of us, as they should. I can think of any number of red wines that I would love to drink with a good hamburger: Beaujolais, Chianti, a California syrah inspired by the northern Rhône, dolcetto—I'm not picky. I would look to see what was around and decide which of the available bottles I would enjoy drinking the most. Simple. For the professionals, it would be something far more obsessively analytical: Is the beef lean, or does it have a high percentage of fat? What are the toppings? Ketchup? Mustard? If pickles, sour or sweet? Black pepper or white? Cheddar or Swiss? What sort of salt? What about the bread? Sourdough? Seeded?

I expect that when I take a sommelier's suggestion in a restaurant it is the result of dedicated fact-finding, tasting through all sorts of combinations with antennas out for the barest of nuances. But just as I don't cook like a restaurant chef at home, I don't want to pick wines like a sommelier. So I act on instinct and learn something each time. Most of us prefer a more casual approach, free of anxiety, I suspect. So take our suggestions. They're good ones. But better yet, explore for yourself and enjoy the journey.

INTRODUCTION

BY FLORENCE FABRICANT

SELECTING A DISH TO ACCOMPANY A PARTICULAR WINE, or category of wines, is not like falling in love. It's more like friending on Facebook; often casual, even haphazard. Participating on the wine panel at the *Times* with Eric Asimov and guest tasters over many years, as well as frequently dining out and entertaining at home, has confirmed that rarely, if ever, is there a single dish that can flatter a wine to the exclusion of all others. The opposite is equally true.

Even classic combinations, like oysters with Muscadet or choucroute with riesling, stand ready for audacious, revisionist thinking. Considering red wine instead of white with these foods is not out of the question but may be daring to accept. The consequences of choices like these are never life threatening.

Indeed, while tasting wines, thoughts often lead to food. The wines that our tasting panels tend to prefer are those that are food-friendly, with a balance of acidity and minerality to offset distinctive fruit and, increasingly, high alcohol. Some even have trouble surviving on their own, needing a plate of seafood, meat, or cheese before revealing their innermost secrets. But wines like this are better by far than overworked bruisers that will knock you out on the first round and suffocate what you are eating.

Food to go with wine is determined not only by the wine but also by geography, the occasion, and the season. After all, long before there was a global wine market, wine and food were local affairs, and when all else fails, you probably cannot go wrong with keeping terroir in mind. Yes, oysters with Muscadet.

What else will be on the menu might be taken into account. The weight of the wine and of the dish should also be in harmony. A delicate red will fade alongside rich osso buco, and a bone-dry Champagne tastes sour with wedding cake. Price is definitely a factor, too. Pizza and Pétrus? I don't think so.

But as symbiotic as Chianti and pappardelle with game might be, what wine will whet your appetite for a plate of curry or a bowl of ramen? The world of food today does pose challenges.

My assignment, in participating on the wine panel, has been to find a recipe for the wines we have been tasting. Sometimes there is an obvious choice, like a dish involving lamb, rosemary, and olives to accompany a meaty Rhône that exhibits whiffs of herbs and olivelike bitterness, or the acidity that a splash of red wine vinegar will contribute to a sauce designed to tame exuberant fruit in a California merlot. Are we tasting rosés? It will be spring or summer and time for food that's more comfortable in flip-flops than fur.

But this approach is also the reverse of the way most people function when it comes to determining food with wine. You decide your menu, then pick the wine. Even in a restaurant, that's usually how it's done. And there are so many options—too many, in fact—that at the end of the day it's hard to make a mistake.

So consider the recipes in this book, each paired with one or another of our wines, as suggestions, interchangeable and forgiving. If a recipe appeals, seems approachable, and appropriate, you might decide to serve its accompanying wine. Or not.

ABOUT THE RECIPES: Most are original, devised and tested by me, in my kitchen. Those that I obtained from chefs I also adapted and tested. The number of people served varies from as few as two up to a dozen, but in many instances, the amount of food can be doubled or tripled, or reduced as needed.

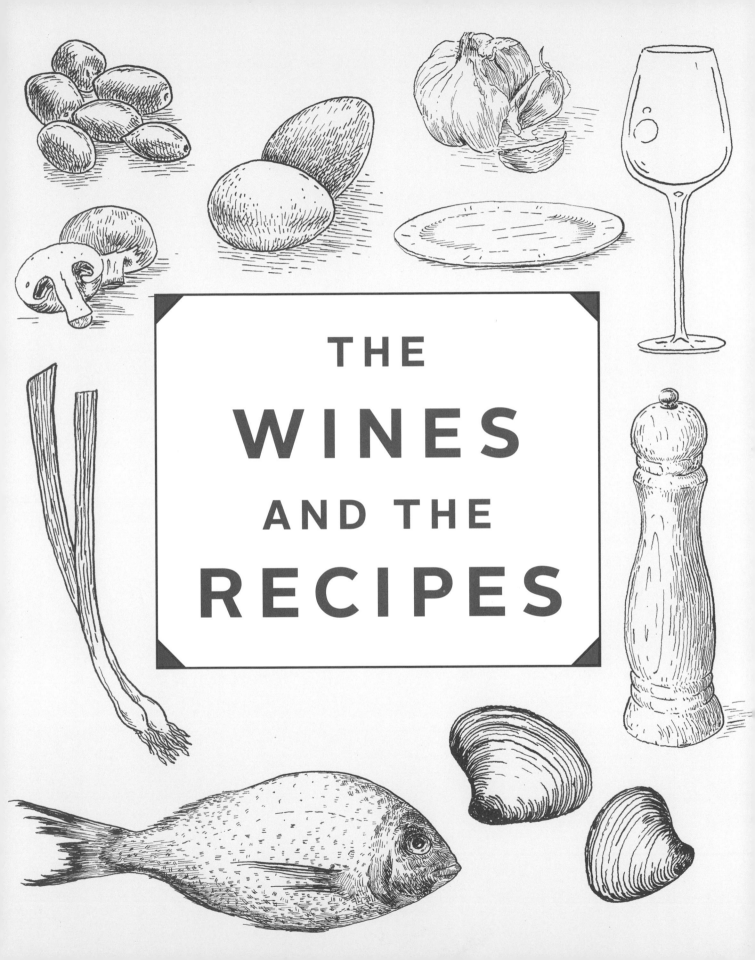

THE
WINES
AND THE
RECIPES

SPARKLERS

The mere act of opening a bottle of sparkling wine creates expectations that still wines never suggest. From the everyday prosecco to that marquee Champagne, wines with spritz make the mood celebratory and festive. Yes, you need some food, but it might not matter precisely what is passed on a platter of canapés or served on your plate as long as you have some carefree bubbles in your glass. They say that Champagne goes with any food and from this point of view, without ever considering taste, there might be truth to that. But to take this issue somewhat more seriously, with sparkling wines the elements to bear in mind when selecting food or even an entire menu, are color, weight, and sweetness. Think of dry sparkling wines as if they were chardonnays, light ones at that, or even leaner, more minerally varietals like sauvignon blanc. A substantial Champagne with some bottle age can stand up to richer foods. Rosé sparkling wines and Champagnes should be regarded as if they were light reds, graceful pinot noirs to serve with anything from smoked salmon to a steak. Then there is also demi-sec, a Champagne category with more dosage, adding sweetness. They have merit as a pour with dessert.

PROSECCO

Nobody drinks sparkling wine as regularly as the Italians do. It's made in almost every Italian wine region, and no meal seems complete unless it starts with a frothing glass of *spumante*, the melodious Italian word for sparkling wine.

In Italy, people generally drink the local bubbly, whatever it is. But here in the United States, no Italian sparkler is more popular than light, faintly peachy prosecco from the Veneto region of northeastern Italy.

Prosecco was made for summer, when you need something blithe, airy, and carefree. It's a light summer dress, a thriller for the beach, an entertainment, not a burden. It's a social drink. You cannot brood over a prosecco.

Drinking prosecco is more like the gentle cooling of a rippling breeze, always leaving you wanting more. Because it's fairly low in alcohol, prosecco is almost meant to be consumed outdoors in the heat or the shade, in the garden, at the beach, up on the roof, or under the boardwalk. It's stylish, too. Millions of Italians can't be wrong about that.

All proseccos are made predominantly of the prosecco grape, sometimes mixed with a small percentage of pinot bianco, pinot grigio, or chardonnay. Some, to be polysyllabically precise, are designated Prosecco di Conegliano-Valdobbiadene. That is the—here we go again—Denominazione di Origine Controllata, or DOC, a designation earned if wines meet certain standards, for example, which grapes are used, where they are grown, and how the wines are aged.

To earn the DOC designation the grapes must come from the hilly area between the communes of Conegliano and Valdobbiadene in the Veneto, the region of Venice and Verona in northeastern Italy, and the wine must be made of at least 85 percent prosecco. And yet it's a tricky issue for consumers. Even if the grapes are not from the designated area, or if the winemakers do not adhere to regulations concerning the proportion of grapes used, the wine may still be called prosecco, but not Prosecco di Conegliano-Valdobbiadene. In this case, the wine must be at least 75 percent prosecco.

Does it really matter? After all, if you think too hard about prosecco, you are defeating the purpose of this breezy, cheerful wine. Whatever the source or proportion of the grapes, the wines are generally made in the same way, and in the end, all of these bottles will be found on the prosecco shelf at the wine shop, regardless of what they are called.

Almost all proseccos rely on the Charmat process, a large-scale method of producing sparkling wines, named for the French inventor Eugène Charmat. The process shortcuts the costly in-the-bottle secondary fermentation that gives Champagne its fizz, price tag, and sense of gravitas. Champagne needs more time to evolve than the more accessible prosecco, and generally seems more austere than friendly.

It's hard to think of another wine with the lightness and easygoing grace of prosecco—maybe a rosé. Aside from being perfect for garden parties, proseccos, like rosés, make excellent aperitifs. One glass, two at most, and you are ready to move on. Unless, of course, you are making Bellinis, the cocktails of sparkling wine and peach puree, for which prosecco is the ideal ingredient. 🍷

POPPING THE CAP OF A BOTTLE OF PROSECCO has none of the ceremony associated with Champagne. Prosecco is a refresher, offering the almost giddy delight that comes from sipping a sparkling wine, but its relatively low alcohol content keeps the buzz in check. It may be the wine of choice for making a Bellini, the perfect summer aperitif, but it stands on its own or accompanies food at brunch, lunch, or a light dinner. Think lunch with this recipe, a delicious open-faced, knife-and-fork sandwich that can also be cut into small pieces and served as hors d'oeuvres. The acidity in a good prosecco is a fine foil for the richness of the crabmeat.

Souffléed Crabmeat Canapés

TIME: 35 MINUTES

6 slices country bread, ½ inch thick

2 large eggs, separated

Juice of ½ lemon

½ teaspoon salt

3½ tablespoons pesto, homemade or purchased

6 tablespoons extra virgin olive oil

¾ pound lump crabmeat

Paprika

1. Heat the oven to 425°F. Place the rack in the center of the oven.

2. Lightly toast the bread and place on a foil-lined baking sheet.

3. Place the egg yolks, 1 tablespoon of the lemon juice, the salt, and ½ tablespoon of the pesto in a food processor or a bowl. While processing or whisking constantly, slowly drizzle in the oil and continue mixing until thickened to a mayonnaise. Transfer to a bowl and mix in the crabmeat. Stir in the remaining lemon juice.

4. Beat the egg whites until they hold peaks. Fold into the crabmeat mixture.

5. Spread the bread with the remaining 3 tablespoons pesto and top each slice with the crabmeat mixture, covering it completely. Lightly dust with paprika. Bake for 15 minutes, until puffed and browned. Cut each slice in half and serve at lunch or as a first course, or cut each slice into 6 pieces and pass as hors d'oeuvres.

YIELD: 12 LARGE CANAPÉS TO SERVE 6, OR 36 SMALL HORS D'OEUVRE CANAPÉS

COOK'S NOTES: Though the most expensive crabmeat, jumbo lump, is not required, it is best to use fresh (always sold pasteurized) rather than canned.

CAVA

Many years ago, I drank cava regularly. I couldn't help it; cava was the cheapest sparkling wine around. My graduate-student parties and celebrations seemed incomplete without numerous bottles of Freixenet Cordon Negro Brut scattered about the room, reflections of dancing candlelight absorbed by the black matte finish of the bottles.

Despite these fond memories, I became disenchanted. While I had repeatedly seen cava cited as an excellent value, the rock-bottom prices never justified the absence of pleasure I experienced. Served chilled, I thought, it was merely cold and bubbly, with little zest or energy. It seemed to lack the sparkling joy of prosecco, or the intrigue of the various crémants, the sparklers of France outside Champagne. In the hierarchy of sparkling wines, I had cava down around the level of the sekts of Germany. Their appeal has long escaped me, too.

All I needed to see the light, though, was one transcendent moment. It came at a tasting with one mouthful of a vintage cava; in particular, Gramona's III Lustros 2001. Its elegant, creamy, nutlike flavors, reminiscent of aged Champagne, demonstrated not only that cava had far more potential than I had given it credit for but also that my experience with good, carefully made cava had been sadly lacking. Oh, did I mention that the Gramona was a sixty-dollar bottle? Maybe not so cheap, though still possibly a good value.

Of course, that is far more expensive than most cavas, which are consumed in quantity, with relish, all over Spain. Most cavas are inexpensive and mass produced, to the tune of millions of bottles each year. Given that scale of production, it's somewhat surprising to learn that cava must be made using the traditional sparkling wine method, with the second, bubble-inducing fermentation occurring in the bottle rather than in large tanks, as with many mass-market sparkling wines.

That leads inevitably to comparing cava with Champagne, which in most cases is unfair. For one thing, the leading cava grapes—parellada, macabeo, and the hyphen's best friend xarel-lo—are completely different from the pinot noir, chardonnay, and pinot meunier used in Champagne, although an increasing amount of chardonnay is making its way into cava. While a top cava like the Lustros can achieve the elegant, rich, toasty quality of Champagne, most tend toward simple, frothy freshness. Exhilarating, yes. Complex? Maybe not.

While most people habitually use cava generically to refer to Spanish sparkling wines, the way spumante can refer to most Italian ones, the name is, in fact, an official designation. Unusually, though, it comes with no geographical requirement. By law, it can be produced pretty much all over Spain, but for all practical purposes most of it comes from the Catalonian region of Penedès, just west of Barcelona.

The biggest problem with cava is inconsistency and freshness. Except for those high-end versions like the Lustros, cavas are made to be consumed young. If left out on retail shelves for too long, they lose their zest and energy. At its best, though, cava is ideal for large parties and brunches, served on its own or in punches and sangrias. Serve cold. 🍷

CAVAS, OFTEN BLESSED WITH NOTES OF CITRUS AND SPRING BLOSSOMS, are genial, versatile sparklers, all the more so because of their modest prices. They can be called on for more than toast-worthy celebrations. In Spain they are the ideal finishing touch for sangria, either red or white. This white sangria, from Tinto Fino, a Spanish wine shop in New York (now closed), is unusual and strong, though white wine in place of manzanilla sherry will moderate the alcohol. The red, contributed by the owner of Pata Negra, a tapas bar in New York, defines sangria as we usually know it. Both are determined to be more refreshing than sweet.

White Sangria

TIME: 20 MINUTES, PLUS OVERNIGHT MACERATING

2 apples, cored and coarsely diced

2 pears, cored and coarsely diced

2 juice oranges, peeled, seeded, and diced

1 cup gin

½ cup triple sec

6 cups manzanilla sherry or dry white wine

½ bottle Cava, chilled

1. Place the apples, pears, and oranges in a bowl with the gin and triple sec. Cover and allow to macerate in the refrigerator overnight.

2. Transfer the fruit and liquid to a large pitcher and add the manzanilla. Stir. Divide the liquid with the fruit among wineglasses and top each glass with some of the Cava.

YIELD: 8 TO 10 SERVINGS

COOK'S NOTES: Gin? In sangria? As a matter of fact, gin is extremely popular in Spain, where a gin and tonic is the mixed drink of choice. 🥛

Red Sangria

TIME: 4½ HOURS, INCLUDING STEEPING

1 bottle (750 milliliters) red wine, preferably garnacha

Juice of 1½ oranges

Juice of 1 lemon

Juice of 1 lime

½ cup Spanish brandy

¼ cup triple sec

1 apple, cored and sliced

1 pear, cored and sliced

1 cinnamon stick

½ bottle Cava, chilled

1. Combine the wine, orange juice, lemon juice, lime juice, brandy, triple sec, and sliced apple, pear, and cinnamon in a 2-quart pitcher. Cover and refrigerate for at least 4 hours.

2. Add 2 cups ice and the Cava, divide among wineglasses, and serve.

YIELD: 4 TO 6 SERVINGS

FIZZ AND ZING, the carbonation and acidity of sparklers, make them excellent foils for lush cheeses, especially full-bodied, irresistibly satiny yet often funky washed-rind examples, like Italian Taleggio. And if you'd prefer a Spanish cheese with your cava, consider torta del Casar. Here the cheese enriches a mushroom tart to serve in place of a cheese course, or as a first course, or, cut like finger food, as hors d'oeuvres.

Taleggio and Mushroom Tart

TIME: 1 HOUR

1¼ cups all-purpose flour, plus more for rolling

Salt and freshly ground white pepper

6 tablespoons cold unsalted butter, plus more for rolling

1 large egg yolk, beaten with 2 tablespoons cold water

1 tablespoon extra virgin olive oil

1 teaspoon cumin seeds

8 ounces shiitake mushrooms, stems discarded, caps sliced

1 tablespoon finely sliced shallots

2 tablespoons crème fraîche

6 ounces Taleggio, rind removed, sliced thin

1. Heat the oven to 400°F. Combine the flour and salt in a food processor. Pulse to mix. Dice the butter and add. Pulse until pebbly. Open the lid and sprinkle with the egg yolk mixture. Pulse about 12 times. If the dough does not come together, add a sprinkle of cold water and pulse a few times more.

2. Gather the dough into a ball, flatten, and roll out on a floured board. Fit into an 8- or 9-inch tart pan. Prick the bottom, line with foil and pastry weights or dry beans, and bake for 10 minutes. Remove the foil and weights. Bake for about 10 minutes more, until the pastry starts to color. Remove from the oven. Reduce the oven heat to 375°F.

3. While the pastry is baking, heat the oil in a 10-inch skillet. Add ½ teaspoon of the cumin seeds. When the seeds pop, add the mushrooms and shallots and sauté, stirring, until the mushrooms start to brown. Season with salt and white pepper.

4. Spread the pastry with the crème fraîche, cover with the mushroom mixture, and top with the cheese. Scatter with the remaining ½ teaspoon cumin seeds. Bake for about 20 minutes, until the cheese melts. Serve.

YIELD: 6 SERVINGS, MORE FOR HORS D'OEUVRES

COOK'S NOTES: To serve as canapés, bake the tart in an 8-inch square baking dish, to facilitate cutting into small portions. This can be done in advance and the canapés can be reheated on a baking sheet before serving. 🥫

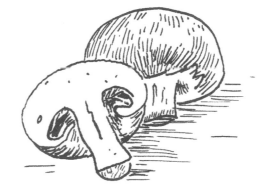

QUANTITIES

How many pours you can obtain from a bottle of wine depends, more than anything, on the capacity of your glassware. I do not have scientific proof, but it has always seemed to me that the bigger the glass, the faster the wine disappears. I remember a river cruise in China where the only decent wine on the list was a Beaujolais and the only wineglasses were thimbles. We made that bottle last the entire meal for ten people! But a single bottle poured into big balloon glasses might be barely enough for two. And there are other guidelines. For example, when serving wine in a cocktail or predinner setting, it's safe to assume each guest will consume a glass of wine in about a half hour. Without being overgenerous, figure about six glasses of wine in a bottle. For Champagne and sparkling wines served in flutes, you can pour nine servings from one bottle. Therefore, how many bottles of wine a dinner will require will depend on your guests and their capacity, and the size of your glasses. For a typical three-course dinner for four, one bottle of wine might be skimpy, so always have a backup ready. For six people you will need two bottles, and it's a good occasion to consider pouring a magnum, always impressive. When you are serving two wines, say a white and then a red, a bottle of each would be fine for four and might do for six. If you plan to serve two wines, the general rule is usually the white with a first course, then your red. But if you have a rich, perhaps sweeter white, you could open it after the red and its main-course partner, serving it with salad and cheese, then on to dessert.   —FF

FRENCH SPARKLERS
No country is so closely identified with sparkling wine as France. Clearly, that's because of the huge, foaming presence of Champagne at so many of life's important events. The tradition of making fine sparkling wines goes beyond Champagne, however, reaching to all corners of the country and taking many different, sometimes surprising forms.

You want a delicate, slightly sweet, pinkish bubbly that can be absolutely delicious before or after a meal? Bugey Cerdon from eastern France is the one for you. Or a fragile, lightly sparkling white wine that is the ultimate in freshness? Maybe something perlant—just a whisper of bubbles—from Gaillac in the southwest. These are, perhaps, obscure examples, but many regions of France make more conventional sparklers that resemble Champagne only in the sense that they can play similar roles.

Like Champagne, these sparklers are wonderfully versatile with food, yet may be delicious on their own. They are usually forcefully bubbly in the manner of Champagne, and therefore can gush forth on ceremonial and celebratory occasions. But in their aromas and flavors they are most definitely not Champagne. Instead, they offer distinctive personalities and characters.

The best of these variations on the bubbly theme are lively and refreshing, distinctive, and with some degree of finesse. This, in fact, is perhaps the chief difference between some of these wines and Champagne.

The elegance and polish that we associate with Champagne is sometimes lacking. Some of these sparklers can seem rustic or, even worse, clumsy. But the good ones offer the tense sense of balance that energizes and animates all good sparkling wines.

This is a prerequisite, but it is not the only thing. Sparkling wines are both sparkling and wine, a notion that seems obvious, or maybe even elusive. But if you try a few of the better sparkling Vouvrays, for example, one of the better categories within the French sparkling genre, they will always express the character of the chenin blanc grape, though perhaps in different ways. One may be complex and savory, dry yet with the telltale touch of honey that to me always indicates chenin blanc. Another may be pure and fresh, with flavors of apples and honeysuckle.

Many French sparklers are made using the same method as Champagne, in which the grapes are fermented into still wines and then bottled. A second fermentation is then induced in the bottle, which produces carbon dioxide that, unable to escape, carbonates the wine. Often, these wines are labeled "crémant." You can find them from Burgundy, Alsace, the Jura, and elsewhere.

By contrast, those labeled "pétillant" are generally made differently, bottled partway through the first fermentation rather than after its completion. As they finish the single fermentation in the bottle, a smaller amount of carbon dioxide is released, producing a pétillant wine, sparkling but with a gentler, more delicate level of carbonation.

Which method is better? It depends. The crémant method, naturally, will produce wines that more closely resemble Champagne in body and bubbles. The pétillants will generally feel more informal. I love them both. But then, I'm bubbles obsessive. 🍷

WITH SPARKLERS, CULINARY INSPIRATION COMES EASILY, especially when a celebratory occasion is involved. It is too obvious, and often too costly, to pop open a tin of caviar. And do you know how to handle an oyster knife? Here's a simpler route, using humble mortadella, the authentic Italian basis for our bologna. Flutes of French sparkling wine are not beachfront property like serious blanc de blancs Champagne, but they are in the neighborhood and are happy alongside this savory mortadella mousse.

Mortadella Mousse

TIME: 20 MINUTES

½ pound mortadella, preferably imported, in one piece, skin removed, and diced

¼ cup mascarpone

⅓ cup freshly grated Parmigiano-Reggiano (about 1 ounce), plus more for dusting (optional)

Pinch of nutmeg, preferably freshly grated

Toast rounds, for serving

Whole shelled salted pistachios or capers, for garnish

1. Place the mortadella in a food processor and process until ground to a paste. Add the mascarpone, grated cheese, and nutmeg. Process until blended. Spread on toast and top each piece with a pistachio or caper, or refrigerate mousse until ready to use.

2. Alternatively, each canapé without the garnish can be dusted with about ½ teaspoon grated cheese, arranged on a baking sheet, and run under the broiler briefly, about 1 minute, to lightly brown the top.

YIELD: ABOUT 50 CANAPÉS, 8 SERVINGS

The best way to keep leftover Champagne and high-quality sparkling wines is refrigerated, with one of those clamp-style stoppers firmly in place. A French old wives' tale suggests that a silver spoon put into the neck of the bottle (handle first) also works, and perhaps it does, but I usually use the stopper. I think the spoon seems effective because good Champagne will not go flat in a hurry anyway.

COOK'S NOTES: This recipe is a simple food processor job.

AMERICAN SPARKLERS

American wines almost all bear a burden, but none more so than sparkling wines. Cabernet sauvignon, chardonnay, and pinot noir all have French ancestors with which they have been endlessly compared. Only zinfandel, a wine that has reached prominence only in the United States, is exempt from the French albatross.

Perhaps these comparisons are unfair. While the grapes grown in the United States and France may be the same, the climate, soil, and cellar practices are often completely different. It stands to reason that the wines should be different, too.

The problem is Champagne. Both in the mouth and in the brain, Champagne's identity is so powerful that it has left little room for American sparkling wines to maneuver.

Practically all the wine-making regions in the world produce sparkling wine, but unlike the American version, most of the wines do not invite comparisons with Champagne. Instead, these regions have carved out their own identities. Spain has its cava, Germany its sekt, and Italy its various spumantes. Even other parts of France—Alsace, the Loire, and Burgundy, to name a few—make sparkling wines that are distinct from Champagne.

With a few exceptions, most regions use local grapes to make their sparklers, rather than the Champagne combination of chardonnay, pinot noir, and pinot meunier. But in the United States, without a competing local tradition, winemakers use the Champagne formula. Sometimes they even use the Champagne name. Luckily, most don't charge Champagne prices.

The grapes may be identical, and the wine-making methods similar, but, in fact, American sparkling wines are quite different from Champagne. Why? Location! The Champagne region is on the cold edge of the wine-making world, where each year farmers struggle to get their grapes to ripen. When they succeed, the result is grapes of great acidity but not a lot of sweetness, not good for still wines but perfect for Champagne.

In California, where most American sparklers come from, the climate is far warmer. The goal is the reverse—to produce grapes that are not too ripe, with sufficient acidity for sparkling wine. This is the reason California wines tend to be fruitier, without the dry, tangy leanness that gives Champagne its liveliness and energy.

Nonetheless, California sparklers have improved greatly in the last twenty years, as growers have learned that the best grapes tend to come from the cooler regions, like the Carneros, which cuts across the southern parts of both Napa and Sonoma, and the Anderson Valley of Mendocino County. And, of course, you can also find good sparkling wines from Oregon, Washington, and New York. I've even had an excellent sparkler from Massachusetts.

It would be wrong to look down on American sparklers. After all, the big Champagne companies themselves thought enough of the potential of California sparklers to make major investments in the state. Since the 1970s, such famous names as Moët & Chandon, Piper-Heidsieck, Mumm, Deutz, and Roederer have planted their flags in California.

Of these hybrids, only Roederer Estate in the Anderson Valley has competed with the best American producers of California sparkling wine, Schramsberg and Iron Horse. There is something to be said for being homegrown. 🍷

WHEN FINANCES WHISPER CAUTION, a holiday gathering can hold its head high if there's good sparkling wine and a little caviar on hand. Think American for both glass and plate. American caviar choices include transmontanus from California, the best of the lot, and hackleback from the Midwest. For a party, the caviar enhances a classic Alsatian tarte flambée. It's not flamed; the name is a corruption of flammekueche, a flatbread baked in a wood-burning oven and topped with soft white cheese, onions, and smoky bacon. For this tarte flambée, I swapped out the bacon for caviar, and in homage to blini, added buckwheat to the pastry.

Tarte Flambée with Caviar

TIME: 45 MINUTES, PLUS RISING

1 packet active dry yeast

4½ tablespoons unsalted butter

1 teaspoon salt

⅔ cup buckwheat flour

2¼ cups all-purpose flour, plus more if needed

2 medium red onions, sliced very thin

1 cup fromage blanc

⅔ cup crème fraîche

2 to 3 ounces caviar or other fish roe

1. Place the yeast in a large bowl, add ½ cup warm water, and set aside for 5 minutes. Melt 3 tablespoons of the butter. When the yeast starts to froth, add the salt, another ½ cup water, and the melted butter. Stir in the buckwheat flour. Mix in 2 cups of the all-purpose flour, a cup at a time, mixing until a ball of dough forms. Add a little more flour, if necessary. Knead on a floured work surface until smooth, elastic, and only a little sticky.

2. Use a little of the remaining butter to grease a 3-quart bowl. Place the dough in the bowl, turning to coat all sides with the butter. Cover and let rise until doubled, about 1 hour. Meanwhile, heat 1 tablespoon of the remaining butter in a skillet on low and sauté the red onions until golden. Set aside.

3. Heat the oven to 450°F. Use the remaining butter to grease a large oblong baking sheet, 11 by 17 inches. Punch down the risen dough and roll and stretch it to fit the pan. Mix the fromage blanc and crème fraîche and spread on the dough. Scatter the onions on top. Bake for about 15 minutes, until the crust starts to brown.

4. Remove from the oven and drop ½ teaspoons of caviar on top in a regular pattern. Cut into portions, or cut the tart into 2-inch squares and put a dab of caviar on each.

YIELD: 4 TO 6 APPETIZER SERVINGS, OR 36 HORS D'OEUVRES

COOK'S NOTES: Though virtually all caviar sold legally is now farm-raised, and can come from a dozen countries, what often determined choices in the past still applies, and that is cost. To garnish a tart, it's not necessary to splurge. If black (sturgeon) is your choice, it pays to shop around and find something that's modestly priced. Step down and there's salmon, though a better choice would be trout, also bright orange pink but with smaller beads. 🗑

CHAMPAGNE

I drink Champagne and sparkling wines year round, with all sorts of foods, for any occasion, and, more important, for no occasion at all.

An estimated 40 percent of Champagne is sold leading into the end-of-the-year holidays, but that does not mean we all must abide by the nonsense of restricting sparkling wines to gatherings and celebrations. The plain fact is that Champagne is one of the world's most versatile and pleasing wines. That's another crucial point: Champagne is a wine, though this may not be obvious to some, and it needs to be thought of in that context.

Too often, sparkling wines are set apart, as if they were a valued set of cuff links brought out only for special occasions, then returned to their plush box. But Champagne goes wherever other wines are capable of going, whenever, with ease. This misplaced perception of Champagne is partly the Champagne industry's fault. It's done such a good job of turning Champagne into an emblem of luxury and black-tie urbanity that it can seem out of place on the kitchen table.

The vast majority of Champagnes are made with some combination of three grapes: pinot noir, pinot meunier, and chardonnay. In theory, at least, pinot noir contributes power, complexity, and a red-fruit quality to the blend. Pinot meunier offers supple fruity and floral aromas, while chardonnay offers elegance, lightness, and citrus and floral flavors. It's a winning combination, but broken down into its constituent parts, Champagne can offer new and varied characteristics that belie the stereotypes of the individual grapes.

Champagnes made solely of pinot noir are rare. They can be more robust and taste distinctly of raspberries and strawberries, yet show great elegance as well. Those made solely of pinot meunier—I'm seeing these more and more—can be surprisingly graceful and subtle, showing complexity and finesse. Those made only of chardonnay, blanc de blancs, are the lightest and most refreshing Champagnes of all, just as right for an August afternoon as for a midnight in December.

As delicate as blanc de blancs can be, they can also have a range of textures, from lean to rich and broad. The best, like good Sancerre and Chablis, can seem transparent, with almost savory herbal and mineral flavors rather than the richer fruit tunes you can find when pinot noir or pinot meunier is dominant.

Rosé Champagnes have skyrocketed in popularity in the last decade, even though they tend to cost more than their equivalent siblings. Of course, it can take an extra step or two to create the myriad colors ranging from onionskin through salmon and ruby. Some winemakers simply add a bit of red still wine to the blend before refermentation in the bottle, the process that produces the fizz. Others allow the juice to macerate briefly with the pigment-laden skins of red grapes, which, ordinarily, are removed from the juice immediately to prevent the addition of color.

I rarely find rosé Champagnes to offer the complexity or finesse of other Champagnes, but they are popular for a reason, and who am I to argue with beauty? 🍷

A CELEBRATORY CHAMPAGNE, especially one that's a shade less than top of the line, is always a good choice for a holiday party. It will kick off the evening on a festive note. Often, however, it shows up at the end of the meal, with dessert; as the year winds down, the new is greeted with bubbles rising in the glass. It's too late for hors d'oeuvres, so what do you serve? With Champagne, dessert pairings are problematic. Brut Champagne will fade and taste acidic alongside popular desserts like chocolate cake, bûche de noël, profiteroles, and crème brûlée. Champagne will certainly hold its own against panettone, the Italian Christmas bread laced with candied fruits. A less obvious but equally felicitous choice is a simple French almond confection called pain de Gênes, or Genoa bread. It's really a pound cake. The story goes that it was created in Paris to honor André Masséna, the general who defended Genoa during Napoleon's wars in Italy. And it's not to be confused with a génoise, a kind of buttery sponge cake that was also named for Genoa, where it originated, but which became a basic in the French pastry repertory.

Pain de Gênes

TIME: 1½ HOURS, PLUS COOLING

9 tablespoons unsalted butter, very soft

2 tablespoons sliced almonds

¾ teaspoon fleur de sel or coarse sea salt

1¼ cups finely ground almonds or almond flour, or 6 ounces blanched almonds

1¼ cups confectioners' sugar, sifted

4 large eggs, at room temperature

2 tablespoons brandy

⅓ cup all-purpose flour, sifted

1. Heat the oven to 375°F. Cut a round of parchment to fit the bottom of a slope-sided 8-inch fluted tart pan that is 2 inches deep, or an 8-inch round cake pan, 1½ inches deep. Use ½ tablespoon of the butter to grease the pan, then the parchment liner. Scatter the sliced almonds and salt over the paper.

2. If using preground almonds or almond flour, whisk in a bowl with the confectioners' sugar to blend thoroughly. Otherwise, grind the blanched almonds in three batches in a food processor with the confectioners' sugar, taking care not to make a paste.

3. Cream the remaining 8½ tablespoons butter in an electric mixer with a paddle beater until light and fluffy. Add the almond-sugar mixture in thirds, beating after each addition, and continue beating until very pale and light. At high speed, preferably with a whisk attachment, beat in the eggs, one at a time. Stir in the brandy and gently fold in the all-purpose flour.

4. Spread the batter in the pan and bake for about 45 minutes, until nut brown and the top is springy to the touch. Remove from the oven, invert on a rack, and remove pan. Allow the cake to cool before peeling off the paper.

YIELD: 8 SERVINGS

COOK'S NOTES: For this pain de Gênes designed to be paired with Champagne, I have tamed the already restrained sweetness of the cake by adding a sprinkling of fleur de sel to the topping. Usually, pain de Gênes is made without salt. But the effect is mouthwatering and tantalizing. I also prefer Cognac in the batter to the usual kirsch. 🍾 Serve plain slices of the cake with chilled Champagne, or add an embellishment alongside: unsweetened whipped cream studded with diced candied fruit peel, or just simple fruit, like pears or pineapple poached in chardonnay. 🍾

LUNCH AT RECH, a classic 1920s Parisian fish restaurant that Alain Ducasse has recently taken over and restored, started with Champagne. Then the waiter brought a small dish of some gray stuff topped with tiny glittering red beads of tobiko (flying fish roe) and slices of toasted baguette. It was a somewhat loosely textured fish spread, mackerel to be exact, an excellent accompaniment for our flutes of blanc de blancs and a nice change of pace from the usual tuna tartare. Where I live, bluefish is easier to find than mackerel and has a similarly rich flavor profile. The fish rillettes, easily prepared, were as lovely a summer hors d'oeuvre with Champagne on a warm evening as they were in Paris.

Rillettes of Bluefish

TIME: 30 MINUTES

1 pound bluefish or mackerel fillets

⅓ cup white vinegar

1⅓ cups dry white wine

2 tablespoons grainy mustard

Juice of ½ lemon

2 tablespoons unsalted butter, softened

2 tablespoons finely minced fresh chives

2 teaspoons finely minced fresh cilantro leaves

Salt and freshly ground white pepper

Scant 1 teaspoon wasabi paste

2 tablespoons flying fish roe (tobiko; optional)

Toasted slices of baguette, for serving

Salad, for serving (optional)

1. Place the bluefish in a sauté pan or a skillet. Pour the vinegar and wine over, bring to a simmer, and remove from the heat. Allow to cool to room temperature.

2. When cool, remove the fish to a cutting board and peel off the skin. Discard the liquid. Place the fish in a bowl, breaking it up with a fork. Add the mustard, lemon juice, and butter and mix. Add the chives, cilantro, and salt and white pepper to taste. Fold in the wasabi.

3. To serve, pile rillettes in a serving dish and, if desired, spread tobiko over the top. Serve with toast. Or fashion mounds of the rillettes on individual plates and garnish with toast and microgreens or some other kind of small salad. Serve as an hors d'oeuvre or a first course.

YIELD: 4 TO 8 SERVINGS

COOK'S NOTES: Though bluefish can be paired as easily with red wine as white, in this context, the addition of vinegar in the poaching liquid, and edgy seasonings like mustard, lemon, and wasabi, called for the sprightly acidity of a white. Here it is provided in spades by Champagne, especially a blanc de blancs with strong citric and green apple notes. It is often said that Champagne can accompany any food. I do not agree. But I will certainly add dark-fleshed fish like bluefish and mackerel, when prepared with an acid component, to my sparkling-friendly list. 🥂

THE EXTRA-FRUITY RICHNESS OF ROSÉ CHAMPAGNE, whether a mere whisper or a shout, gives the wine what it takes to accompany meaty dishes, from first-course beef carpaccios and plates of prosciutto or other charcuterie, to roast veal, game birds, and pork. Its vivacious acid notes make it a felicitous foil for fatty foods. There you have my reasons for loving it with foie gras, especially a seared, beautifully burnished little slab of fresh fat duck liver. On the plate, foie gras can always use a matchmaker, a partner to bring the flavors into focus. In autumn, slices of tender honey-baked quinces, sweetened to give them a mellowness without thoroughly taming them, are ideal. The pink of the quinces and of the Champagne create visual harmony, too. And if searing foie gras seems too daunting, the quinces and Champagne can always team up with slices of purchased cooked foie gras terrine.

Foie Gras with Baked Quince

TIME: 1½ HOURS

1 tablespoon Champagne vinegar

6 tablespoons mild honey

Sea salt and coarsely ground black pepper

3 quinces (about 1½ pounds)

6 slices fresh duck foie gras, each 2 to 2½ ounces, about ½ inch thick, or 6 slices prepared duck foie gras terrine, each about ½ inch thick

1. Heat oven to 325°F. In a medium bowl, mix the vinegar, 5 tablespoons of the honey, ½ teaspoon salt, and ¼ teaspoon pepper. Quarter, core, and peel the quinces. Cut each quarter into 4 slices, placing them in the honey mixture as they are cut and turning to coat completely.

2. Arrange the coated quince slices in a shallow baking dish, such as a 9-inch glass pie pan. Pour over any honey mixture left in the bowl and drizzle with the remaining 1 tablespoon honey. Cover with foil and bake for 30 minutes. Uncover, baste, increase the heat to 400°F and bake for 20 minutes more. Keep the quinces warm for seared foie gras; allow to cool to room temperature for terrine. If prepared in advance, refrigerate until ready to serve, and bring to room temperature or warm in the oven at serving time.

3. If using fresh raw foie gras, season the slices with salt and pepper. Heat a cast-iron skillet to very hot, sear the foie gras for about 30 seconds on each side until browned, and transfer to six warm plates. Sprinkle the foie gras with a little sea salt and spoon the quinces alongside. Alternatively, slices of prepared foie gras terrine can be served with room-temperature baked quinces.

YIELD: 6 FIRST-COURSE SERVINGS

COOK'S NOTES: Quinces are seasonal, and when they are not in the market, consider pears or ripe but firm apricots instead. 🛢

ROSÉS

Rosés are lighthearted, yet often serious, especially when they have a nice, slightly bitter finish. Serve them in warm weather, of course, and consider a large bottle format, like a magnum, to enjoy throughout a dinner. They can also be appropriate aperitif wines at any time of year. In recent years rosé winemakers have surmounted a major hurdle. Their wines are no longer regarded with disdain, as silly compromises or simply warm-weather coolers. But they still tend to be the bottles you'd open in summer rather than, say, that bruising Châteauneuf-du-Pape. As to food, almost anything goes. I have enjoyed a glass of rosé with oysters and especially with clams on the half-shell. Salads, egg dishes, seafood, and chicken are all suitable, as is barbecue, since the acidity and bright verve of many of the better rosés balance richly fatty foods. Then there are those deeper, heavier examples; they will take you dancing with grilled pork, lamb, a burger, and even filet of beef.

ROSÉS FROM PROVENCE

Few wines are both as beloved and belittled as rosé. Since its return to fashion in the first decade of the twenty-first century, the public has embraced rosé as a wine of summer.

Yet bottles of rosé seem to come with neon-red warning signs admonishing consumers that they run the risk of pomposity if they dare to critically assess the wines. Why is this? Part of the great appeal of rosé is that it's not considered a serious wine. Everyone can let down their guard and feel free of any demands to demonstrate sophistication by issuing trenchant analyses of what's in the glass. We can relax and enjoy, like swapping officewear for shorts and huaraches.

By all means, breathe easy—all wines, not just rosés. Still, this call to abandon critical faculties is an insult, both to rosé and to us, the consumers. If we've learned nothing else since the beginnings of the American food revolution, we have learned to pay attention to small, seemingly insignificant things. The quality of ingredients, no matter how humble, is crucial to the perception and enjoyment of a meal. Even in the most modest surroundings, quality is never insignificant.

Why should rosé be different, especially those from Provence, a region inextricably associated with the lazy pleasures of rosé?

Good Provençal rosés ought to be fresh and lively. With rare exceptions, they should be dry, free of noticeable residual sugar. Ideally, good Provençal rosés offer a chalky minerality that can be both tremendously bracing and intriguingly textured, compelling repeated trips back to the glass because it simply feels so good to drink.

These wines, generally made of the region's usual grapes like mourvèdre, grenache, cinsault, carignan, and occasionally syrah, are more about texture than ripe fruit, though light berry and citrus elements can add to their appeal. Yet, we sell rosé short to think it must be only young and carefree. Provençal rosés from Bandol estates like Tempier and Pradeaux, or Château Simone of Palette, are deep and complex and can improve for years.

Other rosés are not so ambitious, which is not a bad thing at all.

Rosé is demeaned partly because most producers choose to make wines that are intended to be drunk young. But is that so bad? Ambition alone has killed as many good wines as indifference. While rosés like Simone, Tempier, and Pradeaux can be awfully good, my guess is that few people would trade the easygoing style of rosé for a slew of wines aged in oak and ultraconcentrated.

Yet easygoing is not a formula for carelessness. Consider the lesson of Beaujolais nouveau: It was embraced uncritically as a seasonal joy until the novelty wore off and the public realized that so much nouveau was confected and banal. Good nouveau is out there, but its poor reputation is a big obstacle to overcome.

Good rosé is out there, too, and not many wines are as transporting. You really don't need to see the seaside shimmering in the heat to enjoy a bottle, or smell the lavender, garlic, anise, and saffron that might be associated with Provence, rosé's fantasy heartland. It's all there in the glass, along with the blues, pinks, and yellows of a pastel sky, and the sounds of the motor scooters chugging over the cobblestones. Those are my images, at least. Good rosés call forth from each of us their own.

A PRETTY ROSÉ WITH FLORAL NOTES and hints of mineral and citrus is not just summer in the glass. No matter where it may have been made, it inevitably hints of the fragrant, sun-drenched landscape of the south of France. To reinforce that sense of place, all you need alongside is a casual sandwich called pan bagnat, or "bathed bread." Assembled with tomato, onion, olives, anchovies, and perhaps canned tuna on a crusty roll rubbed with garlic and olive oil, it is pressed—but not heated—so the moisture in the ingredients softens and drenches what is often day-old bread. I remember it on picnics, or as a substantial snack bought in a market in Nice, and I assure you that back in the day, the tuna was not de rigueur. The singular liberty I have taken here, aside from the touch of fresh basil, is to make it on a ficelle, a skinny baguette, and to cut it into small portions to serve as hors d'oeuvres while I sip that rosé with friends.

Pan Bagnat "Sliders"

TIME: 20 MINUTES, PLUS 1 HOUR PRESSING

1 ficelle (thin baguette), 20 to 24 inches long, split lengthwise

1 garlic clove, split

¼ cup extra virgin olive oil

4 teaspoons black olive paste (tapenade)

6 to 8 anchovy fillets, preferably "white" (marinated) anchovies

2 thin slices sweet onion, halved and taken apart

6 to 8 fresh basil leaves

½ cup canned tuna in olive oil, drained but not thoroughly, broken up

1 medium ripe tomato, halved lengthwise and sliced

Freshly ground black pepper

1. Place the baguette halves next to each other on a sheet of foil longer than the bread. Rub the cut sides with the garlic and brush with the oil. Spread a thin film of tapenade on each. Place the anchovies down the length of one side. Top with the onion pieces, basil, tuna, and tomato slices. Season with pepper.

2. Cover the filled side with the other half of the bread. Wrap the sandwich tightly in the foil. Press down on it, then place a large cutting board on top and weight it with cans of food or other heavy objects. Set aside for 1 hour or longer, turning the sandwich once during this time.

3. Unwrap and slice the sandwich into sections 1 inch or so wide. Skewer them with picks, arrange on a platter, and serve.

YIELD: ABOUT 20 HORS D'OEUVRES

COOK'S NOTES: The sandwiches can become picnic fare if the filled, pressed bread is cut in four equal portions.

ROSÉS OF THE WORLD
When the weather is hot, the wine is indeed pink. The people have spoken, and they've said, in the summer, they want rosé.

Make that rosado, or rosato, or cerasuolo, or, God forbid, even "blush" wine. For simplicity's sake, though, let's call it rosé.

Rosé comes in many flavors and languages, from just about every wine-producing region of the world. It's made from all sorts of red grapes, and even a few white ones, and it comes in many hues, as well. The pale salmon of Provençal rosé is the most familiar. From Spain and from Italy, from the United States and from all points of France, other rosés tend to be darker. But you can't rely on color to transmit much information about the wine.

Garnacha, for example (or grenache, as the French say), can easily yield big, powerful, dark rosés that can be clunky and chunky. But when made with care, as with many good Spanish rosés, they can be steely, tangy, earthy, and awfully attractive.

One of the great rosés of the world comes from Irouléguy, in the Pyrenees in the extreme southwestern corner of France near the Spanish border. It's made by Domaine Ilarria. The color's a shimmering, translucent garnet. On the palate, it's as fierce as rosé ever gets, made of tannat and cabernet franc, and it tastes like liquid rock, combined with iron and blood.

Rosés made from pinot noir, from Burgundy, the Loire, and California, tend to be softly fruity, though the Burgundy may be more floral and the California a tad sweet. A Bordeaux rosé may be sumptuous, with predictably a little more heft to it. Meanwhile, in the Abruzzi region of Italy, cerasuolo wines have a gorgeous cherry color, almost like red wines bleached a shade paler.

What makes a wine a rosé? One crude method is simply to blend white and red wines to achieve pink. Other than many rosé Champagnes, few good rosés are made this way anymore. But I can name at least one that is, a rosato from La Porta di Vertine, a small producer in the Chianti territory. This wine is made of a mixture of the red sangiovese and canaiolo grapes and the white trebbiano and malvasia. The fermentation is allowed to proceed at its own pace. The 2009 took six months to ferment, rather than the matter of days for industrial rosés. The result is a richly hued, textured, juicy yet substantial wine that smells like pressed flowers.

Most rosés nowadays are made from red wine grapes. The winemakers briefly macerate the grapes, then remove the skins, which contain the pigments that make wines red. The juice is then vinified as if to make white wine.

Sometimes rosés are simply by-products of red wine production. As the grapes begin their maceration, a small amount of the juice is bled off and sold as rosé. Often the purpose of this *saignée* technique is to concentrate the red wine, so these rosés can feel somewhat second class.

Most good rosés are dry, but occasionally you find lightly sweet versions, epitomized by the once-famous rosé d'Anjou and, of course, white zinfandel. When a rosé d'Anjou is balanced, it can be quite delicious. As for white zinfandel, well, I had a bone-dry, light-bodied version made, counterintuitively, by Turley Wine Cellars, which is better known for its big, brawny wines. It was delicate and delicious. Who knew? 🍷

AT BAR BOULUD, one of chef Daniel Boulud's New York restaurants, a plate of oysters came beautifully nestled on ice, punctuated with a scattering of pink peppercorns. Usually, I enjoy my oysters plain, with no condiments. But the pink peppercorns intrigued me, so I dropped some on the oysters. It was a delicious combination. And it suggested a sprightly dish to serve with a glass of rosé.

Oysters would be fine here, but in their place I opted for translucent slices of fresh, sweet fish like fluke, raw and garnished with the pink peppercorns. I added pink grapefruit for their rosy tint and some notes of modest bitter sweetness along with some high-toned radish slices. "Nearly naked" is a nod to the beach, where a glass of pretty rosé is always welcome in a café.

Nearly Naked Fluke with Grapefruit

TIME: 30 MINUTES

2 pink grapefruits

2 tablespoons sherry vinegar

2 fluke or flounder fillets, each about 6 ounces

6 large red radishes, sliced paper thin (about ¾ cup)

1 tablespoon minced fresh chives

2½ tablespoons fruity olive oil

Sea salt

1 tablespoon whole pink peppercorns

1. Use a sharp knife to remove all the peel and pith from the grapefruits. Holding each over a medium-large shallow bowl to catch the juice, cut out the segments between the separating membranes. Place the segments in a separate bowl. Squeeze the membranes over the bowl of juice to extract any remaining juice. You should have a scant ½ cup juice. Add the vinegar and set aside.

2. Cut each fillet in half down the middle, along the dark "seam." Holding a sharp knife at an angle, slice each fillet half into 2-inch pieces. Remove 2 tablespoons of the grapefruit juice mixture and set aside. Place the fish in the bowl of juice and set aside for 15 minutes.

3. Pour the reserved juice over the grapefruit segments in the other bowl and fold in the radish slices and chives. Fold in 1½ tablespoons of the oil. Season lightly with salt and set aside.

4. Toss the fish with about ½ teaspoon salt, or to taste. Arrange the pieces of fish in a circle on each of four large salad plates, leaving space in the center. Season with a little sea salt. Pile the grapefruit and radish salad in the middle of each plate. Scatter pink peppercorns over the fish, drizzle the fish with the remaining 1 tablespoon oil, and serve.

YIELD: 4 APPETIZER SERVINGS

COOK'S NOTES: Though fluke, a sashimi staple, is the fish of choice to serve raw, there are other suitable choices, including flounder, arctic char, and hamachi, a Pacific fish that is also called yellowtail. 🥫

ALWAYS A CROWD-PLEASER, spaghetti with lobster is also a dish that few wines, either red or white, cannot complement. In this context, rosé is not a compromise. And when it offers fruitiness and lively acidity, it makes a match in tune with rich seafood and tomatoes kissed by the sun, sweet yet endowed with a tartly palate-pleasing edge. It is a summer dish, when lobster prices tend to be reasonable and tomatoes are at their finest.

Lobster Spaghetti with Fresh Tomatoes

TIME: 45 MINUTES

½ cup fruity extra virgin olive oil

2 large garlic cloves, sliced thin

2½ pounds ripe tomatoes, peeled and very finely chopped

Salt and freshly ground black pepper

Four 1-pound lobsters, cooked and shelled, or 1½ pounds cooked lobster meat (see page 65)

3 tablespoons finely slivered fresh basil leaves, plus sprigs for garnish

1 pound spaghetti alla chitarra or spaghettini

Red chile flakes

1. Heat 3 tablespoons of the oil in a 5-quart sauté pan or wide saucepan. Add the garlic, cook over low heat until it softens, and then add the tomatoes. Bring to a simmer and cook for 3 minutes over medium heat. Season with salt and pepper and remove from the heat.

2. Bring a large pot of salted water to a boil.

3. Meanwhile, dice the lobster meat. Place 1 tablespoon of the oil in a small saucepan over low heat. Add the lobster and cook until just warmed through. Fold in 1½ tablespoons of the basil. Cover and set aside.

4. When the water boils, add the spaghetti and cook until barely al dente. Drain and place in the pan with the tomatoes. Stir in the remaining ¼ cup oil. Cook, stirring gently over low heat, for about 5 minutes, until the pasta and tomatoes are warmed and well incorporated. Season with salt and pepper and fold in the remaining 1½ tablespoons basil.

5. Transfer to six shallow soup plates. Top each portion with lobster, garnish with basil sprigs, and serve, with red chile flakes on the side.

YIELD: 6 SERVINGS

COOK'S NOTES: Once the spaghetti has been cooked, as with many pasta dishes, it's important not to shortcut stirring it in a large pan with the sauce ingredients to finish the cooking and blend the flavors. And instead of mixing the diced lobster with the sauce, I find it preferable to warm the lobster separately with olive oil and slivers of basil, then use it to top each portion of pasta. It retains its integrity that way and the presentation is more impressive.

ALL YOU NEED TO ACCOMPANY A NICE ROSÉ is a warm summer day. Actually, this is a recipe I learned in winter, while in the Grenadines, where a local woman whipped up conch fritters by the dozen. Four of us scarfed them down with glasses of rosé late one afternoon. Back home up north, conch was not so easy to find, but squid made an excellent substitute.

Squid Fritters

TIME: 30 MINUTES

½ cup finely chopped red bell pepper

½ cup finely chopped green bell pepper

4 scallions, trimmed and finely chopped

2 tablespoons minced cilantro

1 pound cleaned squid, finely chopped

1 large egg, beaten

1 cup beer (preferably lager)

1½ cups flour

⅛ teaspoon ground cayenne

½ teaspoon baking powder

Salt and freshly ground black pepper

About ⅔ cup vegetable oil, for frying

Tartar sauce and/or hot sauce, for serving

1. Combine the red and green bell peppers, scallions, cilantro, and squid in a large bowl. Mix in the egg. Stir in half of the beer. In a separate bowl, whisk the flour with the cayenne and baking powder. Add to the squid mixture. Add the remaining beer and mix well. Season to taste with salt and black pepper.

2. Heat the oven to 200°F. Line a baking sheet with foil and spread several layers of paper towels on a work surface.

3. Heat a large cast-iron skillet on medium-high. Add oil to a depth of about ¼ inch. When the oil is hot, drop heaping tablespoons of the fritter batter into the pan, lightly flattening the mixture to make oval pancakes about 3 inches long. Turn when deep golden brown on one side, fry the second side, then place the fritters on the paper towels to drain. Repeat with the remaining batter. As they are done, transfer the cooked, drained fritters to the baking sheet and place in the oven to keep warm. Serve with tartar sauce and/or hot sauce.

YIELD: ABOUT 30, SERVING 6

COOK'S NOTES: Unlike typical fritters, which are deep-fried, these are sautéed in oil, flattened, more like little pancakes. They emerge nice and irresistably crispy. 🧂

WHITES

We assume you do not pay attention to that cliché—"white wine with fish"—though plenty of seafood does extremely well alongside a glass of white, almost any white as a matter of fact. But while the rule-breakers delight in red wine with fish, even oysters (page 141), there are instances when white wine is preferable. White wines come in more styles than you'll find in Macy's shoe department, and many are a good fit with a number of foods. Some dishes do beg for a white. Briny, acid sauerkraut in a choucroute garni is one that comes immediately to mind. Sumptuously creamy specialties like coquilles Saint-Jacques or mac and cheese are a couple of others. You might select a rich, heavy white—a Burgundy or Napa Valley chardonnay, for example—or a riesling with kabinett credentials, to serve with white asparagus or turbot in hollandaise sauce. But then again, you might just prefer to challenge the dish with a leaner, more acidic sauvignon blanc or fiano. Let your taste be the final arbiter. Acidity in the dish, not just the wine, is also a necessary component in making a good match. To give a gratin or a sauce a more wine-friendly profile, regardless of the choice of wine, do not forget that final, finishing splash of lemon juice or vinegar.

SANCERRE AND NEIGHBORS Just say

the word "Sancerre" quietly and you'll get an initial sense of the built-in appeal of this white wine from the Loire Valley. The soft sibilance, the internal alliteration, the smooth completion, whether you give it the clipped French pronunciation or simply ease off the word American style—it's a beautiful sound, suggestive of beautiful wines.

Sancerre is a place, too, on the eastern end of the Loire Valley, which cuts from the Atlantic and Nantes on the west, eastward against the current through Anjou, Saumur, and Touraine until you reach the heart of France. This is Sancerre territory, centered around the villages of Bué and Chavignol (very little wine comes from the town of Sancerre itself). Here, and across the Loire in the Pouilly-Fumé region, many of the greatest sauvignon blanc wines in the world are made.

Sancerre—the place—produces much more wine than Pouilly-Fumé. It is the place that gives these wines their distinctive beauty, and it is the place that makes them Sancerre and not merely sauvignon blanc. In contrast to sauvignon blancs from elsewhere, and particularly from New Zealand, good Sancerres are characteristically restrained rather than exuberant, perfumed with citrus and chalk rather than bold fruit. The aromas and flavors are of lime, grapefruit, and lemon, of flowers and sometimes of herbs, and of minerality, a kind of catchall impressionistic description of a quality found in many great wines.

They also have a texture and depth to them that bely the widespread notion that sauvignon blanc can produce only simple wines.

Often, the best are reminiscent of Chablis. It's interesting to notice on a map that Sancerre is much closer to Chablis than it is to its Loire sibling, Vouvray, and shares some of the same soil characteristics. A good Sancerre can have a lot in common with a good Chablis.

While I love Sancerre, I don't always love paying Sancerre prices. In the last twenty years, as the quality of viticulture and wine making in the Loire Valley has risen, so have prices. What used to be an inexpensive bistro wine now generally costs a minimum of twenty-five dollars for a good producer's basic cuvée, and often ten to fifteen dollars more.

One excellent solution is to shop Sancerre satellites, appellations within the orbit of Sancerre that also make sauvignon blanc wines. This primarily means Pouilly-Fumé, well known in its own right, but also the smaller Loire appellations of Menetou-Salon, Quincy, and Reuilly.

Pouilly-Fumé in particular can be as racy and stimulating as good Sancerre, and at its best can display a similarly dazzling minerality that testifies to the felicitous combination of sauvignon blanc with chalk, flint, and limestone soils. And with one notable superstar exception, Didier Dagueneau, they are generally at least a few dollars cheaper. The other appellations, while perhaps not as exalted as Pouilly-Fumé, can also be excellent sources of delicious wines.

What always comes through in the best wines is a sense of vitality, in both the wines and the region. No matter how well you think you know the sauvignon blancs of the Loire Valley, they are always worth knowing better. 🍷

EVERYONE TALKS ABOUT THE CHICKEN FOR TWO AT NOMAD IN NEW YORK. But even before you get to the chicken, there is the snow pea salad, delicately crisp, brightly flavored, and as light as a spring breeze. I let the chef, Daniel Humm, make his chicken for me, but I feel the home cook has a good shot at preparing the salad. For a crisp white, the equally crisp snow peas dressed in lemon couldn't be better.

Snow Pea Salad

TIME: 45 MINUTES

1½ pounds snow peas

¾ cup lemon-flavored olive oil

¼ cup fresh lemon juice

Salt

1 tablespoon extra virgin olive oil

2 ounces pancetta, finely diced

½ cup finely diced onion

¼ cup fresh mint leaves

Freshly ground black pepper

1½ ounces pecorino, shaved (about ½ cup)

1. Trim the ends of the snow peas and pull off the strings. Stack about a dozen of the snow peas at a time on a cutting board and use a sharp knife to cut them at an angle into a thin julienne. Place the sliced snow peas in a bowl of ice water.

2. In a small bowl, whisk the lemon oil, lemon juice, and 1 teaspoon salt, or to taste, together and set aside.

3. Heat the plain olive oil in a 12-inch skillet over medium heat. Add the pancetta and cook until the fat is rendered. Do not allow the pancetta to brown. Add the onion and cook on low until soft and transparent. Remove from the heat. Drain the snow peas and add to the skillet. Return to medium heat and cook, stirring just enough to warm and slightly wilt the snow peas, about 5 minutes. Remove from the heat.

4. Whisk the lemon dressing to re-emulsify and pour it into the pan. Add the mint and toss. Season with salt and pepper. Transfer to shallow bowls, scatter the cheese on top, and serve.

YIELD: 4 TO 6 SERVINGS

COOK'S NOTES: The job of slicing the peas is best done on an angle, making it a simple task that takes only about 15 minutes. The salad can be prepared in advance except for adding the dressing, which should be done at the last minute so its acid does not dull the verdant color of the peas and mint. 🗑

NEW ZEALAND SAUVIGNON BLANCS

The sauvignon blanc grape owes a lot to New Zealand. Thirty years or so ago nobody knew much about it at all. Sure, it was a component of white Bordeaux, and yes, it was part of the blend in the great sweet wines of Sauternes. It made wonderful white wines in the Loire Valley, particularly in Sancerre and Pouilly-Fumé, as it still does. But the grape's name never appears on those French labels. Even in California, the grape gained popularity only after it was rechristened fumé blanc by Robert Mondavi.

In the 1980s, when New Zealand started to produce bold, pungent, invigorating sauvignon blanc wines, the name of the grape became something that people sought out. So great was New Zealand's success that the rest of the world could not help but embrace the grape.

South Africa began making delicious sauvignon blancs, as did Chile. California reevaluated whether sauvignon blanc was best suited for the oaky pseudo-chardonnays it was making and opted for the leaner New Zealand style instead. Bordeaux took note, too, and the good, inexpensive sauvignon blanc wines bottled as basic Bordeaux blanc offer a restrained Gallic nod in the direction of the Antipodes.

The question is, how much does New Zealand owe to sauvignon blanc?

The reason for this question is that sauvignon blanc is rarely viewed as capable of making great wines. Many ambitious New World regions are not content with making good, enjoyable wines. They strive for greatness. In this context, sauvignon blanc is often seen as a cash cow, an easy source of profits to finance the more important ventures, like making world-class pinot noir.

The problem is that the cash cow often suffers. Why worry about excellence when the public laps up New Zealand sauvignon blanc? The tendency is to take the easy way out rather than push to make the best possible wines.

It's sad to say, but New Zealand sauvignon blanc is no longer a go-to bottle. Once, confronted with a dull wine list or a menu of dishes not traditionally associated with wine, you could happily count on New Zealand sauvignon blanc for its piercing, vivacious refreshment. You can still find a fair number of wines like that. But consumers now face the burden of determining which producers still take sauvignon blanc seriously, and which are simply moving boxes.

I still like Cloudy Bay, though the wine is no longer head and shoulders above the others, as it was once. Villa Maria, Palliser, Greystone, Astrolabe, and Muddy Water are also reliable producers. 🍷

THE SPIRITED, CITRUSY, OFTEN HERBACEOUS FLAVORS of New Zealand sauvignon blancs are appetite whetters. The wines beg for companionship, at the very least a little cloud of fresh goat cheese on a cracker, some marinated white anchovies on buttered bread, or blanched asparagus to dip into lemon mayonnaise. Above all, plan a menu of light, fragrant dishes. A well-perfumed, savory seafood soup with an Asian accent is in elegant harmony with the wine. Fresh cilantro, ginger, scallions, and limes provide the flavor benchmarks for the mix of seafood, some mushrooms, and bok choy. And the Japanese spice called sansho pepper, which will contribute pungent, citrus notes, will add a distinctive touch. It's actually not a kind of pepper, despite the name; but it comes from the prickly ash, which is also the source of Sichuan peppercorns.

Asian Noodle Soup with Seafood

TIME: 40 MINUTES

3 ounces soba noodles

3 cups fish stock

1 tablespoon peeled, slivered fresh ginger

1 tablespoon soy sauce

1 tablespoon Thai fish sauce (nam pla)

4 ounces fresh oyster mushrooms, sliced

8 littleneck clams, scrubbed

12 mussels, scrubbed and debearded

½ pound medium shrimp, peeled and deveined

1 tablespoon fresh lime juice, plus 1 lime, quartered, for serving

2 tablespoons chopped fresh cilantro leaves

4 scallions, trimmed, halved lengthwise, and slant-cut

2 baby bok choy, sliced lengthwise

Red chile flakes or Japanese sansho pepper

1. Bring 2 quarts water to a boil, add the soba noodles, and cook until tender, about 5 minutes. Drain and rinse briefly under cold water. Set aside, covered.

2. Gently heat the stock in a large saucepan. Add the ginger, soy sauce, fish sauce, and mushrooms and simmer for 10 minutes. Add the clams and mussels. When they open, add the shrimp. When the shrimp turn pink, stir in the lime juice, cilantro, scallions, and bok choy. Stir in the noodles.

3. Return the soup to a simmer, then transfer to a deep serving bowl and dish portions into individual bowls, first serving the noodles with tongs, then using a ladle for the remaining ingredients.

4. Pass red chile flakes and lime wedges at the table and have an empty bowl available for shells.

YIELD: 2 TO 4 SERVINGS

COOK'S NOTES: On a dinner menu, this soup recipe could serve four as a first course; it could be the main event at lunch. 🧂

SAUVIGNON BLANCS FROM CALIFORNIA AND ELSEWHERE

Sauvignon blanc is rarely the most expensive wine at any California winery. Few producers are best known for their sauvignon blanc and truthfully, it's rarely the wine of which they are most proud. But in the depths of summer, when the weight of the heat hangs heavy around the shoulders, it's hard to think of a more refreshing choice from California than a chilled sauvignon blanc.

Case in point was an unaccountably hot February day once in the heart of Napa Valley—I mean Fourth of July hot. The occasion was a tasting for the twenty-fifth anniversary of Spottswoode Estate, which makes one of Napa's finest cabernet sauvignons. After sampling cabernets from each of the twenty-five Spottswoode vintages, the crowd repaired to an outdoor lunch at tables under a clear plastic canopy. As if it were a lab experiment, the canopy focused the heat of the sun on the perspiring guests who, even though some of the best cabernets of the day were served, thirsted only for Spottswoode's excellent sauvignon blanc. The clear bottles, glistening with beaded moisture in the broiling sun, were quickly emptied, and the cry went up for more.

Sauvignon blanc often suffers as an also-ran wine. Like Miss Congeniality, everybody likes it but few give it any respect. Yet it is made successfully all over the world: in France, Italy, and South Africa; Chile, Argentina, and New Zealand; and, of course, California, where for years many winemakers demonstrated their attitude toward sauvignon blanc by trying to vinify it as if it were chardonnay, draping it with sweet oak flavors that served only to bury the grape's charm.

Those days are thankfully long gone. Having seen Americans embrace sauvignon blanc in all of its bracing pungency in styles ranging from the subtle minerality of the Loire to the brassy, grassy, fruity intensity of New Zealand, California winemakers have largely stopped trying to turn sauvignon blanc into something it's not. Instead, they are making wines that for the most part are summery charmers, fulfilling the imperative to refresh, while in the best efforts offering character and substance.

As for sauvignon blancs from the rest of the world, well, Chile makes fresh, aromatic sauvignon blancs in the Casablanca Valley and sells them at excellent prices, while South Africa and Israel have gotten in on the global act. Other pockets of sauvignon blanc production exist in Italy, Slovenia, Spain, and Australia. And please, let us not forget Bordeaux, which makes a light, crisp style of sauvignon blanc as well as, from Pessac-Léognan, some of the greatest white wines in the world, especially when blended with sémillon or sauvignon gris.

Sauvignon blanc can make wonderful wines, particularly in those historic regions like Pessac-Léognan and certain parts of Sancerre and Pouilly-Fumé. These wines can truly be said to express their terroir, and often they will be among the most expensive sauvignon blancs you will find. That's not to say you can't find sauvignon blancs from California, New Zealand, and Slovenia that also reflect a sense of place. But for the inexpensive wines, the grape-growing and wine-making practices are more important than where the grapes come from, provided, of course, they are grown in suitable sites. At the least you will find wines that are vivacious. 🍷

THERE ARE WINE LOVERS who think it's cool to open Château Lafite with a burger. But most of the time, when matching food and wine, a better sense of proportion suggests that wines with impressive pedigrees deserve important dishes, just as modest wines are often more suited to simpler fare. Expense plays a role. I would not splurge on langoustines with the generally unassuming, though crisp and nicely structured sauvignon blancs, many of which can do little damage to the budget. And if it's summer, I opt for the first glossy zucchini from the farm stand to accompany the wine. The zucchini, sautéed until tender, bolstered with garlic, pine nuts, and grana padano, and mingled with fresh pasta, deliver the right herbal, vegetal notes to show off the wine.

Fettuccine with Zucchini

TIME: 1 HOUR 20 MINUTES

1 pound medium zucchini (about 6), trimmed and diced

Salt

4 tablespoons extra virgin olive oil

1½ cups minced onions

3 garlic cloves, slivered

1 cup pine nuts

1 pound fresh fettuccine

Freshly ground black pepper

3 tablespoons minced fresh flat-leaf parsley leaves

½ cup grated grana padano cheese

1. Place the zucchini in a colander, toss with salt, and set to drain in the sink or over a bowl for 30 minutes. Meanwhile, heat 3 tablespoons of the olive oil in a heavy sauté pan. Add the onions, garlic, and pine nuts and sauté over low heat for about 10 minutes, or until the onions are soft and the pine nuts start to brown. Rinse and drain the zucchini and add to the pan. Sauté until tender, about 20 minutes.

2. Bring a large pot of salted water to a boil. Add the pasta, cook for about 3 minutes, and drain, reserving about 1 cup of the pasta water. Add the pasta to the sauté pan, and cook over low heat for about 5 minutes to blend the ingredients, adding the reserved pasta water as needed. Season with salt and pepper. Fold in the parsley, cheese, and the remaining 1 tablespoon oil and serve.

YIELD: 6 SERVINGS

COOK'S NOTES: I prefer to use zucchini in summer and early fall, when they are farm fresh, glossy, and unwaxed. At other times of year, you can substitute diced butternut squash, quartered Brussels sprouts, or broccoli florets.

DRY GERMAN RIESLINGS

Many Americans assume all rieslings are sweet. In fact, most rieslings, whether from Austria, Alsace, Australia, or the United States, are dry. Even more surprising is that many German rieslings are dry, too, and that the preference in Germany today and for the last twenty-five years has overwhelmingly been for dry rieslings. But the most surprising thing to me is how delicious dry German rieslings have become.

When I first encountered the German dry riesling phenomenon on a trip to the Mosel and Rhine wine regions in the late 1990s, I was appalled. So many of the dry wines were tart and shrill, parching the mouth and creating thirst rather than quenching it. Now, I'm enchanted with dry rieslings like those from Keller in Rheinhessen, wines that reveal and frame the great mineral soul of the riesling grape, exalting it yet doing so gently without any of the sharp edges of the dry rieslings I so ruefully remember.

How did they get so good?

Among the first American importers to bring in dry German rieslings was Stephen Metzler of Classical Wines, who began working with Georg Breuer of the Rheingau in 1996. Even back then, Breuer was making great dry rieslings, and for years Breuer, along with a few other producers like Dr. Bürklin-Wolf and Koehler-Ruprecht in the Pfalz, were the lonely vanguard, carrying the torch in America for dry German rieslings.

Back then, Mr. Metzler suggested, when the German thirst for dry wine was more fad than anything else, many producers simply fermented the sweetness out of their wines and forgot about the importance of low yields, balance, and careful winemaking. Now, a new generation of German winemakers reared on dry wines is pursuing the style with thought and care. Oh, and global warming, which has made it possible to ripen grapes more fully in this extreme northern grape-growing region, hasn't hurt.

The producers making top-flight dry rieslings are legion these days. They would also include Knebel, von Kesselstatt, Karthäuserhof, and A. J. Adam in the Mosel; Schäfer-Fröhlich and Dönnhoff in Nahe; Wagner-Stempel in Rheinhessen; Ratzenberger in the Mittelrhein; and Rudolf Fürst in Franken.

Could the preference for dry rieslings be so strong that the rieslings with residual sugar will be crowded out? It's a good question, and the prospect of losing those wines should be cause for great concern. Still, I can't help but think that dry German rieslings are singular, combining grace, delicacy, and power in a way unlike rieslings from anywhere else. One can only hope that the world's taste for German rieslings with residual sugar will keep those styles in business, even if Germany itself no longer cares. ♟

SERIOUS WINE LOVERS would no sooner pour a fine wine with artichokes than they would drink it from a paper cup. Artichokes contain cynarin, a compound that delivers an oddly sweet aftertaste and can distort the flavor of wine, especially red wine. Because most of the cynarin is in the leaves of an artichoke, not the flesh, a recipe that relies on the hearts and stems, not the leaves, will be more compatible. Also, a touch of sweetness on the palate might even help round out some of the leaner bone-dry rieslings. And so it was with broiled artichokes slathered with garlic butter, cheese, and bread crumbs that prickly Miss Artichoke gave her heart to modest Mr. Riesling. This recipe comes from what is arguably the most boldface dining room in the Hamptons on New York's Long Island —Nick & Toni's.

Artichokes with Garlic, Chives, and Cheese

TIME: 1 HOUR 15 MINUTES

Juice of 1 lemon

6 large globe artichokes

8 tablespoons (1 stick) unsalted butter

⅓ cup chopped garlic

2 tablespoons minced fresh chives

Salt

⅓ cup toasted panko bread crumbs

¼ cup grated pecorino Romano

1. Place the lemon juice in a large pot of water. Remove the outer leaves from the artichokes. Cut each artichoke in half vertically. Use a sharp paring knife to remove the inner core, with all the purple leaves and fuzz. Pull off the leaves down to a couple of layers of inner ones. Pare the base and stems down to the flesh. Place the artichokes in the pot of water as they are trimmed. Bring to a boil, reduce the heat to a simmer, and cook until tender, 15 to 18 minutes. Drain the artichokes, and place on paper towels to cool.

2. Melt the butter in a skillet over medium-low heat. Add the garlic and chives. Cook, stirring occasionally, until the butter and garlic begin to brown, about 5 minutes. Remove from the heat.

3. Heat the broiler. Place the artichokes, cut side up, in a shallow baking dish that can go to the table. Season with salt. Place under the broiler until the edges of the artichokes start to brown. To serve, spoon the bread crumbs over the artichokes, then the garlic butter, then the cheese. Place back under the broiler for about 1 minute, until the cheese softens but has not melted. Serve.

YIELD: 6 SERVINGS

COOK'S NOTES: Select big globe artichokes, green and perhaps tinged with purple, but with no signs of browning. Those with long stems are best because the stem can be peeled and served intact with the hearts. The parboiled artichokes can also go on the grill. 🍶

GERMAN KABINETT RIESLINGS

With so many grapes grown in so many places around the world, even experts may be forgiven for mistaking, say, a South African sauvignon blanc for a Chilean sauvignon blanc. But a good German riesling from the Mosel region is like no other riesling in the world. It is simply one of wine's singular glories.

In my ideal world, the wine in the glass I raise each year to the coming of spring is a Mosel kabinett riesling. It is a wine of gorgeous delicacy, as fragile as the petals on those first tentative blossoms, yet possessing a tensile strength that comes of perfect balance. It is a captured moment, evocative more than impressive, fleeting rather than penetrating, whispered nuance, not high volume.

Nonetheless you might find some people who ask what all the fuss is about. That's because, for all its joys, kabinett riesling is also one of the least understood, least respected of wine designations. Why? First, let's understand what the term means. *Kabinett, spätlese*, and *auslese* are all designations for the ripeness of the grapes when they are harvested. Kabinett grapes are picked at an early point of ripeness, spätlese grapes at a later point, and auslese grapes even riper than that.

The misunderstanding arises from a tendency to regard these ripeness levels in an ascending order of hierarchy, as if spätlese were always better than kabinett, and auslese better than both. It's easy to see why this happens. The longer grapes are left out on the vine, the riskier the proposition. Rather than chancing bad weather—especially in the old days, when forecasting was more like guesswork—timid growers would harvest earlier, and prices would be higher for the more difficult late-harvest wines. Prices still rise in proportion to ripeness levels.

This notion of a hierarchy of quality has been reinforced for years by the wine trade. Often when I've sought a kabinett riesling in a restaurant or shop, the sommelier or merchant would recommend a bottle because "it's actually declassified spätlese," meaning a desirable combination of spätlese quality and kabinett price.

No! Leaving aside the issue of "declassified," such a response indicates a complete lack of appreciation for the worthiness of kabinett and the importance of context in selecting wines. The modestly sweet and light kabinett rieslings deserve to be valued, not thoughtlessly denigrated.

Complicating matters is that true kabinetts have been in short supply in recent years because of warmer temperatures. Increased warmth speeds the production of sugar in the grape. By the time the other elements of the grape have developed, the sugar content is already at the spätlese level, if not higher. You have to reach back to years like 2008 and 2001 for examples of a true kabinett riesling.

But when you find the real thing, kabinetts are beautiful, with a lovely tension between sweetness and acidity that makes them taste as if they were dry. What's more, the best wines are full of the slatelike mineral aromas and flavors that are so characteristic of Mosel rieslings. Trust me, they will lead even the most skeptical toward sweet wines and down the path of pleasure. ☙

A SAVORY TART, its silky custard thickly studded with crabmeat to pick up the sweetness of the wine, and asparagus to tame tropical fruit and citrus flavors with vegetal and mineral notes, makes for a lovely lunch or a predinner snack. Come summer, some diced zucchini can replace the asparagus. The tart also delivers a kick, not in the filling but in the pastry. There's no heat from the subdued alcohol in the bottle. But the cayenne in the crust makes up for it.

Crab and Asparagus Tart

TIME: 1½ HOURS

1¼ cups all-purpose flour, plus more for rolling

Salt

½ teaspoon cayenne

7 tablespoons unsalted butter

4 large eggs

1 tablespoon minced shallots

½ bunch medium asparagus, ends snapped off, spears halved vertically, cut into 1-inch pieces

8 ounces lump crabmeat

1 tablespoon fresh lemon juice

1 tablespoon minced fresh chervil

¾ cup half-and-half

4 ounces soft goat cheese

1. Heat the oven to 400°F. Whisk the flour, ½ teaspoon salt, and cayenne in a bowl or blend in a food processor. Add 6 tablespoons of the butter and cut in or pulse until the size of peas. Beat 1 egg with 2 tablespoons ice water, scatter on the flour mixture, and mix with a fork or pulse until the dough can be gathered together. Add a little more water, if needed. Form into a disk and roll on a lightly floured surface to line an 8- or 9-inch straight-sided tart pan. Place the dough in the pan.

2. Trim the edges, line with foil, and weight with pastry weights or dry beans. Bake for 10 minutes, until starting to look dry. Remove the foil and weights and bake for 10 to 15 minutes more, until lightly browned. Remove from the oven. Reduce the heat to 350°F.

3. Melt the remaining 1 tablespoon butter in a skillet, add the shallots, and cook on medium for 1 minute. Add the asparagus and cook for about 2 minutes, until starting to soften. Remove from the heat. Fold in the crabmeat, lemon juice, and chervil. Season with salt. Spread in the pastry.

4. Whisk the half-and-half and cheese until smooth. Beat in the remaining 3 eggs until well blended. Pour the egg mixture over the crab and asparagus, place the pan in the oven, and bake for about 40 minutes, or until set and lightly browned. Allow to cool for 15 minutes, remove the sides of the pan, and serve at once or cooled to room temperature.

YIELD: 6 TO 8 SERVINGS

COOK'S NOTES: With this recipe you have the option of baking individual tartlets in 4-inch shells, or even making cocktail tidbits, baking the filling in homemade or purchased little pastry cups. 🥂

GERMAN SPÄTLESE RIESLINGS

Despite endless efforts to explain, simplify, and demystify, the riddle of German wines endures. Confronted with the bewildering nomenclature of so many German wine labels, many people simply shake their heads in confusion and give up. Rather than add to the babble, we concede straight out that understanding German wines is hellishly difficult.

To that, I say, so what? The wines are worth it. And in some cases, what people fear most about German wines is one of the things that makes them so great: their sweetness. Yes, some German rieslings are sweet. But some are not, and consumers are confounded by the need to determine which are which. (If you do manage to master the label terminology, you can tell which German rieslings are sweet and which are dry, as you cannot from the labels of most wines from, say, Alsace.)

Nothing is wrong with sweetness in German rieslings. In fact, unlike many other wines where a little sweetness is unwelcome, well-made German rieslings turn sweetness into a strength. If it is carefully balanced by other qualities, like a lively acidity, you end up with a high-wire balancing act in which the harmony between sweetness and acid is refreshing and thrilling.

Let's take one of those words that causes some consumers to recoil in abject horror and reach for a beer: spätlese. It is pronounced "SHPAYT-lay-zuh," and simply means that the grapes were harvested ripe enough to make a wine that potentially is more than a little sweet, but not enough to make it powerfully sweet.

Notice I said "potentially." Spätlese, like kabinett for less sugary grapes and auslese for later-picked grapes, refers only to the ripeness level. It is up to winemakers whether they want to halt fermentation midway, to leave residual sugar in the wine, or ferment it until all the sugar turns into alcohol and the wine is dry.

In Germany, many winemakers are choosing to make dry rieslings, which German consumers have preferred for some time. I love dry German rieslings, the good ones at least. But I love the sweet ones, too, especially so because no other place in the world can make sweet rieslings with the same exhilarating combination of delicacy, complexity, and taut intensity as Germany. Yet, increasingly, these wines are made primarily for the export market.

It's hard to argue preferences, but well-balanced spätleses are unrivaled and are wonderfully versatile with food. And, with generally no more than 8 percent alcohol, German spätleses can be perfect for the sorts of feasts that last for hours and encompass a wide range of savory and sweet foods.

They are not cheap, but even at twenty-five to fifty dollars, given the difficulty of farming these vineyards, often on impossibly steep slate hillsides rising up from the Mosel river, they can be great values. 🍷

YOU CAN ENJOY A GLASS OF GERMAN SPÄTLESE RIESLING with nothing more demanding than a sun-dappled afternoon. But when it comes to food, there are not many dishes that will daunt these rieslings. Cheeses, like funky washed-rind Époisses and Munster, will be well matched with delicately sweetened yet citric wines so well endowed with acidity. They will shine alongside this simple carrot soup that can be served either hot or cold and is seasoned Moroccan style, like a carrot salad. Subtle sweetness (carrots), acidity (lemon), spice (cumin), fragrance (cilantro), and a touch of salinity (mussels) mirror the very aromas and flavor notes that the best of these wines deliver. The soup can also be made without the mussels.

Moroccan Carrot Soup

TIME: 1 HOUR

2 tablespoons extra virgin olive oil

1 medium-large onion, coarsely chopped

2 teaspoons ground cumin

2 bunches carrots, peeled and cut into 1-inch pieces

Salt and freshly ground black pepper

Juice of 1 lemon

1 pound mussels, scrubbed and debearded (optional)

½ cup finely chopped fresh cilantro leaves

1. Heat ½ tablespoon of the oil in a 3-quart saucepan. Add the onion. Cook over low heat until the onion starts to soften. Stir in the cumin, and cook briefly, stirring. Add the carrots and 6 cups water. Bring to a boil, lower the heat, and simmer, covered, until the carrots are very tender, about 20 minutes. Cool briefly. Puree in a blender in two batches. Return the soup to the saucepan, season with salt and pepper, and add the lemon juice. Set aside until shortly before serving.

2. If using the mussels, place them in a shallow 2-quart saucepan or sauté pan. Add ½ tablespoon of the oil, toss over high heat for about 1 minute, reduce the heat to low, cover, and cook until the mussels open, 7 to 8 minutes. Remove the mussels, draining well so the juices stay in the pan. Discard any that do not open. When the mussels are cool enough to handle, shuck them into a bowl, discard the shells, and toss the meat with the remaining 1 tablespoon oil and the cilantro. Strain the mussel broth and add it to the soup.

3. Reheat the soup if serving it hot; otherwise, leave it at room temperature. To serve, place a few mussels in each of six soup plates, warmed if serving hot soup. Serve the plates to your guests. Ladle the soup over the mussels at the table. If not using mussels, fold the cilantro into the soup, ladle the soup into bowls, and drizzle each portion with some of the remaining 1 tablespoon oil.

YIELD: 6 SERVINGS

COOK'S NOTES: In place of olive oil for garnishing, consider green cilantro oil or toasted Moroccan argan oil. 🫙

GERMAN AUSLESE RIESLINGS All right,

people, take a deep breath, relax, and gather around. Are you ready? Now we're going to talk about riesling. Not just any riesling, but German riesling—auslese riesling, to be specific—quite simply the most perplexing great wine around.

Perplexing? Absolutely. Ausleses are beloved by wine critics, who praise them but almost never tell you what to do with them. Even some confirmed lovers of German rieslings are befuddled by ausleses. Are they dessert? Can they be enjoyed with food? Are they best ignored? They are sweet, right?

Unraveling arcane German wine lingo requires time, incentive, and a taste for banging your head against stone walls. Nonetheless, cracking the code will pay off with the opportunity to enjoy wines that not only are absolutely delicious and sometimes profound, but are among the most reasonably priced great wines in the world.

The most important thing about auslese is not how it's pronounced (OWS-lay-zuh), nor what it means. No, the first crucial thing to know about auslese wines is how good they are with food.

A spicy Indian vindaloo or Thai curry? A young, balanced auslese will surround the heat and envelop it in a gentle cushion of apricot, peach, and mineral flavors. Duck breast with a sweet fruit sauce? Ah, young auslese to the rescue again. How about Sichuan smoked duck or an earthy venison medallion? A ten-year-old auslese riesling is a wonderful match. And finally, in the realm of the sublime, a perfectly ripe Vacherin Mont d'Or, oozing with funky fruit aromas, is just the extraordinary thing to eat with a fifteen- to twenty-year-old auslese, which by then has developed a singular smoky aroma actually reminiscent of kerosene. It makes me sigh to think about it.

The wines are light, often 7.5 to 8.5 percent alcohol, with an intensity that seemingly belies their delicacy.

So what's the problem?

Oh yes, people are afraid it's going to be super sweet. But the thing to remember, as the riesling impresario Paul Grieco has said, is that good auslese is not a sweet wine but a balanced wine.

Even though an auslese riesling may come with a lot of residual sugar, it will not necessarily taste sweet, at least most of the time. Why? Because of great acidity, the glowing signature of the riesling grape. Sweetness in a wine is like a couture gown, and acidity is like exquisite bone structure. Put the equivalent sweetness in a wine with little acidity, like a viognier, for example, and you have a frumpy, clumsy wine. But in a good auslese riesling the combination of sweetness and acidity gives you Heidi Klum.

So, what seems perhaps like a strange category of wines is, in fact, a brilliant category of wines. The trick is to try them.

If it's not the sweetness that discourages, it's often the nomenclature. Yes, I know it's difficult, and knowing that auslese means the grapes were harvested even riper than spätlese or kabinett grapes is only part of it. Some bottles are designated with special cask numbers, others with gold capsules around the cork, and even some with long gold capsules to set them apart from the ordinary gold capsules. Often these wines are made from grapes afflicted with botrytis, the noble rot, which gives the wines a wonderful, honeyed sweetness that indeed differs from the ordinary ausleses.

I have sometimes been surprised by botrytis in an ordinary bottle. You can curse the unpredictable nature of German wines, or you can chalk it up as one of life's pleasant surprises. 🍷

CHEESE Some cheeses, like chèvres, are designed to be paired with white wine. If you serve cheeses with the hors d'oeuvres, chances are you will be pouring a white wine anyway. But what about cheese after the main course? Though the conventional wisdom is to accompany a cheese course with red wine, presumably the red that was served with the main course, there is a compelling argument for switching to a white wine. The fat and salt in most cheeses will often numb the flavor of a good red wine, while they will be balanced by the fruit and acidity in a white. But how do you follow a red wine with a white? Select the white wine with care. The best choice may be a riesling; a spätlese, or even an auslese, with a little residual sugar to round it out should do the trick.   —FF

GERMANS MAY ENJOY AUSLESE RIESLINGS with a steak, but don't tell that to a cabernet lover. Ausleses are difficult wines, enjoyable on their own, especially considering their gentle alcohol content. But with food? Give me cheese. Still, when a vintage displays piercing acidity, which tames sweetness, other options come to mind. Challenging foods, like asparagus and eggs, can find happiness alongside the tart yet mellow rieslings. Add that cheese and you could assemble a soufflé, an omelet, a quiche to serve at lunch, or bake asparagus with cheese and park a poached or fried egg on each portion. Or consider this riff on spaghetti carbonara, made with asparagus and no pork. It's easily a lunch dish or, as a primi, it can be followed by something hefty, with a red wine to match. Or more riesling.

Penne with Asparagus Carbonara

TIME: 45 MINUTES

1 pound medium-thick asparagus

3 tablespoons extra virgin olive oil

3 large garlic cloves, sliced

3 large eggs

10 ounces penne

Salt and freshly ground black pepper

1 cup grated pecorino (about 2 ounces)

2 tablespoons minced fresh tarragon leaves

1. Snap off the ends of the asparagus. If the stalks are thick, peel the bottoms. Slant-cut the asparagus into 1-inch pieces. Heat 2 tablespoons of the oil in a large skillet. Add the garlic and cook on medium-low until the garlic is fragrant. Add the asparagus and stir-fry until al dente, about 5 minutes. Remove from the heat. In a medium bowl, beat the eggs enough to blend them.

2. Bring a large pot of salted water to a boil. Add the penne and cook until al dente, about 10 minutes. Gradually whisk ½ cup of the hot pasta water into the eggs. Drain the pasta and add it to the skillet. Add the remaining 1 tablespoon oil and toss with the asparagus over low heat just enough to combine and warm the ingredients. Season with salt and pepper. Remove from the heat.

3. Very slowly stir about half the egg mixture into the pasta and asparagus, mixing everything constantly. Don't worry if some of the egg scrambles a bit. Remove from the heat. Quickly stir the cheese into the remaining eggs, pour over the ingredients in the skillet, and mix. Fold in the tarragon. Serve at once.

YIELD: 4 SERVINGS

COOK'S NOTES: The trick, when it comes to carbonara, is to blend all the ingredients without overcooking the eggs. Quick work is required. But there is also a cheater's trick: Blend a teaspoon of cornstarch with cold water and stir that into the egg mixture before adding it to the pasta. The starch will stabilize the eggs.

THIS HERBAL, SLIGHTY TANGY GOAT CHEESE GALETTE has a nuttiness, thanks to the whole wheat pastry and the walnut topping. It will flatter the wine and vice versa. When to serve it depends more on the wine, which can be an aperitif or a glass at the end of the meal. The galette suits either scenario. Serve it directly from the oven as a first course or, in place of cheese before dessert, parking a tangle of sweet mâche in vinaigrette alongside. Divide it in slender wedges and you have an hors d'oeuvre to accompany an aperitif. A glass of riesling anyone?

Goat Cheese and Walnut Galette

TIME: 1 HOUR

1½ cups whole wheat pastry flour, plus more for rolling

¾ teaspoon salt

8 tablespoons (1 stick) unsalted butter, in pieces

2 eggs

1 garlic clove, peeled

2 scallions, coarsely chopped

¼ cup flat-leaf parsley

12 ounces plain goat cheese

Freshly ground black pepper

¼ cup chopped walnuts

1. Heat the oven to 400°F. Place the flour and salt in food processor and pulse briefly to mix. Add the butter and pulse until it is reduced to pea-size pieces. Separate one egg and mix the yolk with 7 tablespoons cold water. Open the food processor and drizzle the liquid over the flour mixture. Pulse as needed until the dough just starts to come together. Add an additional tablespoon of water if needed. Form into a ball. Roll the dough on a floured surface to make a circle about 14 inches in diameter. Trim the edges neatly. Place the dough on a baking sheet lined with parchment.

2. Whether you wash out the food processor at this point is your call; I don't bother. Turn on the food processor and drop in the garlic through the feed tube to mince it. Add the scallions and parsley and process until finely minced. Beat the egg white and remaining whole egg together. Add to the processor along with the goat cheese. Process until smooth. Season liberally with pepper.

3. Spread the cheese mixture in a 10-inch circle on the pastry, leaving about a 2-inch border all around, then fold the border over the edges of the filling, pleating it evenly as you go. Scatter the walnuts on top of the filling. Bake about 30 minutes until the filling is set and the pastry is lightly browned. Serve hot or at room temperature.

YIELD: 6 OR MORE SERVINGS

COOK'S NOTES: When it comes to a galette instead of a classic tart, I tend to prefer using whole wheat pastry flour. Perhaps the very rustic nature of the galette is the inspiration. But be sure to use whole wheat *pastry* flour, which has a finer texture than regular whole wheat flour. And if you can find only the regular kind, then use half whole wheat and half all-purpose. 🥄

AUSTRIAN RIESLINGS

When I think of Austrian rieslings, I think of dry, structured wines with stony, pure, shimmering mineral flavors that dominate the palate, yet are never heavy or out of balance. I think of green and yellow fruits, and complex flavors etched with laserlike precision. Finally, I think of wines that are phenomenally refreshing, tangy, and energetic, with textures that feel so good in the mouth that you simply do not want to stop drinking the wines.

Because Austrian rieslings have certain linguistic traits in common with their German counterparts, people tend to lump them together. But they are very different. German rieslings, particularly from the Mosel, tend to be sheer, lacy, and fine, whether they are dry or have a pleasing sweetness to them. Austrian rieslings are almost always bone dry, and are characterized by power and richness. They have great texture, presence, and weight, yet are rarely heavy.

They are closer to the rieslings of Alsace, but even that comparison is not quite right. Alsatian wines can be even fuller and richer, yet paradoxically, the driest rieslings from Alsace can also seem more austere. The truth is, the wines vary too much depending on site, vintage, and the intent of the producers for one to generalize effectively.

It's hard even to speak broadly about Austrian rieslings alone. Rieslings from Wachau tend to be the richest and most concentrated, though the best are refined and graceful, too. As with many German rieslings, those from the Wachau may carry nomenclature indicating the level of ripeness at the time of harvest, with *steinfeder* at the lower end, *federspiel* meaning riper yet, and *smaragd* the most ripe.

Many fine rieslings also come from Kamptal and Kremstal. While those three regions are the best known, other regions are showing what they can do with riesling as well, like Wagram and Weinviertel, although any rieslings from Weinviertel will most likely be labeled "Niederösterreich," a vague, generic appellation that's used because Weinviertel officially permits only grüner veltliner among white wines.

Even Vienna is producing some fine rieslings, believe it or not. Vienna is the only great metropolis to be a significant grape-growing region, with almost two thousand acres of vines within its borders and its own appellation, Wien. After years of producing mediocre wines that were consumed locally, energetic young growers and producers have made great strides. Now, not only are the rieslings of Vienna worth drinking, you no longer have to go there to find them. 🍷

ERIC RIPERT, THE CHEF AND CO-OWNER OF LE BERNARDIN IN NEW YORK, once pointed out that for a salty shellfish broth you need clams. With mussels, your broth will be sweeter, he said. I had that advice in mind with lemony Austrian rieslings that also had an alluring, fruity mellowness combined with a persuasive, clean finish. The mellowness suggested mussels, and the sweet richness of their broth. Instead of standard moules marinières, I decided to try some diced unpeeled apples with shallots as the base for the white wine broth, with excellent results. The apples became just tender enough as they cooked in the white wine with the mussels, still retaining their identity and contributing the perfect suggestion of fruity acidity to the dish.

Mussels in Green Apple Broth

TIME: 45 MINUTES

2 tablespoons extra virgin olive oil

1 cup minced shallots

1 Granny Smith apple, cored and diced

1 teaspoon grated lemon zest

3 fresh thyme sprigs

Freshly ground white pepper

2 cups dry white wine

3 pounds mussels, scrubbed and debearded

1 tablespoon unsalted butter

1 tablespoon minced fresh flat-leaf parsley leaves

1. Warm the oil in a heavy 4-quart saucepan. Add the shallots and cook over low heat until soft but not browned, about 8 minutes. Stir in the apple, lemon zest, and thyme. Season with white pepper. Add the wine and bring to a simmer.

2. Add the mussels, cover, and cook over medium heat until they open, about 10 minutes. Use a slotted spoon to transfer the mussels to a bowl, leaving the broth in the saucepan. Some of the apple will cling to the mussels, some will remain in the saucepan; that's fine. Cover the mussels. Stir the butter and parsley into the broth and bring back to a simmer.

3. Spoon the mussels into soup plates, ladle the hot broth over, and serve.

YIELD: 3 TO 4 MAIN-COURSE OR 6 APPETIZER SERVINGS

COOK'S NOTES: Some of your riesling is the obvious choice for the broth, though dry hard cider to complement the apples would be another fine option. 🥂

FINGER LAKES RIESLINGS

You can search all over the United States and find some pretty good rieslings. They're made in Washington, in Oregon, in Napa Valley, even in Michigan. But no American wine region is making better rieslings than the Finger Lakes of New York, where cool-climate viticulture is not just a talking point but a reality.

The lakes, deep claw marks left in the earth of west-central New York by glaciers moving south from the Hudson Bay, are crucial to the wine-making culture. The great depth of their waters nudges this otherwise inhospitable region to a level of bare tolerance for the fine wine grapes planted on the lakes' slopes. In winter, the lakes almost never freeze, moderating harsh cold to protect the dormant vines, while in summer they air-condition the vineyards.

The lakes themselves, of course, are gorgeous, long, and among the deepest in North America, but never so wide that you can't see across to the other side. Much of the wine activity is clustered around three of the central lakes, Keuka, Seneca, and Cayuga, where the best vineyards are planted on the surrounding slopes.

No particular style of riesling prevails in the Finger Lakes. You will find deeply minerally dry rieslings as well as lightly sweet rieslings patterned on the kabinetts and spätleses of Germany. Mostly, it depends on a producer's inclination, and many producers make an assortment of styles.

The triumph of Finger Lakes riesling is a recent phenomenon, given the long history of grape growing in the area. Plantings of vines in the region took off in the nineteenth century, but most were either native grapes like concord and catawba, or French-American hybrids like cayuga, rather than vinifera grapes, which originated in the Old World and account for almost all of the world's fine wines.

Not until the 1950s, when Konstantin Frank, a refugee from Ukraine, arrived in the Finger Lakes and started his Vinifera Wine Cellars, did a concerted effort begin to demonstrate that vinifera grapes could grow in the cool, wet climate. Dr. Frank planted dozens of grape varieties to see which would thrive. But it was Hermann J. Wiemer, in the 1970s and '80s, who insisted on emphasizing riesling.

In the twenty-first century, Wiemer, which has been passed on to a new generation of managers, along with Ravines and a half dozen other producers, are making world-class rieslings. Even so, it's clear that producers still have plenty of room for improvement. Yields are often high; lower yields would increase complexity. And for riesling, machine harvesting is the general rule, with exceptions like Ravines and Wiemer. It is cheaper and easier than harvesting by hand, but it gives winemakers less control over the quality of the grapes that go into the wine.

Nonetheless, if the destination is still in the distance, the Finger Lakes region has already come a long way. 🍷

WHITE CLAM PIZZA IS A FAVORITE IN THE NORTHEAST where hard-shell clams yield an abundant harvest. Bacon and cheese are all the pizza needs in addition to chopped clams. Using the pizza as my inspiration, I made clam quesadillas that I seared on the grill. Still sizzling hot, with the mellow cheese starting to ooze, I cut them into wedges that disappeared almost as fast as the quenching glasses of wine. They were lunch, but could as easily have been the centerpiece for a late-afternoon gathering.

White Clam Quesadillas

TIME: 30 MINUTES

2 ounces smoky slab bacon, diced fine

4 garlic cloves, slivered

1 large jalapeño, seeded and slivered

2 scallions, finely chopped

1 teaspoon ground cumin

12 cherrystone clams, opened, drained, and meat coarsely chopped

4 wheat flour tortillas

4 ounces young Asiago cheese, slivered

1 tablespoon chopped fresh cilantro

2 tablespoons extra virgin olive oil

1. Light a grill, preferably charcoal. (Quesadillas can also be cooked on a griddle on top of the stove, or under the broiler.) While the grill is heating, sauté the bacon in a small skillet on medium heat until lightly colored. Add the garlic, jalapeño, and scallions. Continue to sauté until the garlic turns golden. Remove from the heat. Stir in the cumin. Transfer the mixture to a bowl and fold in the clams.

2. Place the tortillas on a work surface and divide the clam mixture among them, spreading it to within an inch of the edge. Scatter the cheese and cilantro over each. Fold the tortillas over and press down. Brush with oil on both sides.

3. Adjust the grill so the coals are moderately hot and not too close to the cooking grates. Place the quesadillas on the grill and use a spatula to press down on them. Watch closely so they do not burn; you may have to move them around a bit, depending on the heat. Grill for 2 to 3 minutes per side, until nicely browned.

4. Transfer to a cutting board and cut each quesadilla into 4 wedges. Arrange on a platter and serve.

YIELD: 4 SERVINGS

COOK'S NOTES: With a small portable grill you can prepare the quesadillas to cook at the beach or in the park. But if the weather does not cooperate, sear them on a griddle or under the broiler.

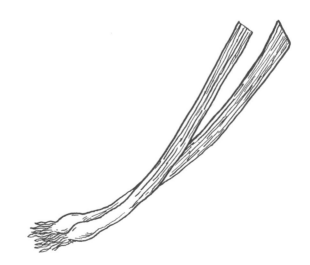

RIESLINGS OF ALSACE

One of the more disquieting issues for wine lovers in the last twenty years or so was the evolution of Alsatian rieslings from dry and somewhat austere to discernibly sweet. Of course, there were exceptions—producers like Trimbach were unwavering in their devotion to dry riesling. But often the presence of residual sugar has been unmistakable.

Now, it may be that the pendulum is swinging back, at least it is in vintages like 2008, which produced a parade of stony, taut, complex, and at times majestic wines.

Why did the wines from Alsace become sweeter? In some cases, no doubt, mass-market producers and *négociants* have intentionally catered to consumers who like a little sweetness, even if they say they prefer dry wines. Many American producers do the same.

Among more conscientious producers, efforts to cut back yields to make wines of greater intensity and concentration can result in grapes of profoundly high sugar levels. These producers also believe in intervening as little as possible in the wine-making, so if the fermentation stopped before all the sugar had been converted into alcohol, well, they believed, that's what nature intended. Making the wines dry might have resulted in absurdly high levels of alcohol in any case. You could say these wines ended up sweet with the best of intentions.

Of course, nothing is intrinsically wrong with sweet wines as long as two conditions are met. First, the sweetness should not come as a surprise. The wines should be clearly labeled as such. The German labeling system, as arcane and complicated as it may seem, ensures pretty much that you know what you are getting.

Second, the wines must be balanced. That is, if a wine does contain residual sugar, it must also contain sufficient acidity to make it invigorating, not flat and fatiguing. Not to belabor the comparison with German rieslings, but they live in a lacy, ethereal world in which, if the residual sugar is high, the alcohol is low, and with enough acidity the wines are delicate and crystalline. In Alsace, where the wines are much more powerful, even wines with residual sugar can have a lot of alcohol, which makes them feel bigger, sweeter, and more voluminous.

To combat this lack of balance, one of Alsace's greatest producers, Zind Humbrecht, altered its viticulture in an effort to produce grapes that achieve ripeness earlier, with less sugar and greater acidity. Its 2008s were complex, minerally, and beautifully balanced.

By any estimation, Alsace is one of the planet's greatest places to grow riesling. Wine lovers will be thrilled to find these wines restored as an option. I personally will still be cautious with Alsace, researching as best I can a particular wine's style before a purchase. But I will be hopeful. 🍷

THOUGH MOST WINES ARE GENEROUS AND FORGIVING, suitable for a wide range of dishes, some classic combinations are too compelling to ignore. Alsatian rieslings and choucroute is a good example. The bracing acidity of the wine is often kissed with a touch of sweetness, and both characteristics can handle tart, briny sauerkraut. But in this recipe, instead of with the usual array of pork and sausages, the sauerkraut is baked with seafood, including some smoked, for a version of the dish I also enjoyed in Alsace at a Strasburg restaurant called Le Crocodil.

Seafood Choucroute

TIME: 1 HOUR

2 ounces smoky slab bacon, diced

8 sea scallops, side tendon trimmed, patted dry

1 cup chopped leeks (white part only)

4 garlic cloves, sliced

1 Granny Smith apple, peeled, cored, and cut into 1-inch dice

1 smoked trout, skinned, boned, and broken into chunks

1 cup dry riesling

1½ pounds sauerkraut, drained and squeezed dry

Salt and freshly ground black pepper

12 small (2-inch) round or oval white potatoes, peeled

12 mussels, scrubbed and debearded

2 fresh trout fillets, about 6 ounces each, skinned

Juice of ½ lemon

1 tablespoon chopped fresh tarragon leaves

1. Place the bacon in a 4-quart stove-top casserole that can go to the table and set over medium heat. When the bacon is lightly brown, remove it, leaving the fat. Add the scallops and sear briefly in the casserole on high. Remove the scallops. Return the bacon to the pan, reduce the heat to low, add the leeks and garlic, and cook until softened. Stir in the apple, cook for about 1 minute, then add the smoked trout. Add the wine, bring to a simmer, and stir in the sauerkraut. Tuck the scallops into the sauerkraut. Season with salt and pepper. Cover and simmer for 20 minutes.

2. At the same time, bring a pot of salted water to a boil. Add the potatoes and simmer until tender, 15 to 20 minutes. Drain and return to the pot. Cover to keep warm.

3. Tuck the mussels into the sauerkraut around the edges of the casserole. Cut the fresh trout into 2-inch pieces and place on top of the sauerkraut. Sprinkle with the lemon juice. Cover and cook until the mussels have opened and the fresh trout turns opaque, about 6 minutes. Scatter with the tarragon and serve from the casserole with the potatoes on the side.

YIELD: 4 SERVINGS

COOK'S NOTES: Choucroute garni, with pork, is usually served with mustard on the side. With seafood, if you want a condiment, consider tartar sauce, mustardy ravigote, or a horseradish sauce.

I FIND CRABMEAT AND RIESLING TO BE AN ESPECIALLY WINNING MATCH. Spaghetti dressed with tart-sweet cherry tomatoes, bracing arugula, and crabmeat is hardly traditional fare for Alsatian rieslings, but it does the trick. And the final dusting of toasted bread crumbs adds to the allure.

Spaghetti with Crabmeat, Tomatoes, and Arugula

TIME: 45 MINUTES

1 cup loosely packed diced sourdough country bread

⅓ cup extra virgin olive oil

1 tablespoon chopped garlic plus ¼ cup sliced

6 fresh oregano sprigs, chopped

Salt and freshly ground black pepper

2 pints small cherry or grape tomatoes (about 50)

12 ounces spaghetti

2 tablespoons unsalted butter

1 pound jumbo lump crabmeat

1 bunch arugula, heavy stems removed (about 2 cups)

1. Heat the oven to 400°F. Toss the bread cubes with 2 tablespoons of the oil and the chopped garlic. Spread in a small baking dish and bake until lightly browned, about 15 minutes, tossing from time to time. Set aside to cool, then grind to make crumbs and set aside. Increase the oven temperature to 450°F.

2. Place 1 teaspoon of the sliced garlic, 2 tablespoons of the remaining oil, and a pinch of the oregano in a bowl. Add the tomatoes and season with salt and pepper. Spread in a baking dish and roast until the tomatoes start to burst, about 10 minutes. Remove from the oven and set aside.

3. Bring a large pot of salted water to a boil. Boil the spaghetti until al dente, about 8 minutes.

4. While the spaghetti cooks, heat the remaining oil and the butter in a large sauté pan on medium. Add the remaining sliced garlic and cook until lightly colored. Add the roasted tomatoes and their juices. Cook on low a few minutes. Fold in the crabmeat and the remaining oregano. When the spaghetti is done, remove 1 cup of the pasta water and add it to the tomatoes. Drain the spaghetti and add to the pan. Toss. Taste for seasoning. Fold in the arugula, and toss all the ingredients together. Transfer to a large warm bowl or individual plates, dust with bread crumbs, and serve.

YIELD: 4 SERVINGS

COOK'S NOTES: Other seafood, like quartered sea scallops, small shrimp, or diced lobster, can be used in place of the crabmeat. If the seafood is raw, cook it with the tomatoes in the sauté pan. 🧂

LET'S ASSUME DRY RIESLINGS HERE, NOTHING LATE-HARVEST. And then you have a wine that offers the right amount of fruit and plenty of acid to pair with ripe tomatoes, sweet corn, and a good dose of lemon. This is a seasonal dish that begs for summer's golden bounty. Excellent served directly, it can also wait a bit and be enjoyed just warm, al fresco, in early evening before the sun slips away.

Chicken Paillards with Corn Salad

TIME: 30 MINUTES

1 tablespoon strong Dijon mustard

¼ cup plus 1 tablespoon lemon juice

2 skinless and boneless chicken breasts (about 1¼ pounds) pounded thin

3 tablespoons extra virgin olive oil

½ cup chopped onion

Kernels from 2 ears corn

1 jalapeño, seeded and minced

1 medium yellow summer squash, diced

Salt and freshly ground black pepper

1 medium yellow tomato, diced

⅓ cup flour

2 tablespoons minced fresh cilantro leaves

1. Mix the mustard and ¼ cup of the lemon juice in a shallow dish. Cut each chicken breast in half, place in the mustard mixture, turn to coat both sides, and set aside in the refrigerator for at least 30 minutes.

2. Heat 1 tablespoon of the oil in a large skillet, add the onion, and sauté on low a few minutes, until softened. Add the corn, jalapeño, and squash and continue to cook until the vegetables are tender. Season with salt and pepper. Remove from the heat, fold in the tomato, add the remaining 1 tablespoon lemon juice, and set aside.

3. Remove the chicken from the marinade and dust with the flour. Heat the remaining 2 tablespoons oil in a large cast-iron skillet or grill pan and sear the chicken, turning once, until just cooked through. Arrange on a serving platter. Add the oil from the skillet to the corn salad, fold in the cilantro, and spoon the salad over and around the chicken.

YIELD: 4 SERVINGS

COOK'S NOTES: Though the recipe is designed to be made with chicken, it works equally well with fish fillets like fluke or flounder. The cooking time will be a couple of minutes less. 🧂

VOUVRAY

Perhaps you have not yet been bitten by the chenin blanc bug and transported to a world of luminous wines made in an astounding range of styles. If this is true, then opportunity is about to pull a cork for you.

The marketplace is awash with a bevy of superb Vouvrays, many priced gently given their high quality, especially in comparison with those other white grapes of note, riesling and chardonnay. If I sound a tad breathless, well, so be it. It's simply that chenin blanc wines offer so much pleasure and intrigue, yet are so underappreciated.

I have no doubt that their time will come soon enough, and not just for Vouvray but for the entire cluster of chenin blancs from the Loire: Savennières, Montlouis, Anjou, Jasnières, and the rest. Consider how long people were trumpeting the virtues of riesling before consumers began to discover them for themselves. But chenin blanc wines seem not to have the determined support that riesling did before it took off.

Chenin blanc has a lot in common with riesling. Both grapes are versatile, making wonderful wines that encompass the range from bone dry to richly, unctuously sweet. And the wines from both rely on a pulsing acidity for structure, balance, and freshness. But when it comes to achieving widespread popularity, riesling has a significant advantage. Distinctive versions come from many places in the world, from Germany and Alsace to New York to Western Australia.

By contrast, apart from a few lonely outposts scattered here and there, chenin blanc shines only in the Loire Valley. And while the wines can differ significantly depending on where along the Loire the grapes are grown and by whom they are tended, only Vouvray has achieved any sort of name recognition beyond the ring of worshippers.

As much as I love Vouvray, the wine is not without its frustrations. While the quality in general is fairly high, particularly because American importers have already edited the selection to a certain extent, it's not easy to tell by looking at the label whether wines will be dry or will display some sweetness.

Because dryness designations are not required, dry Vouvrays are sometimes, but not always, labeled "sec." Compounding that problem, there is a lot of wiggle room between sec and "demi-sec," which can have quite a bit of residual sugar. Many wines end up in an in-between area known unofficially as "sec-tendre." Only occasionally will you see this term, or simply "tendre," on a label.

Aside from the confusion that consumers may experience, the difficulty in determining which Vouvrays are truly dry is not necessarily a bad thing. The crucial point rests on that much-abused term "balance." Chenin blanc, with its powerful acidity, can sometimes be punishingly austere. With proper balance, Vouvrays with a little sweetness can still feel dry and be thoroughly refreshing. In fact, some people make the argument that a demi-sec Vouvray may be the truest expression of the wine. Well, I like Vouvrays all ways.

One last great thing about Vouvray: Even the best producers tend to be moderately priced. This, alas, is a consequence of the grim lack of demand for chenin blanc wines in general. You may as well take advantage of it. 🍷

ASIAN RESTAURANTS OUGHT TO PAY MORE ATTENTION TO DRY VOUVRAYS. Like rieslings, which are frequently poured with Thai, Vietnamese, and Chinese dishes, Vouvrays knit bright minerality into their alluring canvas of citric and floral aromas and flavors, sometimes kissed with spice or sugar. They are ready for action the minute the fragrances of ginger, coriander, and lemongrass waft from the serving bowl. Seafood complements the wine and broccoli adds crunch and color.

Thai-Style Scallops and Broccoli

TIME: 30 MINUTES

2 tablespoons chopped shallots

1½ tablespoons chopped fresh lemongrass (cores of 2 bulbs)

1½ tablespoons chopped peeled fresh ginger

1 large garlic clove, chopped

2 teaspoons Thai shrimp paste or anchovy paste

1 teaspoon coriander seeds

Grated zest and juice of ½ lime

2 tablespoons vegetable oil

½ pound broccoli florets (from about 1 bunch)

1 pound sea scallops, side tendon removed

⅓ cup fish stock

2 tablespoons unsweetened coconut milk

½ teaspoon Sriracha (Thai red chili sauce), or to taste

Salt

1 cup jasmine rice, steamed

1. Combine the shallots, lemongrass, ginger, garlic, shrimp paste, coriander seeds, lime zest, and lime juice in a food processor (a small one works best) or a large mortar. Thrash to a paste.

2. Heat the oil in a heavy sauté pan on high. Add the seasoning paste and cook, stirring, for 1 minute. Add the broccoli, stir, and add the scallops. Reduce the heat to medium and cook, stirring gently, for 3 minutes more. Add the fish stock, coconut milk, and Sriracha, and simmer for 2 minutes more. Add salt to taste and serve with steamed jasmine rice.

YIELD: 3 TO 4 SERVINGS

COOK'S NOTES: This recipe, a template for many Thai dishes, starts with a seasoning or curry paste of some kind, which is heated and becomes the foundation for a stir-fry. Almost any stir-fry. It does require some ethnic shopping, though most of the ingredients have become mainstream. 🥫

VOUVRAYS HAVE A PARTICULAR AFFINITY for sweet-and-sour flavors. A Venetian classic, fish in saor, is a wonderful summer dish. It can be made in advance and left to marinate, then served at room temperature alongside an elegant Vouvray. "In saor" refers to the sweet vinegar and onion marinade for the fish. For this variation I used cipollini onions and fresh local fluke, though any mild, white-fleshed fish will do.

Venetian-Style Fluke in Saor

TIME: 45 MINUTES, PLUS AT LEAST 30 MINUTES COOLING

18 cipollini onions, trimmed and peeled

½ cup golden raisins

1 cup dry white wine

½ cup all-purpose flour

Salt and freshly ground black pepper

2 pounds fluke fillets, in 6 pieces

¼ cup extra virgin olive oil

2 tablespoons pine nuts

1 tablespoon capers, drained

1 tablespoon white wine vinegar

1 teaspoon sugar

Fresh flat-leaf parsley for garnish

1. Place the onions in a saucepan, cover with water, and simmer for 10 minutes. Drain. Meanwhile, place the raisins in a bowl, cover with ¼ cup of the wine, and set aside. Season the flour with salt and pepper. Dust the fillets with the flour.

2. Heat the oil in a large skillet. Add the fish and sauté over medium-high heat, turning once, until golden and cooked through, about 10 minutes. Transfer the fish to a warm platter.

3. Add the onions and pine nuts to the skillet and sauté until lightly browned. Remove from the pan and scatter around the fish. Add the raisins, all of the wine, including the wine used for the raisins, and the capers, vinegar, and sugar to the skillet. Cook over low heat until the mixture has thickened slightly. Season with salt and pepper and spoon over the fish. Allow to cool to room temperature. Serve garnished with parsley, or refrigerate, then bring to room temperature before serving.

YIELD: 6 SERVINGS

COOK'S NOTES: This can be turned into a vegetarian dish using slices of firm tofu or cauliflower in place of the fish. Omit the flour.

TEMPERATURE

What's the best way to get the most out of your glass of wine? Serve it at the proper temperature. Simply put, most good white wines are served too cold.

It's basic science: Raising the temperature at which a wine is served allows the various flavor compounds in a wine to evaporate and rise, thus adding to a wine's aroma, which contributes greatly to enjoyment on the palate. Yet, because we have come to expect white wine to be served at refrigerator temperature, good wines are often over-chilled, depriving us of the complex aromas and delicious flavors in the glass. I emphasize "good," because chilling a mediocre wine often hides its flaws, turning it at least into a pleasant refreshment.

For me, a good white wine need never be more than lightly chilled, say fifty-five degrees, fifty at the coolest. If you want to be fine about it, you can adjust temperature by weight, serving lighter-bodied white wines like Muscadets or Mosel rieslings a little cooler than, say, white Burgundies, but I wouldn't be too obsessive about this.

Restaurants often pose difficulties. White wines often come to the table straight from the refrigerator and head straight for the ice-water bucket. Many sommeliers know better, but they are accustomed to consumers who want to keep white wine a notch below freezing. You must take control of the situation and request that the bottle be kept on the table.

Some people might argue that sparkling wines need to be served colder than dry still whites, but I'm afraid I must take the other side. I feel about sparkling wines the same as I do about still whites—if the wine is complex and balanced, its personality will be hidden if served too cold. But if the sparkling wine is not that good, allowing it to warm up from refrigerator temperature will only reveal its flaws.

Similarly, red wines are often served too warm. The conventional wisdom that red wine should be served at room temperature is absurd. Is that particular room in a Louisiana bayou in July or in a stone cellar in Scotland in November? Who knows?

If served too warm, even a good red wine can taste flat and inert. In general, reds should be served less cool than whites, but most definitely not warm. Even so, sometimes weather and mood call for a red served very cool. In those cases you don't want a big, tannic wine, but a softer, simpler, more accessible wine, which will take to the cold far better.

One day more restaurants will understand that ice buckets are better suited for cooling off reds than overchilling whites.

—EA

SAVENNIÈRES

Savennières is a demanding wine. The characteristics that make it so distinctive and beautiful require attention and thought, which is perhaps more effort than many people would wish to devote to a beverage.

But that is the trade-off. Savennières, from the Anjou region of the Loire Valley, is intense and austere, and not quickly accessible. Unlike Sancerre, its Loire cousin, which comes with an easy Cliffs Notes explanation—It's just sauvignon blanc!—Savennières does not lend itself to the sort of high-concept simplification by analogy that can appease the puzzlement of studio executives and wine novices alike.

Sure, one could describe Savennières as 100 percent chenin blanc, but what does that get you? Chenin blanc is one of the most underrated and underappreciated grapes in the world, achieving greatness only in the Loire Valley, though promising wines do come from South Africa and isolated pockets of the United States. Many people may have heard of Vouvray, a chenin blanc wine from the Touraine region of the Loire east of Savennières, but I doubt many people can summon an impression of what the wines are like.

Even if Vouvray were to strike a flash of recognition, it offers a very different expression of chenin blanc from that of Savennières. Vouvray is generally easier and friendlier, less of a cerebral wine than Savennières.

I don't mean to suggest that some consumers don't have the ability to appreciate Savennières. Not at all. I'm just saying that it is not for everybody. It can't be. Very few producers make Savennières, and only small amounts are available. But if you decide to try it, and are patient enough to savor a bottle over the course of a meal, the pleasures of Savennières are many.

Great Savennières offers a spectrum of unusual flavors: beeswax, citrus, and spice, with a mineral, saline quality thrown in for good measure. Combine this with the floral, honeysuckle edge that I often find in chenin blanc, and a texture that is typically and paradoxically rich, viscous, and wonderfully light, and you have one complex, unconventional wine that is a long way from chardonnay and sauvignon blanc.

These wines practically demand to be served with food. They are also excellent candidates for decanting, as the air seems to help bring the flavors to life. In fact, Nicolas Joly, the most prominent Savennières producer, recommends opening bottles of his wine a full forty-eight hours before serving, not really a practical notion, especially if you encounter a bottle in a restaurant.

Savennières can age beautifully, but it has a maddening habit of shutting down for a few years after its period of youthful liveliness. Predicting a trajectory is not easy, given the differences in producers and vintages. Committed Savennières lovers solve this problem by buying it by the case and perhaps sacrificing a bottle midway in hopes of succeeding with the rest. 🍷

SAVENNIÈRES MIGHT BE CONSIDERED THE ULTIMATE EXPRESSION of the chenin blanc grape, and not just from the Loire Valley. Some consider it to be among the greatest white wines in the world. So what will do justice to a glass or bottle of Savennières? I'd opt for lobster. It's got cachet and succulence to spare for wines that deliver elegant mellowness wrapped in penetrating acidity that stands up to the sumptuously creamy, garlicky seafood stew from the south of France.

Lobster Bourride

TIME: 45 MINUTES

2 cups fish stock

Large pinch of saffron threads

12 thin slices baguette

1½ cups extra virgin olive oil

6 large garlic cloves, 2 of the cloves sliced

1 large egg

Juice of 1 lemon

Salt

Cayenne or Espelette pepper

1 medium fennel bulb

1 cup finely chopped leeks (white part only)

1 red bell pepper, cored, seeded, and finely chopped

1½ cups dry white wine

2 tablespoons pastis (Pernod, Ricard, or absinthe)

Four 1-pound lobsters, cooked, cooled, shelled with meat in 2-inch chunks

1. Warm the stock in a saucepan, add the saffron, and set aside. Lightly toast the baguette slices and brush with 1 tablespoon of the oil.

2. Turn on a food processor. Drop 4 of the garlic cloves into the feed tube and process until minced. Scrape down the sides of the bowl. Place the egg in the bowl and process briefly. With the processor running, slowly pour in 1 cup of the oil. The mixture will thicken to a mayonnaise. Add 2 tablespoons of the lemon juice, process briefly, and season with salt and cayenne. Refrigerate.

3. Mince fennel fronds to make 1 tablespoon. Discard the fennel stems and remaining fronds. Trim and finely chop the bulb.

4. Heat the remaining oil in a 3- to 4-quart casserole. Add the chopped fennel bulb, leeks, bell pepper, and the sliced garlic. Sauté on low heat until soft. Add the wine and pastis. Simmer briefly. Add the fish stock with saffron. Season with salt and cayenne. Set aside until 10 minutes before serving.

5. Ten minutes before serving, bring the broth to a simmer. Add the lobster. On low heat, gradually whisk in the reserved mayonnaise. Heat to a gentle simmer but do not boil. Place 2 baguette toasts in each of four soup plates, spoon in the bourride, and top with another toast and some minced fennel fronds. Serve.

YIELD: 4 SERVINGS

COOK'S NOTES: You can buy shelled lobster meat for this recipe—you'll need about 1½ pounds—but I find that buying and cooking whole small lobsters is much more economical. Boil your one-pounders for about 10 minutes.

MÂCONNAIS
The wines of the Mâconnais region of France are nobody's idea of a new discovery. Back in the 1980s, when I began drinking a lot of wine, they were a reliable source for fresh, crisp, inexpensive whites, and they have remained so. Yet the wines that used to define the Mâconnais are just a part of a much wider range of styles today, though a large part. This ungainly region in southern Burgundy, where chardonnay is the white grape just as in the Côte d'Or, now produces far more interesting wines than those simple bistro guzzlers.

For almost twenty years, a growing number of Mâconnais producers have been approaching their viticulture and wine making with a seriousness of purpose once reserved for more exalted regions. At the same time, celebrated Burgundy producers like Dominique Lafon of Comtes Lafon, the renowned Meursault estate, and Anne-Claude Leflaive of Domaine Leflaive, another top white Burgundy producer, sensed the untapped potential of the region and invested in it. And they are now making excellent Mâconnais wines.

This regional metamorphosis has not been widely recognized. Only in the more enlightened French restaurants, for example, will you find good Mâconnais wines. But for people who love white Burgundy and dread its expense, the Mâconnais offers an introduction at a much lower price point than what the Côte de Beaune, the heart of white Burgundy, has to offer. If the Mâconnais is well beyond discovery, it's fair to say it is ready for rediscovery.

Unlike the Côte d'Or, where the vineyards are ranked in a meticulous hierarchy, the Mâconnais offers only a rudimentary sense of vineyard quality. Plain Mâcon is the lowest rung of the ladder. A step above is Mâcon-Villages, or Mâcon followed by the name of a particular village, or Viré-Clessé, two villages combined into a single appellation. And that's it.

The Mâconnais also includes the Saint-Véran area on the southern end of the region, just north of Beaujolais, and wines centered around the town of Pouilly, which will be addressed elsewhere. I often find Saint-Vérans to possess a bit more structure and complexity than the Mâcon wines, though there is by no means a consensus on that.

Modern Mâconnais offers a diversity of styles and approaches. The best are lively, vivacious, and energetic with taut minerally flavors. Others can be rich and lightly fruity, or surprisingly oaky. And, of course, the familiar crisp, clean, easygoing wines are common as well.

One might see this variety of styles as regional inconsistency, and to lament that consumers won't know what they are getting when they buy. Yet it suggests as well that we can no longer think of the Mâconnais as a homogeneous region. It is a union of many varying terroirs that will display different characteristics if the grapes are grown and the wine is made with care.

While it's perhaps flattering to link these Mâconnais wines to their siblings in the Côte de Beaune, might it be demeaning as well because the comparison diminishes their own identity? Perhaps. But the Mâconnais wines are stuck in the white Burgundy context, and right now they don't look too shabby. 🍷

GOING BACK THIRTY OR FORTY YEARS, when wine drinking in America was an uptight affair and never by the glass, white, from France, was the usual choice with sole Véronique or sautéed chicken breasts. And a Mâcon, notably Mâcon-Lugny "Les Charmes" or a Mâcon-Villages from a reliable négociant like Drouhin, would often be the white to order or to open. Did we even know these were chardonnays? Today, the traditional Mâcons are worth remembering. On the heels of a bourride (see page 69), here you have a chicken bouillabaisse to serve with a graceful Mâcon. Except that it's made with chicken instead of fish, with a broth bolstered by chicken stock instead of fish stock, the components of this dish are exactly like a classic bouillabaisse: fennel, saffron, some ripe tomatoes, garlic, thyme, white wine, anise-flavored pastis, and the French garlic mayonnaise aioli.

Chicken Bouillabaisse

TIME: 1½ HOURS

1 cup chicken stock

½ teaspoon saffron threads

6 chicken thighs, with bones

3 chicken breast halves, with bones, each cut in two

4 tablespoons extra virgin olive oil

1 cup chopped leeks (white and light green parts only)

1 cup chopped fennel bulb

3 garlic cloves, minced

2 cups finely chopped peeled ripe tomatoes

⅓ cup dry white wine

¼ cup pastis (Pernod, Ricard, or absinthe)

6 fresh thyme sprigs

Salt

Cayenne

Boiled small potatoes, toasted baguette slices, and garlic mayonnaise (aioli), for serving

1. In a saucepan, heat the stock to a simmer, remove from the heat, add the saffron, and set aside. Dry the chicken pieces.

2. Heat 2 tablespoons of the oil in a large casserole or sauté pan. Add the chicken, skin side down, and sear over high heat until golden, turning once. Remove from the pan and set aside on a platter. Discard any fat left in the pan. Add the leeks, fennel, and garlic. Lower the heat and cook until soft. Add the stock and saffron, scraping the bottom of the pan. Add the tomatoes, wine, pastis, and thyme. Bring to a fast simmer and cook for 20 minutes.

3. Return the chicken to the pan along with any accumulated juices from the platter and simmer for about 30 minutes, until cooked through. Lower the heat, season with salt and cayenne, and add the remaining 2 tablespoons oil. Serve in soup plates or deep bowls and pass the potatoes, toast, and aioli alongside.

YIELD: 6 SERVINGS

COOK'S NOTES: Using chicken in place of seafood makes this dish more forgiving because overcooking is not as important a consideration. Double the recipe and you have a fine party dish for a buffet. 🍶

CHABLIS

Let's please take a moment to recalibrate our taste buds and expectations. We're about to leave a world of size and power to journey into the realm of fine distinctions, where subtlety, balance, and keen precision hold sway. We'll need some quiet, because the journey at first requires concentration. But soon effortless comprehension will set in, as aromas and flavors become easier to distinguish. Breathe easy, because this exploration carries its own reward: Chablis.

We've come a long way from the days when wine writers were required to insert the obligatory disclaimer differentiating real Chablis, made only in the Chablis region of Burgundy and only from chardonnay grapes, from the cheap generic stuff produced in California that for so long was unworthy of the name. Yet, what does it mean to say Chablis is 100 percent chardonnay? It doesn't resemble California chardonnay, or even chardonnay from the rest of Burgundy. In fact, Chablis, the region, is closer to Champagne than to the Côte d'Or. Really, it's like no other chardonnay in the world. That's part of its beauty.

To understand Chablis, naturally, you have to drink it. This takes a particular kind of patience that maybe isn't so evident in an era that seems to prefer more obvious, flamboyant wines. Chablis, especially young Chablis, can be stark, stern, and austere—steely is a common description—with flavors and aromas that do not connote lavish cornucopias of tropical fruit. Instead they bring to mind minerals, oyster shells, and stones; apple and citrus fruits; and occasionally herbs like tarragon and anise.

Bad versions can be cramped and miserly, and even a fine bottle can offer a fairly narrow spectrum of possibilities. Yet the effect can be deep and intense. As with the compressed complexity of a still life, the greatness of Chablis lies in the exquisite details rather than in the piling up of themes in a larger canvas.

Good Chablis often has a pale yellow color, bordering on green, and chalky aromas, bringing to mind images of earth—white earth—the sort of limestone soils and fossilized oyster beds found in the best Chablis plots. It is bone dry and has an aroma more savory than sweet.

While all good Chablis wines share these characteristics, they can be subtly different stylistically, even at the village level, which, in the Chablis totem pole, is near the base, just above Petit Chablis and under the midlevel premier crus and the top-of-the-heap grand crus. As you ascend to the premier cru and grand cru levels, the wines get richer and more detailed, though always with their distinctive chalky minerality. They also need more time to develop, but can often last for twenty years or so. Because good Chablis is subtle, it is crucial not to serve it too cold, which will mask the flavors. Barely cool is just about right.

Despite the historical inclusion of Chablis with Burgundy, the wines often remind me more of blanc de blancs Champagne and even Sancerre. The best sites in all three regions share the same chalky soils, as do the white cliffs of Dover, for that matter. Despite what sets the wines apart—Sancerre made from the sauvignon blanc grape, and blanc de blancs a chardonnay with fizz—the best versions all seem to display the characteristics of their shared soil more so than their differences. 🍷

TALK ABOUT WHITE CLIFFS OF DOVER—here's a very English predinner nibble, something that I enjoy in London, especially at Scott's, an elegant, classic seafood restaurant in Mayfair. It's perfect with a glass of Chablis. Potted seafood, almost like confit, is designed for keeping, thus having the advantage of being something to prepare days in advance. In England, the shrimp of choice are small brown ones. Tiny red Maine shrimp are a perfect substitute, as are rock shrimp.

Potted Shrimp

TIME: 20 MINUTES, PLUS 3 HOURS CHILLING

1 lemon

1 small onion, quartered

1 bay leaf

½ teaspoon whole black peppercorns

Salt

¾ pound peeled shrimp, as small as possible

12 tablespoons (1½ sticks) unsalted butter, softened

½ teaspoon ground mace

⅛ teaspoon cayenne, or to taste

2½ tablespoons anchovy paste

Freshly ground black pepper

Whole wheat or pumpernickel toast

1. Cut the lemon in half. Juice one half and set aside; cut the other half into 4 pieces. Place the cut lemon pieces, onion, bay leaf, peppercorns, and 1 teaspoon salt in a saucepan with 2 cups water. Bring to a simmer and cook for 10 minutes. Add the shrimp. When the water returns to a simmer, remove the shrimp, drain, and set aside to cool briefly. If the shrimp are not tiny ones from Maine or rock shrimp, chop them fairly fine.

2. Place the butter in a saucepan with the lemon juice, mace, cayenne, and anchovy paste. When the butter melts, whisk to blend and cook at a low simmer for 3 minutes. Remove from the heat. Stir in the shrimp. Season with salt and pepper.

3. Transfer the mixture to an 8-ounce crock or ramekin and refrigerate until the butter is solid, at least 3 hours. The dish will keep, refrigerated, for a week. Serve with toast.

YIELD: 8 TO 12 SERVINGS

COOK'S NOTES: Lump crabmeat, bits of lobster, or diced smoked trout or mackerel can replace the shrimp, if desired. 🗍

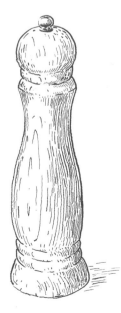

POUILLY-FUISSÉ When I was first learning about wine in the late
1970s, people had a word for Pouilly-Fuissé. It was "joke."

It was the go-to wine of the ignorant and the pseudosophisticated, attractive for its mellifluous, if not-easy-to-say French name, and little else. White wines were then ascendant, and Pouilly-Fuissé was a proto pinot grigio, in demand for every reason except for what was in the bottle.

Pouilly-Fuissé's problem was not its popularity. While the area around the towns of Pouilly and Fuissé, in the southern Mâconnais region of Burgundy, was blessed with great chardonnay vineyards, the 1970s were a nadir in French wine making. The industry had latched on to the notion of better wine making through chemistry and technology. The result was a profusion of herbicides and fertilizers, which produced overly abundant grapes, harvested early by mechanical pickers because growers feared the risk of waiting for optimal ripeness. It was a formula for diluted, acidic wines, which were also overpriced. Not every Pouilly-Fuissé fell into the sinkhole, but the reputation stuck.

While that reputation has been hard for Pouilly-Fuissé to live down, things have most definitely been looking up. A new generation of growers and producers is treating the land and the wine making with more respect, and the wines have improved greatly. It is still possible to find insipid, overpriced wines besmirching the name, but it is also just as easy to find delicious wines that speak of their terroir and do the region proud.

Rather than emphasize pronounced fruit flavors, the best Pouilly-Fuissés show a mouthwatering "drink me" texture and the sort of mineral flavors that Burgundy lovers prize. In general, Pouilly-Fuissés divide roughly into two main styles. One is the crisp, somewhat steely style associated with Mâconnais wines, with added depth and substance in the better versions. The other is a richer, more concentrated barrel-fermented style, like the whites of the Côte de Beaune.

This is partly a matter of winemaker inclination, but it can also be explained by geography. Wines from the northern Pouilly-Fuissé territory, around the town of Vergisson, which has a longer growing season, tend to be richer and more succulent, while those from the south, closer to the town of Chaintré, are usually leaner with more minerality. Incidentally, a small percentage of the wines known collectively as Pouilly-Fuissé may be called Pouilly-Vinzelles or Pouilly-Loché, after two other towns in the area.

Just as producers have everywhere else in France, those in Pouilly-Fuissé have learned that what sells internationally is quality. Americans who have long turned up their noses at Pouilly-Fuissé should take on a new challenge: proper pronunciation. For the record, it's pwee-fwee-SAY. 🍷

AH, POUILLY-FUISSÉ. I remember ordering it in the age of New York's grand French restaurants, back when La Caravelle was fresh and new, and a favorite for my husband and me was Café Argenteuil. Those memories return whenever there is Pouilly-Fuissé in my glass. And what did I eat back then? Why, sole Véronique with green grapes in a cream sauce. Someday I might try the sole again. But for now, I'm opting for a first course of baby pumpkins filled with mushrooms and a creamy sauce—a dish adapted from Las Ramblas, a rustic little Spanish restaurant in New York's Greenwich Village.

Baby Pumpkins with Mushrooms

TIME: 1½ HOURS

6 Jack-Be-Little mini pumpkins

2 tablespoons light brown sugar

2½ tablespoons unsalted butter

20 small cremini mushrooms, halved

Salt and freshly ground white pepper

1 tablespoon all-purpose flour

1⅓ cups heavy cream, scalded

¼ medium onion stuck with 8 whole cloves

½ cup Spanish tetilla or other semisoft cheese, like fontina Val d'Aosta, diced

2 teaspoons finely minced fresh chives

1. Heat the oven to 350°F. Use a sharp knife to cut the tops off the pumpkins, leaving about an inch of pumpkin around the stem. With a spoon, scoop out the strings and seeds. Put 1 teaspoon brown sugar into each pumpkin, restore the tops, and place the pumpkins in a baking dish. Add water to come up 1 inch. Place in the oven and bake until tender, about 1 hour.

2. Meanwhile, melt 1½ tablespoons of the butter in a small skillet. Sauté the mushrooms until just cooked through. Season with salt and white pepper. Set aside, covered.

3. Melt the remaining 1 tablespoon butter in a saucepan. Whisk in the flour, then slowly add the cream, whisking. Bring to a simmer and cook a few minutes until the sauce has thickened. Add the onion and simmer gently for 10 minutes. Strain the sauce and discard the onion. Return the sauce to the pan, add the cheese, and cook gently until it melts. Season with salt and white pepper.

4. When the pumpkins are done, divide the mushrooms among them. Add the sauce. Replace the tops. Just before serving, return the pumpkins to the oven for 10 to 15 minutes to heat through. Lift the tops, sprinkle the filling with the chives, replace the tops, and serve.

YIELD: 6 SERVINGS

COOK'S NOTES: Baby pumpkins are seasonal. The dish can also be baked in 4-ounce ramekins.

CÔTE DE BEAUNE BLANCS

The Côte de Beaune, the slender southern end of Burgundy's fabled Côte d'Or, is the spiritual home of chardonnay. Yes, chardonnay is now grown all over the world, but the reason for its special affiliation with the Côte de Beaune is evident in any good bottle of white Burgundy. It was the greatness of white Burgundy that inspired so many ambitious winemakers elsewhere to try their hands at chardonnay. Later on, the commercial success of these international chardonnays inspired even more plantings around the world. But, while many laudable expressions of chardonnay have been achieved, nothing is quite like the white Burgundy of the Côte de Beaune.

The most famous names roll off the tongue: Puligny and Chassagne with their grand cru caboose Montrachet; Meursault and Corton-Charlemagne. What makes the wines so magnificent?

Ample richness must be taken for granted among the best wines. The flavors are savory, nutlike, and mineral rather than pronouncedly fruity. Most important is the fine detailing of the land, etched with grace and articulation on the raw surface of the chardonnay.

It's a delicious education in terroir to stand in the cellar of, say, a Meursault vigneron and to sample in succession the youthful wine from each separate parcel. Starting with the village wines, you taste the broad outlines of the appellation. Then, perhaps a few individual village vineyards, and some *lieux-dits*, particular sites within vineyards in which the vigneron has detected specific traits. Moving up to premier cru, the more famous names begin to unfold: Les Poruzots, Les Genevrières, Les Charmes, Les Perrières, the traits becoming more distinct, the minerality becoming more pronounced, the sensations more focused and more intense. Each vigneron has a particular hierarchy in which you will taste the wines, each with a rationale arrived at over generations, perhaps over centuries.

Then come the grand crus, not in Meursault, which possesses none, but in Puligny, Chassagne, and Corton. Aficionados have their personal favorites. I love the fullness of Chassagne, the stoniness of Corton-Charlemagne, the precision of Puligny. Is any white wine greater than those of Le Montrachet itself? Well, riesling lovers may have an argument, as may those who find a greater consistency in Chevalier-Montrachet, a neighboring grand cru. Would that we could all study the issue in depth to arrive at our own conclusions.

These are the greatest names, but many more affordable white Burgundies come from the Côte de Beaune. Wines from Saint-Aubin, Saint-Romain, Auxey-Duresses, Monthélie, and the various Beaune appellations may not offer the magnificence of their more famous siblings, but they can be tremendously satisfying in their own right.

Not that white Burgundy is without serious problems. By all rights, these wines should age for decades. But since the mid-1990s the region has been bedeviled by the horror of premature oxidation, in which seemingly random bottles go bad years before their time. Many vignerons are struggling with this issue, which, by the way, is not entirely restricted to Burgundy but is most apparent there because these are the most age-worthy wines. For now, consumers must continue to be wary with their investments. 🍷

I THOUGHT SNAIL BUTTER, AN UNDERAPPRECIATED EMBELLISHMENT HERE, might bedazzle winter's harvest of precious bay scallops like emerald earrings with pale satin Vera Wang. Snails in snail butter are as Burgundian as it gets. Scallops are an easy alternative for a quick, festive first course to accompany whatever white Burgundy your wallet can manage. An advance detail can handle the snail butter and croutons, leaving the final baking to serving time.

Bay Scallops in Snail Butter

TIME: 30 MINUTES

4 garlic cloves

⅔ cup packed flat-leaf parsley leaves

8 tablespoons (1 stick) unsalted butter, softened

Salt and freshly ground black pepper

2 cups fresh ½-inch square croutons, preferably sourdough

1 pound Nantucket or Peconic Bay scallops

Juice of 1 lemon

1. Heat the oven to 500°F. Turn on a food processor. Drop in the garlic through the feed tube and process until minced. Scrape down the sides of the bowl. With the machine running, add the parsley through the feed tube. Scrape down the sides of the bowl. Add the butter and process until blended. Transfer the snail butter to a small bowl and season with salt and pepper.

2. Place the croutons in a single layer in a 9-by-13-inch baking dish. Place in the oven and bake until very lightly toasted, about 5 minutes. Remove the croutons from the dish.

3. Spread the snail butter in the warm baking dish. It will partly melt. Return the croutons to the dish. Season the scallops with salt and pepper and add to the dish in a single layer.

4. Place in the oven and bake for 5 minutes. Stir around to coat the scallops and croutons with the snail butter, rearrange in a single layer, and bake for 5 minutes more. Sprinkle with the lemon juice, toss lightly, and serve.

YIELD: 6 FIRST-COURSE SERVINGS

COOK'S NOTES: To serve with panache, use individual shallow ramekins for the final baking, and present by placing each on a folded napkin on an underplate. 🫙

OREGON CHARDONNAY

In the beginning, there was chardonnay, and it was not good. This was a blow to the pioneering wine producers of Oregon, who regarded their land as a sort of new Eden. Back in the 1960s and '70s, when the firmament of the Oregon wine industry was created, a lot of chardonnay was planted. And why not? Chardonnay was the single most popular fine white wine among Americans. It made sense to want to produce it. After all, pinot noir, the red grape of Burgundy, showed such promise in the Willamette Valley, Oregon's leading wine region. Wouldn't chardonnay, the white grape of Burgundy, do well, too?

But much of the chardonnay was planted without considering the particular conditions in Oregon and how they differed from those in California, where much of the popular chardonnay was grown. The leading chardonnay clone in Oregon then was more suitable for the warmer California weather and ripened too late for the shorter Oregon growing season. The result, for the most part, was mediocre wines. By the 1990s, the focus in Oregon had shifted to other white grapes like pinot gris. Meanwhile, Oregon wine producers mostly wanted to talk about pinot noir.

Nonetheless, dedicated chardonnay producers pressed on. Realizing their initial error, they carefully studied the characteristics of alternative clones. They deliberated over the proper rootstocks for the Willamette soils. The discussion of how best to grow chardonnay in Oregon was furthered by the arrival of Domaine Drouhin, one of the leading names in Burgundy, which established an Oregon outpost in 1987. Drouhin was followed by a new generation of Oregon producers, who had worked in Burgundy and had seen what could be achieved when vines and place were matched properly.

As a result, a second wave of Oregon chardonnay has appeared in the twenty-first century, the product this time of conscious decision-making and more confident winemakers. Naturally, the wines arrived complete with renewed marketing efforts—"the rebirth of Oregon chardonnay," that sort of thing.

In this case, however, it has not been all hype. The best versions show freshness, balance, and a subtle use of oak. Unusually for West Coast white wines, the better Oregon chardonnays do not emphasize bountiful fruit flavors. Rather, they are characterized by enticing textures with the occasional citrus, herbal, or floral accents. In sum, they show the attributes of cool-climate wines: liveliness and restraint rather than extravagance.

Nonethess, as far as chardonnay goes, Oregon remains a region in transition, still experimenting stylistically, like a sculptor chipping away at a block of marble, waiting for the terroir of the Willamette to reveal itself. Until it does, the wines seem to me more Mâconnais than Meursault.

That's not at all a criticism. The Mâcon is widely underrated. Good versions are rich with inviting textures and mineral flavors, not unlike the best of the Oregon chardonnays. 🍷

OREGON BORROWS FROM BURGUNDY'S PLAYLIST in vineyards planted with pinot noirs and chardonnays. That part of France also inspired dinner. The iconic coq au vin, replacing Chambertin with chardonnay, couldn't be a better idea. I went light with it, however, omitting bacon lardons. And I gave a nod to Oregon's truffle crop by finishing the sauce with a gloss of black truffle butter. It's a modest investment that elevates the dish, though a generous dollop of unsalted butter, especially if it's high-fat European-style, could also bolster the sauce, though with less foxy intrigue.

Coq au Vin Blanc

TIME: 1 HOUR 20 MINUTES

1 tablespoon grape seed oil

One 3½-pound chicken, cut into 10 pieces, backbone removed, patted dry

Salt and freshly ground white pepper

8 ounces white pearl onions, blanched for 3 minutes and peeled

1 medium onion, finely chopped

¼ cup finely chopped celery

4 garlic cloves, sliced

9 ounces oyster mushrooms, trimmed, clumps separated

¾ cup chardonnay

1 tablespoon fresh lemon juice

2 tablespoons black truffle butter or unsalted butter

1 tablespoon minced fresh tarragon

1. Heat the oil in a 4-quart stove-top casserole or sauté pan on medium-high. Add the chicken, skin side down, using as many pieces as fit comfortably. Cook until lightly browned on one side, season with salt and white pepper, and turn to brown the other side. Remove to a platter when done and repeat with the remaining chicken pieces.

2. Add the pearl onions to the casserole and toss in the remaining fat until lightly browned. Remove to a plate. Reduce the heat to low. Add the chopped onion, celery, and garlic, and cook until softened. Stir in the mushrooms. When they have wilted, add the chardonnay, bring to a simmer, and season with salt, white pepper, and the lemon juice. Return the chicken with any accumulated juices from the platter to the casserole. Baste, cover, and cook for about 30 minutes, basting a few times until done. Remove the chicken pieces to a platter.

3. Increase the heat to medium-high and cook the sauce and mushrooms until the sauce has thickened slightly, about 5 minutes. Lower the heat, and add the pearl onions and butter. When the butter has melted, check the seasonings, return the chicken to the casserole, baste, and simmer for a few minutes. Serve directly from the casserole or transfer to a deep platter. Scatter the tarragon on top before serving.

YIELD: 4 SERVINGS

COOK'S NOTES: Cold-pressed grape seed oil is my favorite vegetable oil to use when olive oil would be too strong. Unlike other vegetable oils, it is not industrially processed with heat and so it is purer than the usual supermarket oils. 🫙

CALIFORNIA CHARDONNAY Collector's cult

object and joke. Rich, flamboyant fruit-and-oak bomb, and lean, lithe, and energetic. Cougar juice and hipster wine. California chardonnay has been so many things to so many people over the years, and to one extent or another all the descriptions seem to fit. No wine has been as loved and loathed, praised and lambasted as California chardonnay. To call it polarizing would be an understatement, yet that's only a small part of a bigger picture.

Winemakers have often referred to the chardonnay grape as a blank slate because it can so easily express both the qualities of the terroir in which it grows and the ambitions and intentions of the winemaker. In this way, few wines have so transparently displayed the whims of fashion as has California chardonnay. Without the spine of tradition that has guided Burgundy, winemakers in California have been free to mold, shape, sculpt, and, indeed, deform chardonnay into a multitude of different wines.

Even in the bad old days of the 1990s, when the predominant style was so exaggerated—a rich, heavy cocktail of tropical tutti-frutti flavors wrapped in oaky layers of buttered popcorn—other, more taut styles of chardonnay existed. Yet they were in such a minority that you had to look hard to find them. That is no longer the case, and thankfully so, for those of us who prefer wines with more balance, refinement, subtlety, and liveliness. These days, the power and richness of a Russian River Valley chardonnay coexists with the energy of a Sonoma Coast bottling. Often, these varied styles are produced side by side in the same appellation, depending on the inclination of the winemaker.

Even after more than a half century of chardonnay production in California, it's too soon to define with certainty the characteristics of the various regions. From the Santa Rita Hills of Santa Barbara County, I've had vivacious wines that emphasize citrus and mineral flavors, and I've had blockbuster wines that combined great complexity with alcoholic heat and power. I've had gorgeous chardonnays from the Santa Maria Valley and the Santa Cruz Mountains, and I've found my share of oaky duds as well.

Nonetheless, the pendulum has swung back toward the center. Even a superstar producer like Kistler Vineyards, famed for its lush, exuberant style, has eased up on the throttle in favor of more finesse. Today, the spectrum of California chardonnay offers something for almost everybody, from the leanest to the most luxuriant. As with so many regions around the world, it all comes down to finding producers whose styles align with your palate. 🍷

CALIFORNIA CHARDONNAY, LIKE SALMON, IS NOT SOMETHING I SERVE VERY OFTEN. Finding the wine in every glass and the fish on every menu has done them in for me. But there are always exceptions. The first fresh Pacific king salmon of the season is worthy of attention. And unless the fish is grilled or served with some hearty seasoning or accompaniment, like tomatoes, that will demand a red wine, it is often best with a rich chardonnay. To underscore the white wine pairing, I prepared the salmon with a lush sauce of creamed cucumbers. The dish is meant to be paired with a satiny and elegant chardonnay from the Russian River, Sonoma Coast, or even Napa, where chardonnay may still be defined by butter.

Slow-Roasted King Salmon with Creamed Cucumbers

TIME: 1 HOUR 15 MINUTES

2 tablespoons unsalted butter

One 2-inch piece fresh ginger, peeled and minced

1 large shallot, sliced

2 English cucumbers, peeled, halved lengthwise, and sliced ¼ inch thick

Salt and freshly ground white pepper

2½ pounds king salmon fillet, preferably center cut in one piece, skinned, pinbones removed

Juice of 1 lemon

½ cup chardonnay

½ cup crème fraîche

1 tablespoon minced fresh chives

1. Heat the oven to 200°F. Melt the butter in a skillet over low heat. Add the ginger and shallot and sauté briefly, until softened. Add the cucumbers, season with salt and white pepper, and sauté until beginning to appear translucent. Spread in a baking dish large enough to hold the salmon. Do not wash the skillet.

2. Place the salmon on top of the cucumbers. Season with salt and white pepper, sprinkle with half of the lemon juice, and pour the wine around the fish. Cover with a sheet of parchment or wax paper. Place in the oven and cook for 45 minutes for medium-rare, 50 to 55 minutes for more well cooked. Because the fish is slow-roasted, it will remain quite red in the center.

3. Transfer the salmon to a large platter with a rim. Transfer the cucumber mixture to the skillet and cook for 5 minutes. Stir in the crème fraîche and cook until the sauce is the consistency of heavy cream. Season with salt, white pepper, and the remaining lemon juice. Pour the mixture around the salmon. Sprinkle with the chives and serve.

YIELD: 6 SERVINGS

COOK'S NOTES: I like to roast a slab of salmon on low heat for nearly an hour. The result is fish that is cooked but retains the bright color of raw salmon and has a tender, moist, almost custardy texture. If you like your salmon more well cooked, you can leave it in the oven for another 10 minutes or so. 🥛

MUSCADET

Let's dispense with the obvious right away: oysters. Most people, if they know one important thing about Muscadet, know that oysters are its natural partner.

True, true, true. Oysters and Muscadet are glorious together, the briny, mineral-laden quality of one enhancing the other. You could say the same thing, though, about Chablis, and about Sancerre, and if the issue may not be quite so cut and dried, about blanc de blancs Champagne, who ever is going to complain about being saddled with oysters and blanc de blancs?

The truth about Muscadet is that its virtues extend well beyond oysters. Many seafood dishes would go well with Muscadet, as well as light poultry preparations and pasta dishes, too, if you are willing to break the ethnic boundaries that channel so many wine choices.

Apart from food pairings, Muscadet is just plain delicious, providing you are open to what it does best. Muscadet, like Chablis and Sancerre, is not a gobs-of-fruit sort of wine. Yes, one can often sense citrus qualities in Muscadet. But more often, it is a stony sensation, felt as much as tasted, along with herbal, saline, and floral aromas that characterize Muscadet.

Texture, I think, is a vastly underrated quality in a wine, and texture is an essential quality of good Muscadet. It's what impels you to take sip after sip, simply because it feels so good.

For all of Muscadet's assets, the best of all might be its price. Given the high quality of the top Muscadets, made by dedicated small producers, they are insanely cheap, rarely more than twenty dollars for current vintages, and often around fifteen dollars. Finding the good ones is the problem. A lot of mediocre bulk wines in the marketplace have contributed to Muscadet's reputation, in some circles, as dull, anonymous, and overly lean.

Muscadet is made on the western end of the Loire Valley from the melon grape, which can be rather thin and neutral. To give the wine added richness and texture, most good Muscadet producers allow the wine to rest for months on the lees, or sediment, that accumulate during fermentation. This process, indicated by the French "sur lie" on the label, softens the wine and gives it greater depth. It can also result in trapping a little carbon dioxide in the wine, which can give it a bit of sparkle.

Not content with the sur lie treatment, some producers are doing even more, fermenting their wine in barrels, or stirring the lees as the wine rests, in the manner of many chardonnay and white Burgundy estates. These experiments seem to have been successful, partly because these producers are not using new oak barrels, which can impart distressing oaky flavors.

Good Muscadet ages exceptionally well, sometimes taking on the kerosene flavor of older rieslings and developing a surprising complexity. But unless you are buying from a store that specializes in Loire Valley wines, I'd be skeptical of bottles older than a couple of years. Chances are they've been sitting around in storage conditions that are less than optimal. 🍷

WHETHER I'M SITTING AT A COUNTER OVERLOOKING THE HARBOR IN VANCOUVER, perched at an oyster bar in London, having lunch at a brasserie in Paris, or waiting for the shucker to finish opening my selection of a dozen oysters at a raw bar in New York, what I want in my glass is well-chilled, pale, fresh, gravelly Muscadet. There's nothing better to escort the lovely bivalves down my gullet. An alternative to raw oysters for those Muscadets, young or more mature, would be these oyster potpies bolstered with cream, butter, and a whiff of anise throughout, from the fennel bulb, the tarragon, and the splash of pastis.

Oyster Potpies

TIME: 1½ HOURS

1½ cups plus 2 tablespoons all-purpose flour

Salt

8 tablespoons (1 stick) unsalted butter

32 oysters, shucked, with their juices

1 cup clam juice or seafood stock, or as needed

3 tablespoons pastis (Pernod, Ricard, or absinthe)

1 cup chopped onions

1 cup chopped fennel bulb

12 ounces Yukon gold potatoes, peeled and diced

Cayenne

1 tablespoon chopped fresh tarragon

½ cup heavy cream

1. Whisk 1½ cups of the flour with ½ teaspoon salt. By hand or in a food processor, cut in 6 tablespoons of the butter until the mixture is mealy. Gradually add 4 to 5 tablespoons ice water, or more if needed, to form the dough. Shape the dough into a disk, enclose it in plastic wrap, and refrigerate.

2. Drain the oysters well over a large measuring cup. Measure the juice and add enough clam juice to make 1½ cups. Add the pastis.

3. Melt the remaining 2 tablespoons butter in a heavy 3-quart saucepan. Add the onions and fennel and sauté over low heat until soft but not brown. Stir in the remaining 2 tablespoons flour, cook briefly, and stir in the oyster and clam liquid. Bring to a simmer for a few minutes until thickened. Add the potatoes, cover, and cook until the potatoes are tender, about 15 minutes. Season with salt, if needed, and cayenne. Add the oysters, tarragon, and 6 tablespoons of the cream. Cook briefly until the oysters firm up. Divide the mixture among four 1-cup ramekins at least 2 inches deep, putting 8 oysters in each.

4. Remove the dough from the refrigerator. Heat the oven to 425°F.

5. Roll out the dough and cut into 4 circles the diameter of the baking dishes. Top each dish with a circle of dough, brush the tops with the remaining 2 tablespoons cream, and cut slits in the tops. Place the ramekins on a baking sheet and bake in the upper level of the oven for 30 minutes, or until the pastry is golden. Serve.

YIELD: 4 SERVINGS

COOK'S NOTES: For convenience, the potpies can be assembled and refrigerated unbaked for several hours. They should be brought to room temperature before baking, so allow about an hour before serving.

FIANO
For one of the more dramatic examples of how the world of wine has changed in the last few decades, consider the white wines of Italy. Back in the 1970s and '80s, a reasonable response to that suggestion might have been to simply laugh or sigh. Soave might have come to mind, and pinot grigio, though neither would have inspired particularly happy associations. Those white wines in bottles shaped like fishes worked better as campy art, while the memorably named Est! Est!! Est!!! and the various forgettable Frascatis offered little pleasure beyond a well-chilled neutrality.

Now, though, the choices are almost embarrassingly rich. Soave has enjoyed a renaissance (try something from Pieropan, for example, to see how good it can be), and the northeastern regions of Alto Adige and Friuli–Venezia Giulia pour forth a river of delectable bottles. Liguria and Sardinia are making delicious vermentinos, while arneis from the Piedmont can be a joy. Even those old standbys pinot grigio and Orvieto can surprise you with their quality these days.

Many of the best Italian whites are made from grapes that were virtually unknown back then, like three from Campania: greco, falanghina, and fiano. These ancient grapes have been cultivated over millennia, but they had largely faded from prominence by the middle of the twentieth century.

The wine industry of Campania has grown enormously in this time, however, and so has its focus on indigenous grapes. Back then, you would have been hard pressed to name even a handful of good producers whose wines made it to the United States. Now there are dozens, and once-obscure grapes like aglianico and the three whites have become far better known.

The most interesting to me is the fiano, partly because it's stylistically versatile. It can play the role of those Italian whites of yore: clean, cold refreshment. But it can offer more.

At base, it has a smoky, nutlike, spicy quality that I find very attractive, along with winning mineral flavors. Many producers have experimented with fiano, not simply to make fiano taste like more popular wines but to determine which methods can make fiano more distinctively fiano-like.

For example, allowing wines to age on their lees, essentially dead yeast cells and other detritus from fermentation, is an old French technique for adding richness to white wines. Occasionally stirring the lees can add even more body. Many producers are using these methods with fiano and the result is a richer texture, offering far more tactile pleasure, as if the wine had been aged in barrels—without the wood flavoring—even if the lees stirring took place in steel tanks.

The best fianos have a captivating energy that can be wonderfully pleasing. Some are beautifully textured as well, possibly as a result of lees stirring, and possibly because of barrel aging. (It's not always clear which methods were used, unless you are in the cellar to observe.) Others are straightforward and juicy, in a sort of polished pinot grigio style.

Most fianos come from the inland area around the town of Avellino, hence the appellation Fiano di Avellino. But they also come from regions closer to the Mediterranean, a warmer climate where the wines tend to be richer and rounder. You might see some bottles with the name Paestum, an ancient Greco-Roman city south of the Amalfi coast. It's a sign, like the rebirth of interest in these indigenous grapes, of a region returning to its roots. 🍷

REGULARDLESS OF WHETHER YOUR FIANO IS LEAN AND STEELY OR VINIFIED IN A RICHER STYLE, several flavors should emerge from what is served alongside. Notes of grassiness, nuttiness, and a hint of bitterness are paramount. Thinking about these tastes led me to matcha, the earthy, powdered Japanese green tea. But how can you eat matcha? The Japanese tradition, using a fine bamboo whisk to emulsify the matcha, which, when done properly, becomes frothy, does not have to be limited to a bowl of tea. Why not add matcha to mussel broth? Against the briny-sweet mussels, the broth offered a touch of wasabi for heat, lime for acidity, and cream for added foamy richness. These elements brought the flavor of the wine, and the matcha, into elegant focus.

Mussel Soup with Matcha

TIME: 30 MINUTES

1 tablespoon vegetable oil, preferably grape seed

¼ cup minced shallots

2 tablespoons minced peeled fresh ginger

2 teaspoons wasabi paste (from a tube or mixed from powder)

Grated zest and juice of 1 lime

½ teaspoon salt

½ teaspoon sugar

1½ cups dry white wine

2 pounds mussels, scrubbed and debearded

½ cup heavy cream

1 tablespoon matcha (Japanese powdered green tea)

1. Heat the oil in a large sauté pan. Add the shallots and ginger and sweat, covered, over very low heat until soft, about 10 minutes. Whisk in the wasabi paste, lime zest, lime juice, salt, and sugar. Add the wine and bring to a simmer.

2. Add the mussels, cover, and cook over medium heat until they open, about 8 minutes. Using a slotted spoon, transfer the mussels, draining well, to 4 shallow soup plates. Cover the plates to keep warm.

3. Whisk the cream into the broth in the pan. Bring to a slow simmer. Sift the matcha into the pan through a small strainer and, using a fine whisk or a hand blender, blend vigorously until the mixture starts to look frothy. Spoon over the mussels and serve.

YIELD: 4 SERVINGS

COOK'S NOTES: You will have leftover matcha powder, which makes delicious green iced tea.

ALBARIÑO

The rocket trajectory of Spain's transition into a modern wine-producing powerhouse makes it highly susceptible to a focus on the next new thing, in which each pleasant discovery quickly overtakes the last. In the 1980s, albariño was one of the first wines to emerge from modern Spain, which in the current scheme of things makes it positively ancient.

By all rights, more recent moments in the spotlight for txakolís from the Basque country and verdejos from Rueda should have hastened albariño toward a rendezvous with the scrap heap of has-been wine fads. Yet albariños remain highly popular, especially in the United States, which continues to be the top export market for these wines. The consistent popularity of albariño is a tribute both to the fundamental appeal of these bright, thirst-quenching wines and to the canny marketing efforts of Spanish winemakers, who made it the signature white wine of the Rías Baixas region of Galicia, in northwestern Spain.

Many albariños reflect two main styles. Some are lean and crisp, with pronounced mineral and citrus flavors. Others are round and plump, retaining the citrus and mineral qualities, but emphasizing peach, cantaloupe, and tropical fruit flavors. Either way, they can be consummate summer wines, a paradox because they come from the Atlantic coast of Spain, where persistent rainfall and mist can make summer fleeting at best.

As enjoyable as albariños can be, most of them are modest wines, easy to enjoy without prolonged analysis. Occasionally you'll have to navigate through some dull, insipid examples as well, not surprising given the category's success. When a wine like an albariño achieves something approaching brand status, some producers may try to capitalize by emphasizing quantity over quality. Yet, when carefully and conscientiously produced, albariño can produce unexpectedly complex wines that are actually capable of aging for several decades. I've had thirty-year-old albariños that were delicious!

For the most part, however, good albariños combine crisp floral, citrus, and mineral flavors with a snappy, tangy liveliness that sort of lifts one up with each sip. To me, this energy is an essential component not only for a summer wine but for great wines of any kind. ♌

A FRIEND CALLED OFFERING STRIPED BASS. Her daughter had gone on a successful fishing trip and the catch was big and very fresh. "Whole?" I asked. "Filleted" was the response. "Skin on then?" "No." Oops. Striped bass is a fish that when filleted is delicious to sear on the skin, then flip and roast. Without skin, even grilling would be tricky. (If it were grilled, I'd prefer it with a red wine to complement its meatiness and char.) But the fillet could be braised. The result was complex, with Indian seasonings balanced by enough acidity from the tamarind paste and lime juice to make the dish friendly to the wine's tartly citric, gingery, and exotic jasmine notes. When preparing fillets from large fish like salmon and striped bass, if you run your hand over the fish you may feel little bones sticking out vertically. These are pin bones. (See also page 81.) Use a needle-nose pliers (I keep a pair in my kitchen drawer) to yank them out.

Curried Striped Bass

TIME: 40 MINUTES

3 tablespoons grape seed oil

1 teaspoon mustard seeds

1 cup finely chopped onions

1 tablespoon slivered peeled fresh ginger

1 jalapeño, seeded and slivered, or to taste

1 teaspoon ground coriander

½ teaspoon ground turmeric

1 tablespoon tamarind paste (sold in fancy food shops and Indian stores)

2 pounds wild striped bass fillets, skinless, cut into 4 portions, pinbones removed

Salt and freshly ground black pepper

1 tablespoon fresh lime juice

1 teaspoon dark brown sugar

1 tablespoon minced fresh cilantro leaves

Steamed basmati rice, for serving

1. Heat the oil in a skillet large enough to hold the fillets without crowding. Add the mustard seeds. When they start to pop, add the onions. Sauté until starting to brown. Lower the heat and add the ginger, jalapeño, coriander, and turmeric. Cook for 5 minutes. Dissolve the tamarind in ½ cup water and add it to the pan. Simmer briefly. Add the fish and baste with the sauce.

2. Cover and simmer for 5 minutes. Baste and add ½ cup water. Cover and simmer for 5 minutes more, or until the fish is just cooked through. Transfer the fish to a platter. Season the sauce with salt and pepper. Add the lime juice and brown sugar and stir. Add a little more water, if needed. Spoon the sauce over the fish. Garnish with the cilantro and serve with rice.

YIELD: 4 SERVINGS

COOK'S NOTES: On the East Coast, wild striped bass is relatively easy to find in fish markets. And note that you do not want farm-raised striped bass, which is bland and a different fish entirely. But there are alternatives, like black sea bass, hake, and halibut. 🗑

PINOT GRIGIO

Just as an especially popular piece of classical music or literature will be rejected by a contingent of connoisseurs simply because of its popularity, pinot grigio from Italy, the most popular category of imported white wine in the United States, has largely been dismissed by serious wine drinkers as bland and insipid, the harmless, gulpable equivalent of a lawn mower beer.

Even if reflexive, the hostility rests on a truthful assessment. Most pinot grigios give many people exactly what they want: a mellifluous, easy-to-pronounce wine that can be ordered without fear of embarrassment and that is at the least cold, refreshing, and for the most part cheap. Most pinot grigios can meet these minimal criteria, yet some offer much more than that. The best versions can be balanced, lively, crisp, and subtle, with mineral foundations that support stimulating citrus and floral flavors.

Just as pinot grigio has been sneered at, so have Italian white wines in general. However, from Alto Adige in the Tyrolean Alps all the way to Sicily in the south, Italy has been producing more and more excellent white wines. Many of them are highly distinctive, made from grapes that prosper nowhere else in the world, from ribolla gialla and tocai Friulano in the northeast to fiano and falanghina in Campania and carricante in Sicily.

Unlike those grapes, pinot grigio is grown pretty much all over the wine-producing world. In France, where it is known as pinot gris, it is a staple of Alsace, where it makes heavier-bodied, spicy, and often somewhat sweet wines of great character that sometimes have a rosy hue to them. It mostly goes by pinot gris in Oregon, where it can make surprisingly interesting wines for modest prices. I've had excellent Canadian pinot gris from British Columbia. You might see the grape in Germany, where it goes by ruländer or grauburgunder, and it is popular in Slovenia and Romania as well.

But for Americans, none of those regions approach Italy as a popular source for pinot grigios. The best come from either Friuli–Venezia Giulia or Alto Adige. Most are fermented and aged briefly in steel tanks, offering not even the faintest whiff of oak. Yet the most imaginative winemakers of northeast Italy, like Gravner, Radikon, and Movia (technically of Slovenia but worthy of this company), have demonstrated that oak aging and carefully managed yields can give pinot grigio rare substance and texture. Producers like these take pinot grigio into another dimension, and their wines are well worth the added expense, though bottles are hard to come by. ♗

IN THE NORTH OF ITALY, where pinot grigio is often the default white, risotto also reigns. Here, the rice dish is done Asian style. Lemongrass, ginger, garlic, and shallots set the flavor profile. And to bolster the exotic geography even more, coconut milk stands in for some of the broth. The dish is easy to vary with other seafood, and even the addition of edamame or peas.

Asian Shrimp Risotto

TIME: 45 MINUTES

2 tablespoons extra virgin olive oil

2 bulbs fresh lemongrass, chopped

1 tablespoon minced peeled fresh ginger

2 garlic cloves, minced

¼ cup finely chopped shallots

2 cups unsweetened coconut milk

2 cups fish stock

1 cup dry white wine

1 tablespoon Vietnamese fish sauce (nuoc mam)

Juice of 2 limes

1½ cups Arborio rice

1½ pounds medium shrimp, peeled and deveined

3 tablespoons minced fresh mint leaves

Salt and freshly ground white pepper

1. Heat the oil in a heavy saucepan. Add the lemongrass, ginger, garlic, and shallots and sauté over low heat until soft.

2. Meanwhile, place the coconut milk, stock, ½ cup of the wine, the fish sauce, and lime juice in another saucepan. Bring to a gentle simmer.

3. Add the rice to the saucepan with the lemongrass and cook, stirring, for 1 minute or so. Add the remaining ½ cup wine and cook, stirring, until it is absorbed. Add ½ cup of the coconut milk mixture, and stir until it is absorbed. Continue adding the coconut milk mixture, ½ cup at a time, as it is absorbed, stirring constantly. The rice should be al dente after about 15 minutes.

4. Stir in the shrimp. Cook until they turn pink, 3 to 5 minutes. Fold in the mint. Season with salt and white pepper and divide among soup plates. Serve.

YIELD: 4 TO 6 SERVINGS

COOK'S NOTES: You may want to pay attention to where your shrimp come from. Try to find fresh wild shrimp. And even though this risotto is Asian, avoid shrimp raised in the Far East, especially Thailand, because they are often not sustainably cultivated and may have been treated with chemicals. 🛢

OREGON PINOT GRIS

Oregon pinot gris is a stealth wine. It occupies a secure spot in the marketplace, but few crave Oregon pinot gris or give it much thought. Yet on the occasions when I spot it on an otherwise unfriendly wine list, I am relieved to have found a somewhat safe haven.

Good examples seem to occupy a sort of middle ground between ambition and indifference, an unusual place to find an American wine. Too many wines are more pretentious than good, and too many more are cheap but insipid. As a result, values in American wine are hard to come by.

The producers of Oregon pinot gris seem to lack ambition for their wine, which is not necessarily a bad thing. The usual trappings—heavy texture, pronounced oak flavors, too much sweetness, and the like—are mostly absent, and prices are fairly moderate. In fact, a few years back I called Oregon pinot gris one of the best wine values on the market.

They still can be. The best of these wines have a lively vitality, yet they have another dimension as well. The best have a stony mineral quality that I especially appreciate in white wines, along with herb and spice flavors rather than overt fruitiness. But too often, the wines seem routine, as if producers are content to make wines that are decidedly ordinary.

Willamette Valley is Oregon's most prestigious region, but good pinot gris, like those from King Estate and Bethel Heights, bear the more generic Oregon appellation.

With the rare exception, like a superb old-vines cuvée from the Eyrie Vineyards, don't expect these wines to age. Most are made to be consumed young, often with a little spritz of carbon dioxide in the bottle. The mild effervescence contributes to an impression of energy and vibrancy in the wine, which can be attractive. But the effect can be ephemeral. The carbon dioxide can dissipate after a few months or a year. If a wine relies on carbon dioxide rather than acidity for its liveliness, it can then taste flat after a while. 🍷

A CRISP YET GRAPY PINOT GRIS CAN BE THE BEST CHOICE for some dishes that are notoriously hard to please. Salad, for starters, and eggs. I remember having both together at A Voce, an Italian restaurant at New York's Columbus Circle. Missy Robbins, the chef at that time, had assembled a salad of bitter greens with a warm pancetta dressing, some shaved cheese on top, and a poached egg. It was almost a deconstructed Caesar salad, needing only anchovies instead of pancetta to fit the definition. And that's precisely how I made it to accompany the Oregon pinot gris, with the minor addition of some toasted pine nuts to echo the nutty finish in some of the wines.

Warm Deconstructed Caesar Salad

TIME: 30 MINUTES

4 tablespoons white wine vinegar

4 large eggs

1 head romaine lettuce, cored, rinsed, and dried

¼ cup pine nuts

6 tablespoons Tuscan extra virgin olive oil

8 anchovies in oil, drained and chopped

1½ teaspoons Dijon mustard

Freshly ground black pepper

2 ounces Parmigiano-Reggiano, shaved with a vegetable peeler

1. Bring 3 inches of water to a simmer in a 2- to 3-quart saucepan. Add 2 tablespoons of the vinegar. Break an egg into a teacup and gently slip the egg into the water. Repeat with the 3 remaining eggs. Cook at a very gentle simmer for 3 minutes, or until the white is firmly set. Use a slotted spoon to lift the eggs from the pan onto a plate lined with paper towels. If desired, use scissors to trim the excess strands of white clinging to eggs. Invert a bowl over the plate of eggs to keep them warm.

2. Shred the lettuce into a salad bowl. Have four salad plates ready.

3. Heat a small skillet to medium, add the pine nuts, and toast them until fragrant, stirring. Remove from the skillet and set aside. Add the oil to the skillet, reduce the heat to low, add the anchovies, and cook, stirring, until they soften and start to fall apart. Whisk in the remaining 2 tablespoons vinegar and the mustard. Pour the dressing over the lettuce, season with pepper, and toss well. Divide the salad among the four plates. Top each portion with a poached egg, scatter the pine nuts and cheese over, and serve.

YIELD: 4 SERVINGS

COOK'S NOTES: Be sure to toss the salad well so the warm dressing wilts the lettuce. 🧂

TORRONTÉS

Torrontés has been touted as the hottest thing to arrive from Argentina since the tango. Or at least since malbec. It's a grape, and a white wine, and some say it will be as popular in the United States as pinot grigio.

Well, one day, perhaps. But first things first. Have you even heard of torrontés? The grape is grown pretty much nowhere else in the world but Argentina. Yes, Spain also has a grape called torrontés, but the two grapes are apparently unrelated. The Argentine grape has been shown genetically to be a hybrid of the muscat of Alexandria and the criolla, or mission, as it's known in English.

The ancestry of the torrontés is interesting only in that the grape most definitely bears more than a passing resemblance to the gloriously fragrant muscat. The best torrontés is highly aromatic, exuberantly floral with a rich, hothouse citrus scent as well. Dip your nose into a glass and you don't know whether it ought to be sold as a wine or a perfume.

Argentina has a talent for obscure grapes. It took the malbec, a red grape that is forgotten in Bordeaux, overlooked in Cahors, and known as côt in the Loire Valley, and turned it into a juicy, fruity, money-generating phenomenon identified purely with Argentina. Can torrontés become malbec's white counterpart? Perhaps, but so far torrontés lacks a clear-cut identity. Some wines are dry, light-bodied, and crisp, like pinot grigios. Others are broad, heavy, and rich, like ultraripe California chardonnays.

All genres of wine have their stylistic deviations, but consumers can often read the cues. Chablis is a chardonnay that one can reasonably assume will be lean and minerally, without oak flavors. One would likewise expect a California chardonnay to be richer, and oaky flavors would not surprise. Exceptions exist, often from labels that have been around long enough to establish an identity of their own. But torrontés so far seems unpredictable.

Wherever the wines land on the spectrum, their level of quality depends on one crucial component: acidity. Whether light or heavy, if the wines have enough acidity, they come across as lively and vivacious. The rest land with a thud.

Just to make torrontés a little more complicated, it turns out the grape in Argentina has three subvarieties: the torrontés Riojano, the best and most aromatic, which comes from the northern province of La Rioja and Salta; the less aromatic torrontés Sanjuanino, from the San Juan province south of La Rioja; and the much less aromatic torrontés Mendocino, from the Mendoza area, which—fasten your seat belts—may not be related to the other two at all.

All this aside, the aromatic exuberance of the best versions is singular and pleasing, with the caution that the wines ought to be consumed while young. As for comparisons with pinot grigio, they seem both premature and misleading. The big-selling pinot grigios are so indistinct that they offend no one but those seeking distinctive wines. Torrontés, on the other hand, are quite unusual, which confers on them the power to offend. In wine, that's often a good thing. 🍷

AN EASYGOING MANNER AND A GENTLE PRICE POINT make torrontés an agreeable choice for many a seafood dish. Here is a simple preparation with a delicate Asian accent and just a hint of heat. The acidity in the wine becomes a terrific foil for the mellow coconut milk in the broth. The word *nage* means "swim" in French, and refers to the souplike nature of this dish.

Cod and Clams in Coconut Nage

TIME: 30 MINUTES, PLUS 2 HOURS MARINATING

2 pounds fresh cod fillets, skinless, in 6 pieces

3 tablespoons fresh lime juice

Salt and freshly ground black pepper

2 tablespoons grape seed oil

6 garlic cloves, slivered

1 tablespoon minced peeled fresh ginger

1 jalapeño, seeded and slivered

1½ cups thinly sliced fennel bulb

½ cup dry white wine

18 little neck clams, scrubbed

One 14-ounce can unsweetened coconut milk, stirred

3 cups steamed jasmine rice (from 1 cup raw rice)

12 mint leaves, slivered

1. Place the cod on a platter, pour 2 tablespoons of the lime juice on it, season with salt and pepper, cover, and refrigerate for 2 hours.

2. Heat the oil in a large sauté pan. Add the garlic, ginger, jalapeño, and fennel and cook over low heat until soft. Add the wine, bring to a simmer, and add the clams. Cover and cook until the clams open, 5 minutes or so. Use a slotted spoon to remove the clams in their shells to a bowl. Cover the bowl.

3. Add the coconut milk to the pan, and bring to a slow simmer. Add the cod—it should be nearly submerged. Cook gently until the fish is just done, about 8 minutes. Use a large slotted spoon to transfer the fish to each of six shallow soup plates. Add a scoop of the rice alongside. Return the clams to the pan, bring to a simmer, add the remaining 1 tablespoon lime juice, and check the seasonings. Place 3 clams in each bowl, ladle coconut broth over each portion, garnish with mint, and serve.

YIELD: 6 SERVINGS

COOK'S NOTES: Canned coconut milk tends to separate. It's easier to use if you either store or open the can upside down.

GRÜNER VELTLINER
Grüner veltliner is one of summer's great, unlikely pleasures. Why unlikely? Well, it may seem shallow, but Americans have always been riveted by the mellifluous, flowing wine names drawn of the Romance languages—the chardonnays, pinot grigios, and Sancerres. Germanic terms, with their umlauts and consonant pileups, have historically posed obstacles, whether gewürztraminer, blaufränkisch (its alternate name, lemberger, is no better), or the ever-popular trockenbeerenauslese.

Yet grüner veltliner from Austria has not only survived but prospered on restaurant lists across the country. It's one of those happily inexplicable things. Years ago I never would have guessed that Americans would fall in love with raw fish, but now sushi bars are everywhere.

One possible reason for grüner veltliner's popularity is that, unlike riesling, it did not have to overcome the assumption that it's sweet. Sure, sweet grüner veltliners are produced, very good ones, in fact. But they are the exception. Consumers can be confident when they order a bottle that it will be dry.

Another is the wine itself. Grüner veltliner can range from crisp and light-bodied to rich and full-bodied, with aromas and flavors of citrus, flowers, and herbs. Perhaps its most distinctive feature is a peppery spiciness. The best can have a kind of crystalline purity and a minerally richness.

Across the stylistic board, though, a dry grüner veltliner should have a refreshing tanginess, borne of good acidity. All told, a good grüner veltliner goes wonderfully with many foods.

As for the name, Americans have found several methods of sliding by. Most common is simply truncating the name, calling it grüner (and softening it to GROO-ner rather than the more correct, diacritical GREWH-ner), and dispensing with the ungainly veltliner (pronounced FEHLT-lee-ner). Some call it simply G.V., and occasionally you'll find sommeliers and industry people who use the insiderish term "gru-ve," pronounced "groovy."

The richest versions come from the Wachau region. The best bottles offer richness without weight and heft. Among Austrian regions, Wachau alone uses specific designations for ripeness at which grapes are harvested. Federspiel indicates the medium ripeness level and steinfeder, the lightest. The ripest Wachau wines are called smaragd (pronounced shmar-AHGD), and they also tend to be the most expensive.

The other leading grüner veltliner regions are Kamptal and Kremstal. The wines from those places tend not to have the richness of those from the Wachau, but they are not necessarily slender wines. As with so many wines, balance is the key. 🍷

IN AUSTRIA, GRÜNER VELTLINERS ARE OFTEN SERVED WITH VEAL DISHES. The New York–based Austrian chef Kurt Gutenbrunner has done a riff on sliders, those popular mini hamburgers, with veal. His are small patties, not served on buns, and are accompanied by a cabbage fondue. The wilted cabbage slaw is a somewhat simpler version, dressed with sour cream.

Veal Sliders with Wilted Cabbage

TIME: 45 MINUTES

1 cup diced crustless stale baguette

¼ cup milk

1 medium onion

2½ tablespoons unsalted butter

4 cups finely shredded cored Savoy cabbage (about ½ head)

Salt and freshly ground white pepper

2 tablespoons white wine vinegar

4 teaspoons fresh marjoram leaves

½ cup sour cream

1 pound ground veal

1 large egg

1 large egg yolk

1 tablespoon finely chopped fresh flat-leaf parsley

3 tablespoons Dijon mustard

¼ cup veal or chicken stock

Slider buns (optional)

1. Place the bread in a bowl, add the milk, and let soak. Finely mince enough of the onion to make 1 tablespoon. Slice the rest thin. Melt ½ tablespoon of the butter in a medium skillet. Add the minced onion and cook on low until soft but not brown. Transfer to a medium bowl.

2. Add 1 tablespoon of the remaining butter to the skillet and add the sliced onion and cabbage. Dust with salt and white pepper and cook on low, covered, until the cabbage wilts, about 10 minutes. Stir in the vinegar and marjoram. Remove from the heat and fold in the sour cream. Set aside in a serving dish.

3. Add the veal to the bowl of minced onion, then add the egg, egg yolk, parsley, mustard, and soaked bread. Mix well by hand or pulse briefly in a food processor. Season with salt and white pepper. Shape into 8 to 12 oval patties.

4. Heat the remaining 1 tablespoon butter in a heavy skillet. Cook the patties on medium until browned, about 4 minutes per side. Larger patties will take longer. Transfer to a platter. Add the stock to the pan and deglaze on medium. Strain the sauce into a small dish and serve with the patties, cabbage, and buns, if using.

YIELD: 4 SERVINGS

COOK'S NOTES: The sliders can be grilled instead of sautéed if the calendar demands outdoor cooking.

SOAVE

On the face of it, Soave would seem to be about as controversial as a carrot. It's a white wine, right? An Italian white, which to many people means a crisp, cold, characterless quaffing wine for knocking back, not for savoring.

This conventional attitude, of course, is way out of date. In recent decades a small cadre of producers in Soave territory, in the northeastern Italian region of Veneto, has taken the wine much more seriously. Instead of the bland mass-produced white of the 1960s and '70s that Americans had become familiar with, these producers were making delicious wines with a pronounced minerality that I have enjoyed tremendously.

What's changed? Instead of the large-scale farming techniques that emphasized quantity over quality, these producers drastically reduced yields in the vineyards, resulting in grapes with more character and intensity. They focused their efforts on the garganega grape, the most interesting of the Soave blend, rather than on the dull trebbiano Toscano. In fact, updated rules for the Soave Classico appellation, which covers the best hillside vineyards, prohibited the trebbiano Toscano and required that Soave Classico be at least 70 percent garganega, with the remaining 30 percent made up of pinot bianco, chardonnay, or trebbiano di Soave, the local name for verdicchio.

Over the years, I've had many good Soaves in strikingly divergent styles. Some are steely and dry, not conceptually different from the Soaves of memory yet startlingly improved in quality. Others can be lavish and golden with fleshy textures, clearly showing the effects of aging in oak barrels, a technique not usually associated with Soave. By effect, I don't mean the overbearing aromas or flavors of vanilla and chocolate that typically come from new oak. I mean the gentle effect of the microscopic amounts of air that penetrate the wood, which adds complexity and richness to the texture of the wine.

To me, this was all to the good. Stylistic divisions in wine are often presented as traditionalism versus modernism, and I regularly find myself on the traditionalist side because modernism is often code for diminishing what makes a wine distinctive. But in the case of Soave, the best examples all over the divide seem to retain their Soave character.

Not everybody will agree with me on this. That's an important reminder of how subjective the perception of wine can be. The good news is that most Soaves are inexpensive enough to warrant taking a chance to find out how you feel about them. ♟

THE BRIGHT MINERALITY AND HINTS OF DILL AND CITRUS that characterize the best of the Soaves suit tender greens, herbs, and vegetables—the springtime palate. A plate of fresh tagliatelle noodles tossed with sweet garden peas and briny clams in a buttered broth of white wine also offers a whiff of fresh basil and a dusting of bread crumbs for texture. You might think of this description as leading to the old standby, linguine with white clam sauce, always suitable for a Soave. But here the dish is dressed with more elegance and grace.

Buttered Tagliatelle with Clams and Peas

TIME: 1 HOUR

1 cup fresh English peas (about 1 pound in pods)

1 tablespoon extra virgin olive oil

3 tablespoons unsalted butter

4 large shallots, sliced vertically paper thin

Salt and freshly ground black pepper

24 littleneck clams, scrubbed

2 cups dry white wine

24 basil leaves, torn

12 ounces fresh tagliatelle or fettuccine

¼ cup dry toasted bread crumbs

1. Bring a small pot of salted water to a boil. Add the peas, cook for 2 minutes, and drain. Set aside.

2. Heat the oil over medium-low heat in a skillet or sauté pan large enough to hold the clams in a single layer. Add 1 tablespoon of the butter. When the butter starts to foam, stir in the shallots and cook until wilted but not colored. Season with salt and pepper. Stir in the clams. Add the wine, cover, and cook gently just until the clams open, about 8 minutes. Remove the pan from the heat. Add the remaining 2 tablespoons butter. Stir in the basil.

3. Meanwhile, bring 4 quarts salted water to a boil. Add the pasta, stir to separate the strands, and cook until al dente, 5 to 6 minutes. Drain, reserving 1 cup of the pasta water. Add the pasta and peas to the clams in the skillet and cook over low heat, tossing enough to combine and warm the ingredients. Add some pasta water if needed; the mixture should be very moist without being soupy. Season with salt and pepper.

4. Divide the pasta, clams, and broth among four warm soup plates. Dust with the bread crumbs and serve.

YIELD: 4 SERVINGS

COOK'S NOTES: The dish has been crafted for fresh garden peas. You could substitute frozen.

RUEDA

The shelves are filled with anonymous white wines. They're fresh, they're inexpensive, they're cold, the kind of generic beverage served in bars as the house white. Usually they require little thought: Pour, serve, drink, and forget. But what if a wine emerged that fulfilled its obligation to be lively and inexpensive, and yet had real character? If you have not already had the pleasure, allow me to introduce you to the Spanish wine Rueda.

Good Ruedas can be mouthwatering wines filled with juicy citrus, floral, and mineral flavors, just the sorts of bottles to have on hand in the refrigerator, ready to open at a moment's notice. Best of all, they tend to be downright cheap.

Rueda is yet another region to emerge triumphantly in the rebirth of the Spanish wine industry after the fall of Francisco Franco. Like Bierzo and Montsant, Toro and Navarra, Rueda is an ancient region that has come of age in the last twenty-five years. While its wine-making history stretches back more than a millennium, making it older than the numerous castles that dot its rugged terrain, only recently has Rueda come to the attention of the rest of the world.

For much of the last thousand years, Rueda, in the Castilian region northwest of Madrid, produced mostly a fortified, oxidized wine not unlike sherry, using the indigenous verdejo grape. Production was interrupted by phylloxera devastation at the turn of the twentieth century. The region's slow recovery, followed by the Spanish Civil War and the ascendance of Franco, contributed to decades of stagnation, during which the verdejo vines were largely replaced by the high-yielding sherry grape palomino.

There things stood until the 1970s, when the Rioja winery Marqués de Riscal sought a region in which it could make a fresh, modern white wine, a wine that it could successfully export to the rest of the world unlike the traditional, oaky white Rioja. With the help of the noted French oenologist Émile Peynaud, the Riscal winery settled on Rueda with the aim of reviving the verdejo grape, which Peynaud felt would be ideal for the purpose. Riscal's experiment was a success, and other producers followed in Rueda, replanting verdejo and building new wineries.

While the verdejo grape makes a rich yet crisp wine on its own, most Ruedas are a blend of several grapes, including sauvignon blanc, which Marqués de Riscal also introduced to the region. Rules of the Rueda appellation require the whites to be at least 50 percent verdejo, with the remainder sauvignon blanc or viura, while Rueda Superior must contain at least 85 percent verdejo. As a result Ruedas can have slightly different characteristics. Those with more sauvignon blanc can take on a brash grassiness, while those that are entirely verdejo or have more viura, the traditional grape of white Rioja, tend to be more minerally and floral with a richer texture.

Rueda's success with verdejo has proved refreshing in many ways. In an era when many historic wine regions have turned away from their indigenous grapes in favor of varietals with proven popularity, Rueda has demonstrated that wines can be made in an appealing yet distinctive style by applying up-to-date viticultural and wine-making techniques to traditional grapes. Isn't the world better off to have a wine that tastes clearly of Rueda rather than, say, one more cheap chardonnay? 🍷

WINE WITH CORN ON THE COB? Thanks, but I'll have a beer. Actually, though, with fresh midsummer corn, a white wine with good acidity and some richness might be the ticket, providing it displays some lean backbone, thus letting the butter drip from the corn, not fill the glass. Seafood is another, more serious food group to consider with the often complex Ruedas. And for corn and seafood together, chupé, a thick chowder from South America, not Spain, comes to mind. Like chowder, chupé can be made with almost anything, but those I have enjoyed in Venezuela and Chile usually included corn.

Corn and Seafood Chupé

TIME: 1½ HOURS

2 tablespoons unsalted butter

1 teaspoon cumin seeds

1 large onion, finely chopped

1 large garlic clove, minced

One 1-inch piece fresh ginger, peeled and minced

1 jalapeño, seeded and minced

24 medium shrimp

6 cups fish stock

4 cups fresh corn kernels (from about 4 ears)

1 pound very small Yukon gold potatoes, peeled and halved

2 medium-small zucchini, about 10 ounces, cut into ½-inch-thick slices

2 pounds halibut fillets, cut into 12 pieces

Salt and freshly ground white pepper

Lime wedges, for serving

1. Melt the butter in a 4- to 5-quart casserole. Add the cumin seeds and cook over medium heat until the seeds smell fragrant. Do not allow the butter to brown. Add the onion and sauté until soft. Add the garlic, ginger, and jalapeño, and sauté another minute or so. Add the shrimp, toss just until pink, remove with a slotted spoon, and set aside.

2. Add the stock and bring to a simmer. Add the corn and potatoes and simmer, covered, until the potatoes are tender, 10 to 15 minutes. Remove the casserole from the heat and set aside until 10 minutes before serving. Peel the shrimp.

3. Reheat the contents of the casserole on medium. Stir in the zucchini. Place the fish on top, cover the casserole, and simmer until the fish is opaque, 5 to 8 minutes. Add the shrimp and simmer, uncovered, a moment longer. Check the seasoning and serve, with lime wedges alongside.

YIELD: 6 TO 8 SERVINGS

COOK'S NOTES: This recipe, which can be made in advance and reheated before cooking the fish, welcomes variations: yellow squash instead of zucchini, other kinds of fish or seafood, a jolt of fiery aji amarillo puree if you can find it, and garnishes like nubbins of queso blanco, or diced avocado marinated in lime juice. 🍶

ASSYRTIKO AND OTHER GREEK WHITES

It's so easy to fall into a wine-drinking rut. We all have wines that we enjoy and look forward to for just about any occasion or type of food, so why even think about choosing a different bottle?

I get it completely. Some people never tire of exploring France, so never daydream about vacationing in Spain. It's just that we are living in a golden age of wine drinking, where so much pleasure is to be had from so many parts of the world that I find it a shame not to branch out occasionally.

In this spirit of exploration, I give you the white wines of Greece, which at the very least will expand your perspective on the popular genre of cool, crisp wines that immediately improve any Mediterranean-style meal. You know the type: wines that are lively and unpretentious, that smack of sunshine, whitewashed walls, and seafood. They are made to be drunk young and they come most often but not exclusively from Italy, France, Spain, and Portugal.

Greece simply offers a subtly different take on these familiar wines. But it's a great take, with unfamiliar, indigenous grapes grown nowhere else. From the windswept volcanic island of Santorini in the Aegean Sea comes the assyrtiko grape, which produces dry, deliciously minerally wines. They offer an almost tactile sensation that prickles the mouth, as if the liquid were condensed from millions of microscopic sea pebbles. The assyrtiko vines, by the way, are trained in little bushlike circles that hug the ground, both to protect them from the wind and so they can absorb the morning dew on this largely dry island.

From the Peloponnese comes the pink-skinned moschofilero grape, which produces highly floral wines that can often have a rosy tinge to them. And there are so many others, like the ancient athiri; the light, citrus-imbued roditis; and the textured savatiano. Of course, this is the modern world, so Greece has a growing proportion of nonindigenous grapes, like sauvignon blanc and chardonnay, but so far they play a supporting role.

I like all of these wines, but the assyrtikos have emerged as the strongest group, ready to take their place along with everything else the Greek islands conjure up: summer, freshness, lemon, capers, fish. The moschofileros, as delicious as they can be, remind me a little bit of gewürztraminer, perfumed of roses and grapefruit, and so may find a smaller, more select audience.

No matter which wines you choose, they all can be delicious and transporting. 🍷

A VELVETY CHILLED CAULIFLOWER SOUP and a glass of assyrtikos will quickly transport you to the Greek Isles. This summer soup from John Fraser, the chef and owner of Dovetail in Manhattan, has been given extra panache with a garnish of green apple, pickled shallots, and oysters.

Chilled Cauliflower Soup with Oyster Garnish

TIME: 40 MINUTES, PLUS CHILLING

2 shallots

2½ tablespoons extra virgin olive oil

1 cup thinly sliced sweet onions

1 garlic clove, thinly sliced

Salt

1 head cauliflower, cored, and diced

3 fresh thyme sprigs

1 bay leaf

Freshly ground white pepper

½ cup white wine vinegar

2 tablespoons sugar

1 green apple

2 teaspoons minced fresh chives

Juice of ½ lemon

18 oysters, shucked

1. Slice 1 shallot thinly. Finely dice the other one. Heat 2 tablespoons of the oil in a 3-quart saucepan on low. Add the sliced shallot, onions, and garlic. Dust with salt and cook until soft but not brown. Add the cauliflower. Tie the thyme and bay leaf together, add them to the pan, and cook until the cauliflower starts to soften. Add 4 cups water and season with salt and white pepper. Gently boil until the cauliflower is tender, about 10 minutes.

2. Meanwhile, in a small saucepan, bring the vinegar, sugar, and ½ teaspoon salt to a simmer and cook until the sugar dissolves. Add the diced shallot, remove the pan from the heat, and set aside for 2 hours to marinate.

3. When the cauliflower is tender, allow it to cool briefly, then puree the contents of the saucepan in a blender until smooth. You will have to do this in two or three batches. Season with salt and white pepper and chill for 4 to 6 hours. Drain the marinated shallot and set aside.

4. Just before serving, core and finely dice the apple and place it in a bowl with the marinated shallot, chives, lemon juice, and the remaining ½ tablespoon oil. Place 3 oysters in each of six flat soup plates. Top each with the apple mixture and serve. At the table, ladle the soup around the oysters.

YIELD: 6 SERVINGS

COOK'S NOTES: If shucking oysters does not happen to be listed on your résumé, you can order them on the half shell. Many markets also sell shucked oysters by the pint. A half-pint should do it. 🥫

DRY GEWÜRZTRAMINER

I'm a pushover for a good, dry gewürztraminer, but its attractions are by no means universal. Its aroma, often described as a combination of litchis, grapefruit, and roses, with a dollop of cold cream thrown in, can have a polarizing effect, like cilantro or licorice. Some people simply hate it. Others are mystified by it because it's so different from the usual run of dry, crisp white wines.

Many winemakers adore it. In California, it's rarely any estate's most important wine, but I've always been surprised by how many producers make a little gewürztraminer on the side, especially because I almost never see people in restaurants actually drinking it. I drink it pretty infrequently myself. Nonetheless, I love dry gewürztraminer with Cantonese food, even if this oft-cited recommendation has become a cliché, and I think gewürztraminer is more versatile with food than its singular aroma would lead one to believe.

Most gewürztraminer hails from Alsace, where it is made into classically dry wines, along with both mildly sweet and unctuous, syrupy-sweet versions. All too often, it's difficult to tell the dry from the semisweet in Alsace, which can be a problem. Outside of Alsace, you might also find some good dry gewürztraminers in Alto Adige, the Tyrolean province of northeastern Italy where German is spoken as often as Italian.

Most often, I've found myself drawn to American gewürztraminers, which at least tend to be reliably dry. Yet, these, too, can be inconsistent. You can find a few good ones from the Finger Lakes of New York and from Oregon. Some noted Napa Valley producers, like Stony Hill, make good versions. Cathy Corison, the noted Napa cabernet producer, makes Corazón from grapes grown in the Anderson Valley of Mendocino County, perhaps the source of the best American gewürztraminers.

It takes courage to brave the Germanic pileup of letters, to select the tapered bottles invariably used in Alsace and California, and to taste the wine after breathing in the singularly exotic aroma. It's a wine so different from other whites—the chardonnays, pinot grigios, and sauvignon blancs—that it almost requires a contrarian personality to order it.

Yet those who love it really love it. Ted Bennett and Deborah Cahn, who established Navarro Vineyards in 1974 in the Anderson Valley, planted thirty acres of gewürztraminer. At first, they found little demand for the wine, but slowly they built up an audience to the point where no California winery is identified more closely with gewürztraminer than Navarro.

"Gewürz is such a great wine because it's so aromatic," Ms. Cahn once told me. "It's so personal and intimate." 🍷

THOUGH DRY AND BOASTING GREAT MINERALITY, in a gewürztraminer there is always a hint of honey lurking. Sweet onions and smoky trout are combined for a simple brunch or lunch preparation that is suited to entertaining and delicious with the gewürztraminers poured alongside. A frittatalike mixture inspired by the Spanish tortilla omelet of potatoes and onions but with the addition of smoked trout is baked, not fried, in individual portions. They can be made in advance and reheated. A salad is all that's needed alongside.

Smoked Trout Frittatas

TIME: 45 MINUTES

2½ tablespoons extra virgin olive oil

1 pound Yukon gold potatoes, peeled and cut into ½-inch dice

Salt

1 cup finely chopped onions

1 ounce speck, finely chopped

1 smoked trout, skin and bones removed

2 tablespoons minced fresh dill

7 large eggs, beaten

Freshly ground black pepper

1 cup sour cream

1. Heat 2 tablespoons of the oil in a 10-inch skillet. Add the potatoes and cook on medium-low until starting to soften, about 10 minutes. Sprinkle with salt. Add the onions, increase the heat to medium, and cook until the onions and potatoes are tender, about 5 minutes longer. Stir in the speck and sauté for another minute. Stir in the trout and 1 tablespoon of the dill. Transfer to a bowl and allow to cool for 10 minutes.

2. Heat the oven to 325°F. Use the remaining ½ tablespoon oil to grease 6 large (8-ounce) muffin cups. Fold the eggs into the trout mixture. Season generously with pepper and add salt, if needed. Spoon the mixture into the muffin cups. Place in the oven and bake for 15 minutes. Fold the remaining dill into the sour cream and place in a serving dish.

3. Unmold the frittatas and serve with the dilled sour cream alongside.

YIELD: 6 SERVINGS

COOK'S NOTES: Speck is a smoked bacon from Germany, Austria, and northern Italy. American smoked bacon can be substituted.

CONDRIEU

The resurrection of Condrieu is one of the more dramatic success stories of the Old World. Today, Condrieu is a somewhat fashionable wine, valued around the world for its lush, voluptuous tropical fruit flavors and rich, seductive texture. Yet only forty years ago the Condrieu appellation in the northern Rhône Valley was barely alive, with only about thirty acres of grapes to its name.

What shook it from its near-death slumber? In a word, "viognier."

Had New World producers not seized on viognier, the grape of Condrieu, in an effort to make it their own, Condrieu might have languished among the forgotten vineyards of old. Instead, the marketing of viognier in the New World created a demand for the original source, and Condrieu was reborn in the 1980s and '90s.

While the New World fervor for viognier may have dimmed, Condrieu is alive and well. From those paltry thirty acres in the early 1970s, plantings in Condrieu are now about three hundred acres—still a tiny amount, comparable to a single large Bordeaux estate, but firmly established nonetheless.

The reawakening of Condrieu has provided an Old World appellation with many of the issues that confront New World producers, except for the most important one, of course: which grape to grow where. In Condrieu, only viognier is permitted. Beyond that, pretty much anything goes.

Without an anchor of tradition holding wine-making styles in place, Condrieu producers, like their New World counterparts, are experimenting with several different styles. As with California chardonnay, you are as likely to find a rich, viscous wine framed with new oak as you are a bone-dry, crisp, minerally wine. A fair amount of sweet late-harvest wine is also being made. Regardless of the style, the wines are exotic and sensuous, and their sheer deliciousness sets a high standard.

Few wines are as texturally interesting as Condrieu, a tribute to the region itself where viognier is able to ripen without sacrificing the acidity that gives it freshness and structure. And while I am not generally a fan of new-oak flavors in any wine, in Condrieu new oak seems to integrate beautifully with the fruit.

The thin soils and hilly vineyards of Condrieu are crucial to its success with viognier. The grape itself is said to be difficult and capricious, and yields must be kept low, particularly because so many vines are young, planted in the last two decades and prone to overcropping. Growers do not consider viognier vines to be in their prime until they are twenty-five years old. The combination of young vines and high yields can result in thin and shallow wines.

The best are sumptuous without being heavy, and while the conventional wisdom is to drink Condrieu young, within three or four years of the vintage, good bottles age surprisingly well.

Condrieu is rarely cheap, which perhaps is the price of scarcity. ☙

I STILL REMEMBER MY FIRST TASTE OF CONDRIEU. It was at the legendary Lutèce in New York umpteen years ago and it accompanied a warm lobster salad. Ever since, to me, Condrieu and lobster were a match. But over time my palate for Condrieu has broadened. Here is a casserole made with dark meat chicken, which retains its succulence better than white for a perfect dinner party dish. A rich viognier with a pedigree—a Condrieu, of course—suits it well, though for a party, a step down to a less exalted viognier from southwest France or California would be fine.

Casserole of Chicken and Fingerlings

TIME: 1 HOUR 15 MINUTES

½ pound cipollini onions

1 head garlic, cloves peeled

12 ounces small fingerling potatoes

1½ cups plus 1 tablespoon extra virgin olive oil

8 fresh thyme sprigs

3½ pounds (approximately) dark meat chicken parts, 8 thighs and 4 legs

Salt and freshly ground black pepper

½ cup viognier or chardonnay

2 cups rich chicken stock, or 1½ cups chicken and ½ cup veal stock

3 tablespoons unsalted butter, preferably high-fat European style

2 tablespoons minced fresh tarragon

1. Heat the oven to 300°F. Arrange the onions on a small baking dish, place in the oven, and roast for 30 minutes. Allow to cool.

2. Meanwhile, place the garlic cloves and potatoes in a saucepan. Add 1½ cups of the oil and the thyme, and cook over very low heat until the potatoes are tender when pierced with a knife, about 20 minutes. Allow to cool in the pan.

3. Season the chicken with salt and pepper. Heat the remaining 1 tablespoon oil in a large sauté pan. Add the chicken and brown on both sides. Remove the chicken, pour off all the fat in the pan, and return the chicken to the pan. Add the wine and stock, bring to a simmer, and braise, covered, for about 20 minutes, until the chicken is cooked through. Meanwhile, peel the onions.

4. Remove the chicken from the pan and cook the liquid over high heat until it has reduced to 1¾ cups. Over very low heat, add the butter, bit by bit, whisking it in. Season with salt and pepper, if needed, and stir in the tarragon.

5. Place the chicken in a stove-top casserole dish that can go to the table. Remove the potatoes and garlic from the oil with a slotted spoon and add to the casserole. Add the peeled onions. Pour in the sauce. Gently reheat the casserole just to a simmer and bring it to the table. Serve in shallow soup plates.

YIELD: 4 SERVINGS

COOK'S NOTES: In place of flat cipollini onions, round little white onions can be used. And for the fingerlings? Small Yukon golds. You may wonder about all that olive oil you used for cooking the potatoes and garlic. Do not discard it. Transfer it to a container and refrigerate it to use for subsequent potato cooking jobs. Adding a sprig or two of fresh thyme to it will only improve it. 🥫

JURA SAVAGNIN
At the turn of the millennium, few Americans had ever heard of the Jura, much less its wines. Now, the wines are among the most coveted in the wine vanguard. Yet little about their popularity smacks of fad or fashion.

The leading whites, made from the savagnin grape, have a nutty, fino sherrylike aroma that many people regard as hopelessly oxidized, but they are actually tangy, complex, pure, and delicious. The most famous example would be the vin jaune, or yellow wine, a powerful, almost punishingly austere white that nonetheless can be spectacularly captivating, especially when paired with one of the local specialties, like chicken with morels or Comté cheese. As the British wine writer Hugh Johnson says, vin jaune is not for neophytes.

That the wines are singular should not be surprising. The Jura is a bucolic green bowl between Burgundy and Switzerland, where the patchwork of vineyards and hay fields is occasionally interrupted by a village of tile-roofed houses or a herd of cows. Roads came fairly late to the region; canals never did. So the Jura evolved, like the marsupials of Australia, in relative isolation, which permitted the planting of grapes like savagnin, poulsard, and trousseau that are grown almost nowhere else, and made into wines with techniques that in most places would be regarded as downright peculiar.

What makes the savagnin wines so different? After the wine is fermented, it is put into barrels. Over time, the wine begins to evaporate and, in contradiction to ordinary wine production, the barrels are not topped off to keep oxygen out. Instead a yeast forms on the surface of the wine, much as in sherry production, which protects the wine and contributes to its characteristic tangy, salty, nutlike flavor. Wines made in this style are said to be made sous-voile, or under the veil.

Jura winemakers tend to bridle at the comparison with sherry. They point out that sherry is fortified, unlike their wines. Yet the savagnin wines made in the sous-voile style do share aspects of the fino flavor profile, in the best possible way.

Not all Jura whites are made in this manner, however. Some, both savagnins and chardonnays, are made in a clean, straightforward style that is not nearly as unusual. But the sous-voile savagnins are the most distinctive, neither New World nor Old World but a world apart. 🍷

AT SOME TASTINGS, the wines display great consistency, which simplifies the choice of a dish to serve alongside. But there are others at which the styles of the wines are all over the map. This situation seems to come up more with white wines than with reds, and the Jura whites, vins jaunes, are a case in point. I mated them with leeks, mellow and sweet, and Roquefort cheese, a classic pairing with sweet white wines. I combined these ingredients in a quiche-like tart that can be served as a first course (or, in small wedges, with an aperitif glass of the wine), or as a luncheon dish.

Roquefort and Leek Tart

TIME: 1 HOUR

Pastry for an 8-inch tart shell (page 49)

1 tablespoon unsalted butter

2½ cups chopped leeks (white and light green parts)

Freshly ground black pepper

6 ounces Roquefort or other blue-veined cheese, crumbled

1 teaspoon fresh thyme leaves

3 large eggs, beaten

1½ cups half-and-half

1. Heat the oven to 400°F. Roll out the pastry and fit it into an 8-inch quiche or tart pan. Line with foil and weight with pastry weights or dry beans. Bake for 10 minutes, remove the foil and weights, and bake until golden, about 15 minutes more.

2. While the pastry is baking, heat the butter in a large skillet. Add the leeks, season with pepper, and sauté over low heat until soft but not browned. Remove from the heat. When the pastry is done, remove from the oven and lower the heat to 375°F.

3. Spread the leeks in the bottom of the pastry shell. Add the cheese and thyme. Mix the eggs and half-and-half and pour over the ingredients in the pastry shell. Place in the oven and bake for 35 to 40 minutes, until the filling feels fairly firm to the touch and has barely begun to brown. Serve warm or at room temperature.

YIELD: 6 SERVINGS

COOK'S NOTES:
Alongside, perfection can be achieved with a small green salad dressed in white wine vinegar and walnut oil, scattered with toasted walnuts. 🫙 In place of Roquefort, another good blue-veined cheese, like Fourme d'Ambert or, from the United States, Maytag Blue, would be fine. The recipe does not need added salt. The cheese takes care of that. 🫙

REDS

Many reds will take no prisoners. They are determined, assertive, demanding. They willingly stand toe to toe with whatever is being served, grabbing the mike and all the attention. A wine-lover about to enjoy a fine bottle of red may consider any food to be of secondary value when it comes to enjoyment. With few exceptions, it pays to throw great food at red wines with pedigree and heft. With these bottles, serve those prime meats, exceptional burgers, properly smoky barbecue, crackling roast chicken, and lobsters sizzled under the broiler or on the grill. There are lighter reds, to be sure, like graceful pinot noirs and delicate Valpolicellas, and even Bordeaux from lesser vintages that are wonderful alongside more subdued dishes. The best rule of thumb, when selecting a red wine and its accompanying menu, is to consider the weight of the wine you have a taste for. Then find a dish with comparable body. A menu that calls for more than one wine should proceed with a lighter red to start and a sturdier one to follow. It's an occasion to consider selecting the wines first, and then the foods to serve with them.

CHIANTI CLASSICO

Chianti Classico is the designation for wines made in the Chianti region's heartland in the hills of Tuscany, the spiritual home of the sangiovese grape. With its cherry and floral aromas, its earthy mineral flavors, its lively acidity, and its sometimes dusty tannins, sangiovese speaks directly from the Italian soul.

At least that's the general idea. Unfortunately, it has not always worked out that way. Like a family constantly at odds, Chianti has seldom been able to present a unified face to the world, except, alas, for those straw bottles that were once emblematic of Italian wine.

A good deal of Chianti's troubles have been self-imposed, as Italian wine bureaucrats have veered wildly in the past forty years trying to define and redefine what makes a Chianti, generally at the expense of sangiovese and its traditional companions, canaiolo nero and colorino. Currently, sangiovese must make up 80 percent to 100 percent of the blend, which can also include the indigenous grapes as well as interlopers like cabernet sauvignon, merlot, and syrah. The best bottles speak not only of the sangiovese grape itself but of the Tuscan hills where sangiovese vines flourish as they do in few other places in the world.

I might ordinarily say that I like the traditional style of Chianti Classico best, but with Chianti, "traditional" is a largely meaningless word. Chianti has generally been a blended wine, made primarily of sangiovese but also with several other red grapes and even some white ones. In fact, the father of Chianti, Baron Bettino Ricasoli, who codified Chianti production methods in the mid-1800s, called for as much as 30 percent white grapes like trebbiano and malvasia.

More than a century later, as the rest of the wine world was modernizing its viticulture and cellar techniques, Italian bureaucrats clung to the old ways, enforcing the formula despite the large number of thin, unpleasant wines being produced. In the 1970s, many serious Tuscan winemakers began to direct their best efforts elsewhere, making wines with grapes or blends unsanctioned by the bureaucracy. These wines came to be known as super Tuscans, and while some showed what Tuscany could do with cabernet sauvignon and the international grapes, others demonstrated what could be done only with sangiovese.

One of these was Sergio Manetti of Montevertine, in the heart of the Chianti Classico region, who was so disgusted with the rules of Chianti that he simply withdrew from the denomination. Today, I might consider Montevertine the greatest Chianti Classico producer of all, except that it still does not call its wines Chianti, even though the current rules would let it.

The rules have changed frequently in the last few decades, though the 80 percent rule has been in force since 2006. Obviously, they leave a lot of room for variation: A Chianti Classico can be 100 percent sangiovese or it can contain 20 percent cabernet, which can dominate the sangiovese. But no longer can it contain white grapes.

Incidentally, Chianti Classicos with the "riserva" designation have received extra aging. These wines tend to be darker, denser, and more oaky. Personally, I generally prefer the freshness and energy of the "normale" bottlings. 🍷

CHIANTI CLASSICO RISERVA IS AN ANYTIME WINE. Steak, often a partner for this wine, also knows no season. Potatoes and garlicky sautéed greens are suitable cold-weather additions to the menu. But to give slabs of thick porterhouse or rib eye on the grill sunglasses and a deck chair, consider a salad alongside. The quintessential Tuscan salad is panzanella, made with garden vegetables and pieces of stale bread in a vinaigrette. Taking advantage of a lighted grill, this version combines seared fennel with cucumbers and olives and grilled bread. Some rosemary addresses the dominant herbal flavor in the wine. And even the salad can be dished up in cold weather because the ingredients, like the meat and the wine, are perennials. There is another panzanella recipe, using autumn vegetables (page 153).

Tuscan Steaks with Grilled Fennel Panzanella

TIME: 1 HOUR

1 medium cucumber, peeled, quartered lengthwise, seeded, and sliced ¼ inch thick

Salt

½ cup pitted Kalamata olives, halved

1 large garlic clove, slivered

½ cup chopped red onion

Leaves from 3 fresh rosemary sprigs

2 tablespoons chopped fresh flat-leaf parsley

Steaks for 4: 2 thick porterhouse, or 2 to 4 thick rib eyes or bone-in strip loins

Freshly ground black pepper

9 tablespoons extra virgin olive oil

2 large fennel bulbs, trimmed, cored, and sliced ¼ inch thick

2 slices country bread, preferably stale

6 tablespoons red wine vinegar

1. Place the cucumber in a medium bowl, add ½ teaspoon salt, toss, and set aside for 30 minutes. Drain the excess liquid. Add the olives, garlic, red onion, rosemary, and parsley to the cucumbers. Heat a grill or broiler. Brush the steaks with a little oil and season with pepper.

2. Massage the fennel slices with 2 tablespoons of the oil. Spread on a perforated grilling pan or on a broiler pan. Grill or broil the fennel, turning as pieces start to brown, until all are uniformly dappled. Remove the fennel to a cutting board.

3. Season the steaks with salt. Place the steaks on the grill or under the broiler and sear, turning once, until cooked to the desired degree of doneness (in Tuscany that means rare). Transfer to a carving board and allow to rest for 15 minutes.

4. Brush the bread with 2 tablespoons of the oil and grill or broil, turning once, until toasted. Coarsely chop the fennel and bread. Add to the salad mixture along with the remaining 5 tablespoons oil and the vinegar. Season with salt and pepper and place in a serving bowl. Slice the steaks and arrange on a platter. Serve with the salad.

YIELD: 4 SERVINGS

COOK'S NOTES: As with roasted meats and poultry, thick grilled steaks also benefit from a resting period of a good 15 minutes after they come off the fire to permit the internal juices to consolidate, making the meat more succulent and tender.

ROSSO DI MONTALCINO

It's been a rough few years in the wine business for Montalcino. First came scandal in 2008, when some producers of Brunello di Montalcino were accused of adding other grapes to a wine that by law must be made of only the sangiovese grape. Then came prolonged debate over whether to change that rule and others, along with soul-searching, breast-beating, garment-rending, and other essential expressions of an acute identity crisis.

It's not as if the region were tampering with centuries of tradition. Brunello di Montalcino was a relative latecomer to the ancient world of Italian wines. Although wines had been labeled "Brunello di Montalcino" since the late nineteenth century, the name was largely the province of one producer, Biondi-Santi. The rules of the appellation were not codified until 1968, and the wines did not explode in popularity until the 1980s.

Even from the outset, the rules for Brunello di Montalcino struck many as being overly rigid. In addition to the 100 percent sangiovese standard, the wines had to be aged at least forty-eight months, forty-two of them in barrels, before they could be released. Over time, the period of barrel aging was reduced to twenty-four months, although producers were still required to age their wines for four years, delaying substantially the return on their investment.

To help ease this burden, back in the early 1980s the authorities created Rosso di Montalcino, a wine that, like Brunello, could be made only of sangiovese but was required to have just one year of aging before it could be sold. In addition to improving cash flow, the new category let producers release as Rosso the wine that didn't make the cut as Brunello or that came from grapes grown outside the areas designated for Brunello.

So far, so good. So, again, why were people unhappy? Brunello made in the traditional manner can yield a wine that is lean and tight, requiring years to unwind, even after its long aging at the winery. While good traditional Brunellos like those made by Biondi-Santi offer a rare combination of purity, depth of flavor, intensity, and finesse, many consumers did not want to make the investment in time.

Rosso is the ideal solution. The best bottles are soulful and elemental, like good trattoria food, with winsomely bitter, citrus-tinged cherry flavors—dusty, earthy, and pure. Naturally, you will find stylistic deviations. Some wines will be leaner and lighter-bodied; others more robust. Some will taste like oak barrels, others just of the grape. As with Brunello, it's left to consumers to determine which producers align with their own tastes. 🍷

WHILE TASTING AN UTTERLY SATISFYING COLLECTION of Rosso di Montalcino wines, my appetite kept turning to chicken livers to go alongside. The chicken livers' edge of bitterness tamed by salt when properly prepared seemed to be on the same wavelength as the wines. In Tuscany, chicken liver crostini, often seasoned with anchovies, are a typical palate whetter. I took my chicken livers in a different direction, with some global spicing, which delivers a brash, curried swagger that can look the more muscular of these wines straight in the eye.

Spiced Chicken Liver Mousse

TIME: 35 MINUTES, PLUS CHILLING

6 to 8 tablespoons chicken or duck fat, or clarified butter

½ teaspoon black mustard seeds

½ teaspoon ground cardamom

1½ teaspoons ground cumin

1 pound chicken livers, connective tissue removed

1 medium onion, chopped

One 1-inch piece fresh ginger, peeled and slivered

¼ cup amontillado sherry

⅓ cup heavy cream

Salt and freshly ground black pepper

1. Melt 3 tablespoons of the fat in a 12-inch skillet. Add the mustard seeds, cardamom, and cumin and sauté until the spices sizzle and are fragrant. Add the chicken livers and sauté over medium-low heat, turning once, until cooked but still pink inside, about 10 minutes. Remove the livers from the pan.

2. Add 2 tablespoons of the remaining fat, the onion, and the ginger to the pan and sauté until soft, about 5 minutes. Add the sherry and simmer until somewhat reduced, about 5 minutes. Stir in the cream and cook until starting to thicken. Transfer the livers and the onion mixture to a food processor and process until smooth. Season with salt and pepper.

3. Spoon the mousse into a crock or bowl and smooth the top. Melt the remaining 2 tablespoons fat in a separate pan and pour it onto the surface of the mousse. Use an additional tablespoon fat, if needed, to seal the surface. Refrigerate for at least 4 hours before serving.

YIELD: ABOUT 2 CUPS

COOK'S NOTES: The recipe is generous and any leftover portion will keep for several days if sealed with more melted fat or with plastic wrap placed right on the surface. 🧂

BRUNELLO DI MONTALCINO

Good Brunello di Montalcino can be a magnificent wine, a pure evocation of the bitter cherry and dusty mineral flavors that are the soul of the sangiovese grape, presented with the combination of grace and intensity that is characteristic of great reds. But Brunello di Montalcino can be many other things, too, some good and some not so.

The core question for the last few decades has been one of identity. Should Brunello di Montalcino be made only of sangiovese, as has always been the law? Or should winemakers have the latitude to add other grapes if they think they will improve the wine—say, cabernet sauvignon or syrah, or even montepulciano? This has been the subject of great debate, and even legal scandal. But whatever Brunello producers believe in their secret hearts, when they had a chance to put it to the ballot, they voted overwhelmingly in favor of retaining the 100 percent sangiovese rule.

Yet even made legally, Brunello di Montalcino offers many different faces. It can be light-bodied, ruby colored, complex, and a little austere; or it can be big boned, dark, plush, and velvety, and marked decisively by the chocolate and vanilla flavors of new French oak. Or it can be anywhere in between. I prefer the lighter, less oaky style, as a clearer, more distinctive expression of sangiovese, while the plusher versions veer toward a more generic international style.

These variations all could be attributed to differences in style and taste, and quite possibly to geography. Brunello di Montalcino, after all, is a fairly recent creation, coalescing as an appellation in the mid-twentieth century. In the last few decades, it has expanded greatly, as have notions of what constitutes the wine. Partly, this is because the Montalcino appellation—or what Italians call Denominazione di Origine Controllata e Garantita (DOCG)—covers a wide and diverse territory.

Bordeaux, for example, recognizes that adjoining territories can have differing characteristics and so distinguishes Pauillac from Saint-Estèphe and Saint-Julien. But as far as Brunello di Montalcino is concerned, it is left to the public to try to recognize which wines come from the lower elevations and clay soils in the south, and which are from the higher, lighter soils in the central area around the town of Montalcino.

All the uncertainty makes it imperative for consumers to figure out which producers align with their own tastes and which do not. From my point of view, good Brunello is dense but not weighty, with pure, focused bitter-cherry flavors buttressed by an underlying earthiness. The wines can be deep, complex, and elegant, but good ones also ripple with acidity and, when young, can be tannic and austere.

They require aging to open up fully, but the wait will be repaid. Yes, these wines can be very expensive. Are they worth it? That's a question only you and your bank account can answer. Meanwhile, for a taste of Brunello, Rosso di Montalcino beckons. 🍷

DECIDING WHAT TO SERVE WITH BRUNELLO DI MONTALCINO is no small challenge. In any vintage, the bold wines from this elite patch of the Tuscan countryside demand serious food. The impressive, fist-size hunks of meat and bone that go into osso buco are a good place to start. But instead of the traditional, somewhat rustic recipe for this Italian specialty, I strike a more elegant note by simmering the veal in a red wine sauce with slices of deeply flavorful portobello mushrooms that add a suggestion of tannin, echoing the character of these long-lived wines.

Osso Buco Portobello

TIME: 2 HOURS

2 tablespoons all-purpose flour

Salt and freshly ground black pepper

4 pieces veal shank, 2 inches thick

4 tablespoons extra virgin olive oil

4 large portobello mushrooms, stemmed, cut into slices ½ inch wide

½ cup finely chopped shallots

4 garlic cloves, sliced

1 cup dry red wine

⅓ cup beef stock

2 tablespoons red wine vinegar

6 fresh thyme sprigs, plus more for garnish

1. Season the flour with salt and pepper. Spread on a plate. Dust the meat top and bottom with the flour. Heat 3 tablespoons of the oil in a 4- to 5-quart casserole on medium-high. Add the meat and brown on both sides. Remove from the casserole. Add the mushrooms and cook, stirring, until they start to wilt and no longer look dry, about 5 minutes. Remove.

2. Add the remaining 1 tablespoon oil to the casserole, reduce the heat to low, and add the shallots and garlic. Sauté until just starting to brown. Add the wine and stock and deglaze the pan, scraping up any bits on the bottom. Season generously with pepper. Stir in the vinegar. Return the meat and mushrooms to the casserole, add the thyme, cover, and cook on very low, basting the meat a few times, until the meat is tender, about 1 hour 15 minutes.

3. Season the sauce with salt as needed. Transfer the meat, mushrooms, and sauce to a warm platter. Garnish with thyme sprigs and serve.

YIELD: 4 SERVINGS

COOK'S NOTES: Serve the osso buco with creamy polenta bolstered with some Parmigiano-Reggiano. Do not forget utensils for scooping out the rich marrow, and, as you savor it, be grateful for the acid balance in the best of the wines. 🍶

CÔTE CHALONNAISE

So close, and yet so far away. I sometimes wonder how it feels to be a vigneron in the Côte Chalonnaise, the hilly region that extends south and slightly east of the southern tip of the Côte d'Or, the great heart of Burgundy. The Côte d'Or, of course, receives all the accolades, the fawning visits, and the money. The Côte Chalonnaise receives the figurative back of the hand because, well, it just isn't the Côte d'Or. But it isn't Beaujolais, either—a different sort of nearby region that is simply linked administratively to Burgundy.

The reds are made of pinot noir, the whites of chardonnay, just as in the famed villages to the north. Yet the wines from the main villages of the Côte Chalonnaise—Bouzeron, Rully, Mercurey, Givry, and Montagny—have always been considered the poor rustic relations, without the elegance, grace, or delineated intensity of their betters. As in all the world's great but stratified wine regions, it must be a bitter thing to realize that regardless of how much commitment one brings to the soil, the grape, and the wine making, respect will always be elusive.

But no matter how vast a chasm separates the Côte Chalonnaise from the Côte d'Or, it is still Burgundy after all, and the spillover potential is alluring. The hope always beckons that for appreciably less money the villages of the Côte Chalonnaise will offer a satisfying glimpse of Burgundy's gorgeous sunlight. This hasn't always been the case. In his book *The Wines of Burgundy*, Clive Coates calls the Côte Chalonnaise "a well-known 'forgotten area,'" suggesting that while people in the wine trade acknowledge that the region is worth investigating, few merchants have actually taken the trouble to explore what the Côte Chalonnaise has to offer. For many years, Americans have effectively not had access to some of the region's best producers.

Yet things are indeed changing for the better. As in so many other regions all over the world, the viticulture and cellar work in the Côte Chalonnaise have improved tremendously in the last twenty-five years. A new generation has taken over, one that has traveled widely and understands that quality is paramount in a global business. And more importers are seriously exploring the Côte Chalonnaise and making some of the better producers more widely available.

In fact, the wines are quite delicious. The whites may not have the heft of those from the great Côte de Beaune villages, but they offer the crystal clarity and mineral flavors that certainly identify them as Burgundies. And the reds, like any good Burgundies, are pretty, aromatic, and seductive. They may not have the fleshy fruit of New World pinot noirs, but the light-bodied grace and intensity of Burgundy is clear.

The best wines of the Côte Chalonnaise are not always easy to find, but as more people recognize the quality of these wines, perhaps that will change. Then, people may no longer speak wistfully about what the Côte Chalonnaise is not, but instead speak enthusiastically about what it has become. 🍷

SWEETBREADS ARE A SUPERB CHOICE WITH RED BURGUNDIES. But here I picked up the cherry flavors that frequently show up in these beautifully accessible wines and I added dried cherries to the braised sweetbreads. There is a certain amount of preliminary preparation—soaking, peeling, and poaching—required before sweetbreads are ready to cook. Some recipes also call for pressing them, but I think that just makes them dry, which they certainly are not in this pinot noir–friendly dish.

Sweetbreads with Cherries

TIMES: 30 MINUTES, PLUS 2 HOURS OR MORE SOAKING AND COOLING

1⅓ pounds sweetbreads

Salt

1 lemon

½ cup dried cherries

⅓ cup dry red wine

3 tablespoons all-purpose flour

Freshly ground black pepper

2 tablespoons unsalted butter

1½ ounces pancetta, in one slice, diced

½ cup finely chopped yellow onion

24 very small pearl onions

⅔ cup chicken stock

1 tablespoon minced fresh tarragon leaves

COOK'S NOTES: If preparing sweetbreads seems too daunting, there are alternatives for this recipe. Chunks of boned duck confit, which is sold already cooked, would be an excellent option, and a classic with a cherry sauce.

1. Rinse the sweetbreads under cold running water. Dissolve 1 tablespoon salt in 2 cups cold water in a 2-quart bowl. Add the juice of ½ lemon. Add the sweetbreads. The water should cover them. Soak for 1 to 2 hours. Place the cherries in a dish, add the wine, and set aside for at least 2 hours.

2. Remove the sweetbreads from the water and use a sharp knife to peel off the translucent membrane and remove any bits of fat. If the sweetbreads separate into sections, that's fine. Place the sweetbreads in a saucepan, cover with cold water, and add almost all the juice of the remaining lemon half. Bring to a slow simmer and poach for 15 minutes. Allow to cool in the liquid, then refrigerate until ready to use.

3. Place the pearl onions in a saucepan, cover with water, bring to a simmer, and cook for 5 minutes. Drain, rinse under cold water, and peel.

4. Remove the sweetbreads from the liquid. Separate them into 1- to 2-inch nuggets. Pat dry. Season the flour with salt and pepper and dust the sweetbreads. Melt the butter in a 12-inch skillet or sauté pan with a cover. Very lightly brown the sweetbreads on medium heat and remove to a dish. Add the pancetta and chopped onion to the skillet. Sauté on medium-low until starting to color. Add the pearl onions and sauté until starting to color. Add the cherries with the wine and the stock. Stir to deglaze the pan. Bring to a simmer, add the sweetbreads, and baste with the sauce.

5. Cover and simmer gently for 10 minutes. Season the sauce with the remaining lemon juice and salt and pepper. Baste the sweetbreads again, add the tarragon, and serve.

YIELD: 4 FIRST-COURSE, OR 3 MAIN-COURSE SERVINGS

CÔTE DE NUITS REDS

The narrow north-to-south strip known as the Côte de Nuits comprises an honor roll of red wine villages that induces panting the world over: Gevrey-Chambertin, Morey–Saint-Denis, Chambolle-Musigny, Vougeot, Vosnes-Romanée, and Nuits–Saint-Georges, along with a few less well-known lights like Marsannay and Fixin. Wondrous reds come from the Côte de Beaune to the south as well, particularly from Volnay, Pommard, Corton, and the Beaune appellations. But for red Burgundy, the Côte de Nuits is the heartland.

These are the wines that weaken the knees as they touch the mind and soul. Few red wines on earth can match Burgundy's combination of intensity and fragility, strength and finesse, complexity and tension. The quality of red Burgundy has never been higher or more consistent. At their best they are precise, graceful, and subtly but firmly structured, offering great pleasure while at the same time transparently showing the characteristics of their particular terroirs. Sadly, these wonderful qualities come at high prices, which seem only to be going up.

Within the Burgundian hierarchy, the grand cru vineyards, with hallowed names like Chambertin and Musigny, Richebourg and La Tâche, are sacred territory, with single bottles ranging from around one hundred fifty dollars to ten times that, depending on the vineyard and the producer. These days even fanatical Burgundy lovers can mostly just fantasize about drinking the best of these wines.

Many astute buyers used to find a sweet spot among the premier crus, the level right below grand cru. Premier cru vineyards are judged to have desirable attributes worthy of being singled out, though the wines they produce, theoretically at least, don't have the potential depth, complexity, and age-worthiness of the grand crus. But prices have also gone up for premier crus, and some wines from the best premier cru vineyards, like Les Amoureuses in Chambolle and Clos Saint-Jacques in Gevrey, can cost several hundred dollars.

For many of us, that leaves mostly village wines from the most vaunted communes as the sole affordable dip into Burgundian terroir. These wines come largely from vineyards not judged to have particularly distinctive characteristics beyond reflecting the villages in which they are situated. So, a village-level Chambolle-Musigny ought to offer the distinctive characteristics of Chambolle, even if it will not permit the deeper parsing of specific vineyard traits so beloved by Burgundy fanatics.

It's often said that Burgundy is a minefield in which consumers never know what they are buying. Nonsense. Red Burgundy, at least, is no more of a crapshoot than any other wine region. In fact, through hard work, it has achieved a far higher level of consistency among good producers than many other top regions that are never assailed by such criticism. Perhaps the stakes are higher in Burgundy because of price and scarcity, but as with anywhere else, learning who the good producers are helps to assure reliability. 🍷

THE LOVELY, OFTEN UNASSUMING RED BURGUNDIES with village appellations are thoroughly food-friendly. They offer excellent structure, good acidity, and alluring earthiness to balance floral and fruity notes. For me, they seemed to be the perfect partner for all sorts of charcuterie, for which Burgundy is famous. Jambon persillé is a Burgundian terrine in which cooked ham and parsley are bound with gelatin, so both the preparation and the finished dish are lighter and simpler than a traditional pork terrine. This recipe was adapted from Gilles Verot, a well-known charcuterie shop on the Left Bank in Paris. Add a tangle of fresh little salad greens with a mustardy dressing alongside, and you're all set.

Jambon Persillé

TIME: 2 HOURS, PLUS OVERNIGHT CHILLING

4 cups chicken stock

1½ cups dry white wine

1 onion, stuck with
2 whole cloves

1 bouquet garni

1 teaspoon whole black peppercorns

1 celery stalk, with leaves

1 pound spareribs

One 2-pound piece boiled ham, preferably jambon de Paris

2 large garlic cloves

2 shallots

1 cup packed fresh flat-leaf parsley leaves

Fine sea salt and freshly ground black pepper

2 packets plain gelatin, softened in ⅓ cup cold water

1. Place the stock, wine, onion, bouquet garni, peppercorns, and celery in a pot. Add the spareribs, bring to a simmer, and cook for 1 hour. Remove the meat and reserve for another use. Strain the broth into a container and refrigerate overnight.

2. Dice half the ham, including all the fat, and place in a food processor with the garlic, shallots, and parsley. Pulse to mince fine, but do not make a puree. Season with salt and pepper. Cut the remaining ham into matchsticks about ¼ inch wide and 1 inch long.

3. Remove all the fat and sediment from the broth. You should now have about 2 cups. Place the broth in a saucepan, add the softened gelatin, and simmer just to dissolve the gelatin. Mix half the broth with the minced ham and spread one third of this mixture in the bottom of a 6-cup loaf pan. Add half the ham sticks, arranging them across the width of the pan. Cover with some of the remaining broth. Repeat, ending with a layer of the minced mixture, and pour all the remaining broth on top. Cover with foil.

4. Heat the oven to 275°F. Cook for 40 minutes. Allow to cool, then refrigerate until firm, at least 6 hours. Unmold and serve in slices.

YIELD: 8 TO 12 SERVINGS

COOK'S NOTES: So what's up with the spareribs? Their role is to enrich the stock; and after your terrine is done, you can simply glaze them and put them on the grill. 🫙 Placing the ham cut into matchsticks across the width of the pan, makes it easier to slice. 🫙

"PINOT NOIR DEMANDS MUCH OF BOTH VINE-GROWER AND WINE-MAKER," said Jancis Robinson, in *The Oxford Companion to Wine*. As challenging as the grape may be, once it is in the bottle, it often becomes the most forgiving of wines. Pinot noirs are safe choices, especially in restaurants, when a party of four, for example, may order a diverse assortment of dishes and seek a wine to accompany them all. There is, in short, no better red wine to drink with fish, especially meaty, rich varieties like salmon, arctic char, tuna, and Alaskan black cod (sablefish). And of these fish, none is easier to prepare than Alaskan black cod, a fish whose high fat content makes it almost impervious to drying out from overcooking.

Black Cod on Wilted Radicchio

TIME: 45 MINUTES

6 tablespoons extra virgin olive oil

1 medium red onion, sliced thin

4 ounces Italian sweet sausage, casing removed, diced

1 large head radicchio, quartered, cored, and shredded

1 teaspoon fennel seeds, crushed

3 tablespoons sherry vinegar

Salt and freshly ground black pepper

2 pounds Alaskan black cod (sablefish) fillets, skinned, in 4 pieces

1 tablespoon French mustard, preferably violet mustard from Brive

1 tablespoon finely chopped fresh flat-leaf parsley leaves

1. Heat the oven to 200°F. Heat 2 tablespoons of the oil in a large skillet. Add the red onion and cook over low heat until wilted. Add the sausage and cook, stirring, until it loses its redness. Add the radicchio and cook, stirring, until it is wilted, about 6 minutes. Stir in the fennel seeds and 1 tablespoon of the vinegar. Season with salt and pepper.

2. Transfer to a baking dish large enough to hold the fillets in a single layer, cover with foil, and place in the oven.

3. Pat the fish dry on paper towels and season with salt and pepper. Add 2 tablespoons of the oil to the skillet. Increase the heat to medium-high and cook the fish, turning once, until very lightly browned and just cooked through, about 3 minutes on each side. Transfer the fish to the baking dish, cover, and return to the oven to keep warm.

4. Dissolve the mustard in the remaining 2 tablespoons vinegar. Stir in the remaining 2 tablespoons oil. Pour the mixture into the skillet and cook briefly, stirring, until warmed.

5. Divide the fish and the radicchio mixture among four plates, drizzle the warm vinaigrette over, shower with parsley, and serve. Or serve the fish directly from the baking dish, with the sauce and parsley added before it is brought to the table.

YIELD: 4 SERVINGS

COOK'S NOTES: The recipe is quick to prepare, but thanks to this most tolerant of fish, it can also be made in advance and kept warm for a good hour in a slow, 200°F oven—a convenience for a dinner party. But it's best to undercook the fish slightly if you plan to hold it in this fashion. Warm the vinaigrette and drizzle it on along with the scattering of parsley just before the dish is served. 🧂

CORKSCREWS

Most people pay corkscrews little mind. They're perfectly content with the gimme corkscrew from the local wine shop; or the cheap double-winged corkscrew, in which you squeeze the arms together to extract the cork; or even the Swiss army knife. Ambitious types can find battery-operated corkscrews or tapered yet cumbersome models the size of restaurant pepper mills, which operate not on the principle of twisting the worm into the cork, but with a press and a pull.

In restaurants the world over, sommeliers, those exacting, extracting professionals, rely overwhelmingly on a simple, handy device known as the waiter's friend or, sometimes, as the wine key. Essentially a knifelike handle with a spiral worm for inserting into the cork and a hinged fulcrum for resistance, the waiter's friend has largely stood the test of time, with modest tweaks and improvements, since it was patented in Germany in 1882. Basic versions go for less than ten dollars.

For most people, who simply want to get a bottle open for dinner, any of these choices is fine. Even if you regularly drink very good wines, the waiter's friend is sufficient for almost every eventuality. Three situations, however, may call for something different.

If you regularly open many bottles and find the routine tiresome, one of the automated openers might be a solution. That's true as well if for some reason you lack the fine motor skills necessary to manipulate the waiter's friend.

If you occasionally open very old bottles, situations where the cork can break or crumble, it may pay to have what is colloquially called an ah-so cork puller, a device with twin flexible prongs that can be inserted between the cork and neck of the bottle. This allows you to pull the cork without further damaging it. The device can also be used if you want to pull the cork without penetrating it, which allows you to taste the wine and then reinsert the cork.

The last possibility is that you may simply like fine tools. Personally speaking, when I pick up my standby home corkscrew, a Pulltaps double-hinged waiter's friend, I'm not wowed by the black plastic handle, flimsy metal fulcrum, and serrated foil cutter. It works fine, but I confess I don't feel much of anything about it. When it breaks, I have others lined up ready to go.

But certain corkscrews, like high-end Laguioles or Code38s, are beautifully designed tools that are a pleasure to handle and to use. They may cost several hundred dollars but may last for years, in which case you may well get your money's worth. —EA

OREGON PINOT NOIR

Oregon had no wine commerce back in 1965 when David Lett arrived in the Willamette Valley, armed with three thousand vine cuttings and a theory that the best wines come from places where the grapes have to struggle to ripen. He and his wife, Diana, planted thirteen acres of vines in 1966 in an old prune orchard in the Dundee Hills that they named the Eyrie Vineyard. Their vines foreshadowed the future of Oregon wine making. Today, the state has more than ten thousand acres of pinot noir.

Even after a half century or so, Oregon remains a young wine region. Pinot noir may be its signature grape, but the slow pace of agriculture cannot be rushed and experimentation continues. Nonetheless, with each year of experience, winemakers in Oregon become better at understanding the combination of climate, vineyard, and cellar work necessary to produce good wines.

The success of this work can partly be seen as the Willamette Valley, the prime Oregon grape-growing region, has been divided into smaller sub-appellations over the years. Time will tell whether names like Dundee Hills and Yamhill-Carlton, McMinnville and Ribbon Ridge, Eola–Amity Hills, and Chehalem Mountains will ever convey the subtle differences in terroir found in the appellations of Burgundy. At least one Burgundy producer, Joseph Drouhin, took the gamble, establishing Domaine Drouhin Oregon back in the mid-1980s.

In a good vintage, Oregon pinot noirs can be balanced and well structured by virtue of their lively acidity. They can be full of delicious red-fruit flavors without being syrupy, over the top, or, to use the dreaded phrase of wine marketers, "fruit forward." They can offer the rare New World combination of fruitiness and restraint. Many of them will be versatile with food.

Yet, it is hard to generalize about the wines. The orthodox view of Oregon pinot noir places it somewhere between the exuberant fruity ripeness found in California pinot noirs and the leaner, more subtle grace characteristic of Burgundy. Such specificity, of course, is almost pointless. Neither California nor Burgundy can be boiled down to a single style, nor can Oregon.

Oregon, in fact, is capable of a wide stylistic range of pinot noirs, just as California and Burgundy are, and any bottle of Oregon pinot noir can defy expectations. I've had big, rich Oregon pinot noirs that, if they don't quite achieve the heights in alcohol that are possible in California, still fill the mouth with opulent sweet fruit. And I've had beautifully delicate pinot noirs, floral and nuanced, that are capable of aging and evolving for decades.

The truth, if I may use such an elusive term, is that Oregon pinot noir is still far more dependent on the stylistic inclinations of the producer than it is on the evocative properties of the land. As with so many regions, it's imperative to learn the names of a few producers whose styles you like. 🍷

A RECIPE TO COMPLEMENT THE SMOKE, EARTH, AND FRUIT IN THESE WINES should offer some of the very same components. Mushrooms are a fine choice. Like pinot noir, they are Oregon's pride, another gift of terroir. I used an assortment; wild chanterelles, if available, and cultivated but exotic customers like majestic maitake and oyster. Some chestnuts intensified the earthy notes. There is even a tempting option to slip in a whisper of black truffle, an increasingly successfully grown native of Oregon.

Mushroom Lasagna

TIME: 1¾ HOURS

4 ounces pancetta, sliced thin and slivered

2 tablespoons extra virgin olive oil

1 medium onion, finely chopped

4 large garlic cloves, slivered

1 pound mixed mushrooms (shiitake, cremini, oyster, chanterelle, porcini, etc.), sliced

12 chestnuts, roasted, peeled, and quartered (use fresh, jarred, or frozen)

12 fresh sage leaves, slivered

Salt and freshly ground pepper

3 cups milk

6½ tablespoons unsalted butter or black truffle butter,

½ cup all-purpose flour

½ pound pasta for lasagna, preferably fresh, parboiled if dry

3 ounces grana padano cheese, grated

1. Place the pancetta in a large skillet over medium-low heat and cook, stirring, until the fat starts to render. Increase the heat and cook a few minutes more, until the pancetta barely begins to brown and crisp. Remove it to a dish. Add the oil to the pan. Add the onion and garlic and sauté until softened. Stir in the mushrooms and sauté over medium heat until they wilt. Stir in the chestnuts and sage. Season with salt and pepper. Remove from the heat.

2. Scald the milk in a saucepan. In a clean saucepan, melt 6 tablespoons of the butter on low heat. Whisk the flour into the melted butter. Cook briefly, then gradually whisk in the warm milk. Continue whisking and cooking until the sauce is thick and smooth. Season with salt and pepper.

3. Heat the oven to 350°F. Grease an 8-inch square baking dish with the remaining ½ tablespoon butter. Spread a film of white sauce in the dish, then place a layer of pasta to cover the bottom of the dish. Spread with half the mushrooms, scatter half the pancetta on top, and sprinkle with one third of the cheese. Spread a third of the sauce on the cheese. Repeat the layers. Cover with the remaining pasta, spread with the remaining sauce, and scatter the rest of the cheese on top.

4. Bake for 40 to 45 minutes, until the top is lightly browned. Serve.

YIELD: ABOUT 8 FIRST-COURSE OR 4 TO 6 MAIN-COURSE SERVINGS

COOK'S NOTES: The lasagna can be made in advance and frozen. Defrost it overnight in the refrigerator and reheat it at 350°F for about 30 minutes. 🧂

NEW ZEALAND PINOT NOIR Pinot noir

production in New Zealand is a relatively recent phenomenon, a couple of decades old. Centuries have gone into understanding Old World vineyards, so it is not an insult to suggest that New Zealand still has a ways to go to discover the intricacies of making wines that express a sense of place. This notion, the idea that the wine you are drinking expresses the specific qualities of a particular place and a particular culture or people, develops over time, as farmers and consumers come to understand the qualities of a piece of land. It is one of the prime reasons that people are drawn to pinot noir wines.

What sort of obstacles does a young viticultural area face? One of the blessings of working with grand cru Burgundy, Aubert de Villaine, a director of Domaine de la Romanée-Conti, once said, is the recorded history of a centuries-long marriage of pinot noir to a particular site. At the least, this offers decades of references for handling in the vineyard and the cellar each vintage's particular characteristics. Experience beats winging it.

And then, the simple fact of a vineyard's age affects the wines. Young vines, growers often say, are like teenagers, ungainly and impetuous in their growth, offering grapes that make bright, fruity, but relatively simple wines. As vines reach an age of twenty years or so, they become more self-regulating, and the wines have a greater chance to show complexity and depth of character.

Nonetheless, New Zealand pinot noirs seem to get better and better. The country's cool climate suits the grape, and if a sense of place can often seem elusive, many of the wines at least are crowd-pleasers, offering plenty of fruity enjoyment without going over the top too often. The best regions for pinot noir include Martinborough, Marlborough, and parts of Otago.

As is so often the case in a youngish region, consumers will find a profusion of styles. Some New Zealand pinot noirs are sleek and graceful, light and elegant. Others are big, dense, and concentrated. You might guess some are from Burgundy and others from the Russian River Valley.

While it is relatively easy to find good pinot noirs from New Zealand, great wines are another matter. The region still awaits its benchmark, a great wine that suggests what New Zealand pinot noir can be at its full potential. Naturally, that takes time. 🍷

A WELL-MADE PINOT NOIR TANTALIZES with notes of the forest and the spice route. It's not hard to complement the wine with food that brings out the same flavors. These pork chops, infused overnight with spice and herbs, are cut thin for quick grilling. No need to worry about whether they will be done enough. They will be. Piled on a platter, with the sauce passed alongside, they make for a terrific late-summer lunch or dinner with sliced tomatoes, potato salad, and corn to round out the menu.

A Mess of Pork Chops
with Dijon Dressing

TIME: 30 MINUTES, PLUS OVERNIGHT MARINATING

20 pork chops, ½ inch thick, preferably heritage breed

Salt and freshly ground black pepper

1 teaspoon ground allspice

1 bunch fresh thyme

1 tablespoon grape seed oil, plus more for grilling

⅓ cup thinly sliced shallots

2 tablespoons Dijon mustard

2 tablespoons soy sauce

Juice of 1 lemon

½ cup dry white wine

1. Season the chops on both sides with salt, pepper, and the allspice. Place thyme sprigs on each. Reserve 1 tablespoon thyme leaves. Place the chops in a large bowl or container, making layers. Cover and refrigerate overnight.

2. Remove the chops from the refrigerator. Light a grill and brush the grates with oil. While the grill is heating, heat the 1 tablespoon oil in a skillet, add the shallots, and sauté until tender and starting to brown. Stir in the mustard, soy sauce, lemon juice, and wine. Bring to a simmer. Season with salt and pepper. Stir in the reserved 1 tablespoon thyme leaves. Set aside.

3. Grill the chops—with thyme sprigs still stuck to them—just a few minutes per side until lightly browned. You may need to work in batches, depending on the size of your grill. Pile the chops on a platter. Warm the sauce and serve alongside.

YIELD: 8 SERVINGS

COOK'S NOTES: Heritage pork, from select breeds, has much more flavor as well as more fat than standard supermarket meat. The difference will show up even with these chops. 🥫

CALIFORNIA PINOT NOIR
California winemakers share a calling with the Cistercian monks of the Middle Ages: a relentless quest to find the best places to grow pinot noir. Over centuries, the monks settled on the heart of Burgundy, now famous as the Côte d'Or, along with a few scattered sites in Germany that may only now be coming to fruition. In California, the search goes on.

Pinot noir experiments worthy of monkish devotion have been taking place in California for years. Why else would someone retreat to a hill of limestone in the middle of nowhere, as Josh Jensen did in establishing Calera in the remote Gavilan Mountains? Or plant vineyards on the gorgeous seclusion of the true Sonoma Coast? Or in the wind tunnel of the Santa Rita Hills of Santa Barbara County? Or on the barely accessible slopes of the Santa Cruz Mountains? Or off the grid in Mendocino County? Each of these sites has made a compelling case for inclusion in the pinot noir pantheon.

As many places as pinot noir is grown in California, just as many styles of wine are made. The dominant style of California pinot noir has been round, ripe, and extravagant, with sweet flavors of dark fruit and alcohol levels approaching and sometimes surpassing 15 percent. But more and more producers are moving in the opposite direction. Instead of power, they strive for finesse. Instead of a rich, mouth-coating impression of sweetness, they seek a dry vitality meant to whet the appetite rather than squelch it. Instead of weight, they prize lightness and an almost transparent intensity.

Suffice it to say, whatever style of pinot noir you enjoy, you most likely will be able to find it in California. But the profusion of styles makes it difficult to discuss California pinot noir as a single coherent subject. Do you prefer lush or light-bodied? Nuanced or jammy? It's all there. As ever, it's imperative for consumers to associate styles with producers, as for the most part winemaker inclination is the determining factor.

But not entirely. Wines from the heart of the Russian River Valley, for example, are apt to be richer and fruitier than those from the Anderson Valley or the Carneros region. Yet perhaps even that generalization goes too far, as I've had fresh, elegant Russian River Valley pinot noirs, and big, powerful Carneros wines.

In the end it's a conundrum that is difficult to simplify. If that puts the burden on consumers, well, at least it's a delightful problem to unravel. 🍷

FIND A RED WINE THAT BALANCES GENEROUS FRUIT WITH WELL-DEFINED STRUCTURE, minerality, and finish and you're on your way to dinner. Pinot noirs, even the fruitier ones that might emerge from California's vineyards, would suit duck, especially if the wine's dark fruit comes cloaked in some acidity to tame the bird's fat. The edgy quince compote with Chinese seasonings to spoon alongside the duck is a simple affair that can be assembled while the duck is in the oven, or even prepared earlier and set aside for reheating.

Duck Breast with Quince Compote

TIME: 1 HOUR 15 MINUTES

2 magrets de canard (duck breasts), about 1 pound each

1 teaspoon Chinese five-spice powder

Salt and freshly ground black pepper

½ cup thinly sliced shallots

2 quinces, peeled, cored, and cut into slices ¼ inch thick

2 tablespoons sugar

1 cup chicken stock

½ cup dry red wine

1 tablespoon hoisin sauce

1. Heat the oven to 200°F. Trim a tablespoon of the fat from the edges of each magret and set aside. With a sharp knife, score the skin into the fat of each magret in a crisscross pattern. Rub the flesh side of each with ¼ teaspoon of the five-spice powder and season with salt and pepper. Place a heavy skillet, preferably cast iron, over medium-high heat.

2. Place the magrets, skin side down, in the skillet and sear a few minutes until the skin is nicely browned, doing both breasts at once or one at a time depending on the size of the pan. Place the magrets in a baking dish that will hold them comfortably, skin side up. Place in the oven and cook for 1 hour.

3. Meanwhile, melt the reserved fat in a saucepan over medium heat. Add the shallots and cook until soft. Add the quince slices, the remaining ½ teaspoon five-spice powder, and the sugar and cook, stirring, a few minutes, until the quinces start to color. Add the stock and bring to a simmer. Mix the wine with the hoisin sauce and add to the saucepan. Cover and cook for about 20 minutes, until the quinces are tender. Season with salt and pepper and set aside.

4. Remove the magrets from the oven and slice them on the bias. Pour any juices into the pan with the quinces. Arrange the duck on a platter. Reheat the quince mixture and spoon it around the duck. Serve.

YIELD: 4 TO 6 SERVINGS

COOK'S NOTES: I sear whole duck breasts (magrets) on the skin side, then slow-roast them for an hour at 200°F. This method is tailored for entertaining, because the duck can go into the oven before the guests are seated, and needs only to be sliced to serve. It is also a foolproof technique that delivers properly medium-rare slices. 🍶

BAROLO AND BARBARESCO

Barolo and Barbaresco have much more in common than they have differences. They are both made solely of the nebbiolo grape. They ideally are grown on hillside vineyards, where the sun can burn through the shrouds of fog (*nebbiolo* means "little fog" in Italian)., in their respective zones in the Piedmont region of northwestern Italy. Good versions of both Barbaresco and Barolo are beautifully aromatic of red fruits, flowers, licorice, and tar. They tend to be electric in acidity and can be fiercely tannic. With aging, they develop complex flavors of truffles and earth. The best offer a mind-bending combination of intensity, finesse, and grace. They are among my absolute favorite wines.

So where do Barbaresco and Barolo diverge? Well, the Barbaresco zone has only about a third of the vineyards as in Barolo, so much less of it is made. And, legally speaking, Barolo must be aged for three years, two in barrels, before it can be released, while Barbaresco is required to be aged for only two years, one in barrels. This can lead Barbaresco to be slightly less tannic and a little more approachable at a younger age.

Indeed, in the way of Romance-language cultures, Barolo is often portrayed as "masculine" to Barbaresco's "feminine." Practically speaking, though, this formulation is fairly pointless. Set out a glass of Barolo and a glass of Barbaresco, and I'd wager most people, even experts, couldn't tell the difference. More important to determining the personalities of the wines are the individual styles of the producers, the particular terroirs within each region, and the vintage characteristics.

Like all great wines, Barolo and Barbaresco appeal both to the head and to the heart. Their complexity and depth reward contemplation, while their sensual aromas and flavors seduce and enthrall. For me, Barolo and Barbaresco are right up there with Burgundy in possessing this thrilling combination of intellectual and soulful attraction, although my cabernet-loving friends scoff that I simply haven't drunk enough great Bordeaux. I'm sure they are right.

For much of the 1980s and '90s, Barolo and Barbaresco were defined by conflict between the so-called modernists and the traditionalists. But in the last decade, these stark stylistic differences have come a long way toward the middle. Or, to put it another way, many of the modernists, who strove to make softer, more approachable wines, partly through the use of small barrels of new oak, have pulled back from the excesses of the past. Oak is still evident, but with far less of the powerful vanilla veneer that used to mar the beauty of the nebbiolo grape. Regardless of the style, Barolo and Barbaresco reward long aging. You often see five-year-old bottles on restaurant wine lists, which is awfully young in nebbiolo terms. Ten years is more like it for the more accessible vintages, and for excellent but long vintages like 1996, even twenty years may not be long enough for the best versions. ♗

FOR MAJESTIC BAROLOS AND BARBARESCOS, a pasta alongside should deliver rich complexity. A beef ragù and truffles would certainly comply. Venison and porcini speak the same language. A good dollop of truffle butter adds the right touch of funky flavor and aroma. This dish requires some last-minute stove work before you can put it on the table and pour that Barolo.

Pasta with Venison and Porcini

TIME: 1 HOUR

1 venison loin (8 to 9 ounces), cut into 1-inch cubes

3 tablespoons extra virgin olive oil

Salt and freshly ground black pepper

6 fresh thyme sprigs

1 ounce dried porcini

½ cup dry white wine

2 teaspoons Dijon mustard

¼ cup minced shallots

1 tablespoon unsalted butter, or half unsalted, half black truffle butter

6 ounces fresh fettuccine or pappardelle

1. Place the venison in a bowl, add 2 tablespoons of the oil, ¼ teaspoon salt, ½ teaspoon pepper, and the leaves from 4 of the thyme sprigs. Mix well and set aside for 30 minutes. Place the porcini in a bowl, add ⅔ cup warm water, and set aside.

2. In another bowl, mix the wine and mustard together. Place a fine strainer over this bowl. Place the porcini in the strainer and press out as much liquid as possible. Mix the mushroom liquid with the wine mixture. Dry the porcini on paper towels and chop.

3. Heat the remaining 1 tablespoon oil in a 12-inch skillet. Add the shallots and the chopped porcini and sauté over medium heat until tender and lightly browned, about 3 minutes. Season with salt and pepper. Remove from the pan. Bring a pot of salted water to a boil for the pasta.

4. Heat ½ tablespoon of the butter in the skillet on medium-high. Add the venison and quickly sear on all sides, about 1 minute. Remove from the pan. Return the shallots and porcini to the pan along with the wine mixture. Simmer for a few minutes, until somewhat reduced. Stir in the remaining ½ tablespoon butter. Remove from the heat.

5. Boil the pasta for about 4 minutes, drain, and add it to the skillet. Simmer briefly, tossing the ingredients together, until heated through. Check the seasoning. Add the venison, toss again, and serve garnished with the remaining 2 thyme sprigs.

YIELD: 2 SERVINGS

COOK'S NOTES: While truffle oils, especially white truffle oils, may simply be test-tube products, with little or no real truffle in them, truffle butters, especially black, are usually more legitimate. I rarely use truffle oils but I find that black truffle butter (you can see the flecks of truffle and smell them) can be a useful, if perishable, staple to keep on hand. You can even simply spread it on toast to serve with drinks. 🫙

AT THE END OF THE DAY, with Barolos and Barbarescos, beef remains the default choice, and here it is, rendered with depth of flavor with Chinese mushrooms and soy sauce.

Beef Braised in Red Wine

TIME: 6 HOURS

2 to 2¼ pounds tri-tip sirloin, in one piece, or other cut of sirloin, chuck or rump

2 cups dry red wine

3 tablespoons soy sauce, preferably mushroom soy

16 dried Chinese black mushroom caps (about 1 ounce)

2 tablespoons extra virgin olive oil

2 carrots, peeled and finely chopped

2 celery stalks, finely chopped

1 large onion, finely chopped

3 garlic cloves, finely chopped

4 fresh thyme sprigs

1 tablespoon red wine vinegar

Salt and freshly ground black pepper

1. Place the meat in a bowl that will hold it comfortably and add the wine. Stir in the soy sauce. Cover and marinate at room temperature for 2 to 3 hours.

2. Remove the meat from the bowl and pat dry on paper towels. Place the mushrooms in the marinade. Heat the oven to 300°F.

3. Heat the oil in a 4-quart casserole on medium-high. Lightly brown the meat. Remove from the pan. Lower the heat, add the carrots, celery, onion, and garlic and sauté until soft. Add the thyme. Pour in the wine marinade and mushrooms, increase the heat to high, and cook until reduced by about half, 8 to 10 minutes. Return the meat to the pan, cover, and cook until fork-tender, about 2½ hours.

4. Stir in the vinegar and season with salt and pepper. Remove the thyme sprigs. Cut the meat into thick slices and arrange on a platter. Spoon on the sauce or serve it in a separate bowl.

YIELD: 4 SERVINGS

COOK'S NOTES: Tri-tip is a sirloin cut I first encountered in California, where it is often grilled for steak. But it has delectable merit when braised. Like most braised dishes, this one will only improve if it's made a day in advance, refrigerated, then reheated on top of the stove. 🗑

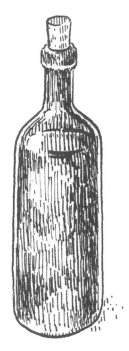

THESE WINES TEND TO BE EARTHY AND SOMETIMES BOLD, with sleek fruit and hints of violets in the ones I like most. The pasta can stand up to these wines, and so can the meaty duck confit that carries the sauce. Its richness is balanced by the acidity in the best of these bottles. Mushrooms contribute earthiness as well, ginger sharpens it a bit, and fresh mint sends it down the garden path. Simple chicken stock, nothing fancier, is all that is needed to put the ingredients in harmony. By the time everything has simmered together, the duck, mushrooms, and seasonings will have done their job, bolstering and thickening the stock so it will coat the pasta.

Pasta with Duck Confit

TIME: 40 MINUTES

2 confit duck legs

1 cup chopped onion

1 tablespoon minced peeled fresh ginger

3 garlic cloves, minced

½ teaspoon ground cardamom

8 ounces shiitake mushrooms, stemmed and sliced

2½ cups chicken stock

10 fresh mint leaves, slivered

Salt and freshly ground black pepper

1 pound whole wheat or farro penne, strozzapreti, or other short pasta

Grated pecorino, for serving

1. Remove the bones, skin, and fat from the confit. Save 2 tablespoons of the fat. Chop or shred the meat.

2. Melt the duck fat in a large skillet. Add the onion, ginger, and garlic. Sauté over low heat until soft. Stir in the cardamom. Add the mushrooms and sauté until wilted. Stir in the stock and duck meat, simmer 10 minutes, and add the mint. Season with salt and pepper.

3. Bring a large pot of salted water to a boil. Add the pasta and cook until al dente, 8 to 10 minutes. Drain, reserving about ½ cup of the pasta water. Add the pasta to the skillet and fold the ingredients together over low heat. Add some or all of the pasta water to moisten the mixture, if necessary. Check the seasonings. Serve with cheese on the side.

YIELD: 4 SERVINGS

COOK'S NOTES: Ready-made duck confit is one of the newer blessings of the market, available from an online purveyor or a fancy food shop. Do not even think of making duck confit from scratch. The shortcut is perfect, and you should consider always having some on hand in the freezer, for pastas like this, or for salads or other dishes. 🗎

RIOJA CRIANZA

What is this word "crianza"? First of all, it is pronounced cree-AHN-tha, though you may be excused if you choose not to employ the voiceless dental "fricative," the linguistic term for the Castilian lisp. A simple "-zah" will do.

Riojas have historically been classified by how long they are aged before the bottles are released. Light and fruity *joven* wines, which are released virtually as soon as their transformation to wine is complete, are rarely seen in the United States. Next comes *crianza*, the youngest of the aged Riojas. By law, crianzas must spend at least one year in oak barrels and cannot be sold until two years after the harvest, though, in fact, some wineries hold on to their bottles longer. The next-oldest Riojas are those labeled *reserva*, which must be aged at least three years before release. Last are the *gran reservas*, with at least five years of aging.

But let's not get bogged down in technicalities. What's important is to understand that no other category of Spanish red wine is as consistently satisfying and as good a value as Rioja crianza. One way to think of crianzas is like ordinary Chianti Classicos, which might be overshadowed by longer-aged, showier riservas and super Tuscans but are just right for ordinary meals. Similarly, the spotlight often falls on the more expensive Riojas, but while they are stored away to wait for properly august occasions, the crianzas are delicious everyday wines.

Like any group of Riojas, the crianzas tend to range stylistically from light, silky, and elegant to dense, dark, heavy, and powerful. We all have our personal tastes; I generally prefer the lighter wines. With their almost tender texture, they are unlike wines made anywhere else in the world. This leanness finds its greatest expression in the gran reserva Riojas, which after years of aging are gorgeously delicate and complex, emphasizing flavors of smoke and leather over fruit. The bolder, plusher wines are nothing to dismiss, but I don't find them as distinctive or interesting.

Part of Rioja's identity is the harmonious evidence of oak, used to accent the berry flavors of the tempranillo grape, which most often forms the backbone of these wines, along with garnacha and graciano. Traditionally, Rioja was aged in large vats made of American oak. Sometimes, the vats were used for many years, softening their influence to a subtle vanilla that cushioned the spicy fruit flavors of the grape. Today, just as many wineries are using small barrels of new French oak, which gives a darker, toastier, more overt flavor to the wine. Some wineries even use a combination of French and American oak.

Regardless of the style, what sets crianzas apart is that they often are great values, no matter how you pronounce their name. 🍷

RIOJA CRIANZAS CAN HANDLE A RUSTIC DISH like this bold, richly succulent barbecued beef tongue. The recipe, from Michael's Genuine Food & Drink, a Miami restaurant, is somewhat surprising. Instead of some kind of slow cooking done over applewood or hickory, the barbecue is contributed by a mere couple of tablespoons of sauce added to the cooking liquid. Once the tongue is done—and it calls for quite an investment in unattended time—it is delicious.

Barbecued Beef Tongue

TIME: 5 HOURS, PLUS 2 HOURS OR MORE CHILLING

1 beef tongue (2 to 3 pounds), rinsed

½ carrot, peeled and diced

1 celery stalk, diced

1 medium onion, diced

2 fresh thyme sprigs

1 cup fresh flat-leaf parsley sprigs (about ½ bunch)

1 teaspoon whole black peppercorns

2 tablespoons Chinese or Thai barbecue sauce

1 quart veal stock

2 quarts chicken stock, plus more as needed

2½ cups bitter greens (arugula or baby spinach)

1 tablespoon red wine vinegar

1 tablespoon extra virgin olive oil

1. Heat the oven to 325°F. Place the tongue in a deep, ovenproof, 5- to 6-quart casserole. Add the carrot, celery, onion, thyme, parsley, and peppercorns. Mix the barbecue sauce into the veal stock and add to the casserole. Add enough chicken stock to cover the tongue. Bring to a boil and reduce the heat to a simmer. Cover and place in the oven until very tender, about 3 hours. Check the liquid from time to time, adding more chicken stock as needed. Remove the casserole from the oven and set aside for 1 hour.

2. Remove the tongue from the casserole. Strain the cooking liquid into a 4-quart saucepan, bring to a boil, and reduce to 3 cups, about 45 minutes. Meanwhile, peel the skin from the tongue, wrap the tongue in plastic wrap, and refrigerate for at least 2 hours or overnight. Refrigerate the reduced cooking liquid if not proceeding with the recipe within a couple of hours.

3. Slice the tongue into pieces ½ inch thick. Arrange the slices, slightly overlapping, in a large skillet. Pour the reduced liquid over, bring to a simmer, and cook until the sauce is syrupy, about 30 minutes. Toss the greens with the vinegar and oil. Transfer the tongue to a serving platter, spoon the sauce over the tongue, and serve with the greens alongside.

YIELD: 4 TO 6 MAIN-COURSE OR 8 TO 12 FIRST-COURSE SERVINGS

COOK'S NOTES: Is there a shortcut for this recipe? The only option would be to reduce by half a few cups of veal stock to which you have added the barbecue sauce and use it with sliced smoked tongue from a store. 🧂

RIOJA RESERVA

It's accepted wisdom today that most wine drinkers do not have the money, the storage space, or the patience to wait years as their bottles age to maturity. Consumers expect wines to be ready, or at least enjoyable, immediately after they buy them. That's a marked departure from the old days, when it might never have occurred to our wine-loving forebears to pull the cork on, say, a decent Bordeaux before it was twelve or fifteen years old. As a result, many producers around the world have altered their methods in an effort to make wines that are more accessible when young.

That's not to say you can't still find young wines that will give you a puckering mouthful of astringent tannins. Plenty are still out there, like Barolo. Even though people say Barolos are more approachable these days, I don't enjoy them young. In fact, if you do have the money, the storage, and the patience, many wines from all over the world will still benefit greatly from prolonged aging. Nonetheless, most people today don't want to take the trouble themselves, and while some restaurants will bear the burden of aging wines, they usually charge forbidding prices for their efforts.

Surely this state of affairs must leave more than a few wine lovers frustrated. Who among us would not like the opportunity to drink aged wines without paying a fortune or waiting them out? What about tonight?

May I humbly offer a happy solution: Rioja reservas.

These wines are not necessarily well aged before they are sold. By law, a Rioja can be labeled "reserva" if it is aged for a minimum of three years (at least one in oak barrels) before it is released. In practice, you can find a lot of Rioja reservas in stores right now from the most recent vintage— fresh, minimally aged young things, mostly.

What's exciting, however, is that some Rioja producers are not bound by the minimal-aging standards for reservas. Bless their hearts, they go above and beyond what's required. This means, happily, that in stores it's not hard to find Rioja reservas that are more than ten years old. These are current releases, and in the great scheme of things, they really don't cost much at all; maybe half what you might pay for a mediocre Napa cabernet.

Rioja, of course, is not the only wine region with requirements for minimal aging. Montalcino, for one, requires Brunellos to be aged four years before they can be released, five for Brunello riservas. Yet even when Brunellos are released, they generally need years of additional aging before they are really enjoyable.

Rioja is different. The old tradition was for producers to age the wines until they were ready to drink, well beyond the minimal requirements. Only a few wineries still offer this service. But when you find such a wine, the difference in complexity and finesse is clear. Even aged Rioja reservas, in a way, are starter wines that merely suggest the ultimate expression of traditional Rioja, gran reservas. These wines must be aged for six years after the vintage and don't come into their own until, as with young adults, their early twenties. But that's another story, and it'll be worth the wait. 🍷

A RAGOUT OF PORK IS MADE WITH CHUNKS OF THE FAT-STREAKED SHOULDER (either the picnic or butt) slowly stewed in wine with buttery white beans and seasoned with orange. The dried beans, given a quick boil and one hour soaking as a shortcut for overnight treatment, will become tender simmered with the pork. Some smoky paprika and a whiff of ground cloves add complexity to the ragout's register of flavors to complement the wine.

Orange Pork Ragout with Beans

TIME: 3 HOURS

1 cup dried cannellini beans, rinsed

3 tablespoons extra virgin olive oil

2 pounds boneless pork shoulder, cut into 2-inch chunks

1 medium onion, finely chopped

3 garlic cloves, minced

1 red bell pepper, cored, seeded, and finely chopped

1½ teaspoons Spanish smoked paprika

¼ teaspoon ground cloves

Grated zest and juice of 2 oranges

1½ cups dry red wine

3 fresh rosemary sprigs

Freshly ground black pepper

Small pinch of red chile flakes

Salt

1 tablespoon finely chopped fresh flat-leaf parsley

1. Place the beans in a saucepan, cover with water by 2 inches, and bring to a boil. Cook for 2 minutes, cover, and set aside to soak for 1 hour.

2. Meanwhile, heat 2 tablespoons of the oil in a 4-quart casserole over medium-high heat. Add the pork without crowding, lightly brown it, and remove. Add the onion, garlic, and bell pepper. Sauté over low heat until soft. Stir in the paprika, cloves, and orange zest. Stir in the orange juice and wine, scraping the bottom of the casserole. Return the pork to the casserole and set aside until the beans have finished soaking. Drain the beans and add to the casserole. Add the rosemary, black pepper, and red chile flakes. Bring to a simmer.

3. Cover and simmer for 2 hours, until the beans are tender. Season with salt. Transfer to a serving dish or serve from the casserole. Drizzle the remaining 1 tablespoon oil over the surface and scatter the parsley on top before serving.

YIELD: 4 SERVINGS

COOK'S NOTES: Dried beans are not forever. They will become tender, faster, as they simmer if they are "fresh," that is, within a year of harvest. Quality purveyors put a date on the package. 🗓

RIBERA DEL DUERO
Ribera del Duero is a paradoxical region, ancient yet thoroughly modern. Its wines embrace the mainstream characteristics that seem so popular around the world. They are plush, opulent, flamboyantly fruity, and powerfully oaky. Yet, while some unavoidably stray into the homogenized international style, the best remain identifiably Spanish.

What makes Ribera del Duero so unusual? Throughout European wine regions over the last fifty years the essential story has been how traditional wisdom and methods, honed over generations of careful observation, have come to terms with modern technology and globalization. This conflict, felt in Old World vineyards and cellars, resonates with consumers around the world. Efforts to appeal to perceptions of global tastes have produced rivers of standard-issue wines, as bland as computer-generated car names. At the same time, a rising appreciation and understanding of fine wine around the world has meant unprecedented access to a wide diversity of wonderfully distinctive wines, some from appellations virtually unknown until a few years ago.

Gaze at Bordeaux and Burgundy, Barolo and Sicily, Rioja and the Rhône, even at Napa Valley, and you can find innumerable examples of this conflict playing out. But if you look at Ribera del Duero, in the geographical heart of Spain, you see a place seemingly set aside from this central clash of cultures. This paradox may seem peculiar against the backdrop of other Old World countries. But then again Spain has always stood apart from European wine-making powers like France and Italy. Because of regional tastes, politics, and civil war, the Spanish wine industry got a far later start on modernization than its neighbors. Despite having grown grapes and made wine for centuries, the wines of Ribera del Duero never achieved high status.

The region had one significant exception. Vega Sicilia was established in 1864, and it rightfully came to be recognized as one of the world's great wines. Beyond Vega Sicilia, it wasn't until the 1980s that the region came to be seen as a source for fine red wines. By that time the Franco era had ended, Spain had joined the European Community, and modernization was well under way.

Unlike Rioja, where many producers had already been established by the early twentieth century, Ribera del Duero, on a harsh, high plain southwest of Rioja, was dominated by cooperatives up until the 1980s. After the pioneering efforts of a few producers like Alejandro Fernández in the 1970s, new wineries began to pop up. Without long-standing traditions of excellence to clash with new and fashionable ideas, modernity was largely unchallenged.

Success and acclaim came swiftly to Ribera del Duero in the 1990s and it was hard not to make comparisons with Rioja. Both make red wines largely from the same grape, called tempranillo in Rioja and tinto fino in Ribera del Duero. The wine critic Stephen Tanzer once said Rioja is Bordeaux to Ribera del Duero's Napa cabernet, and I think the analogy remains apt. Equally appropriate might be to think of these big, modern wines as the malbecs of Spain.

In the end, it pretty much comes down to taste. If you enjoy modern California cabernets, Argentine malbecs, and new wave Riojas, these wines should be just right for you. If you prefer old-school Riojas, classic Rhônes, and wines that show an herbal touch now and then, these may not be for you. Better to wait and to hope for a benefactor to pour you a glass of Vega Sicilia someday. 🍷

TIMING IS EVERYTHING. I WAS AT CASA MONO, a Spanish restaurant in New York, lapping up every drop of the sauce from a little cazuela of delectable piquillo peppers stuffed with oxtails. The next day I was tasting Ribera del Duero wines and could think of no better dish for them than those meaty, slightly fruity peppers with their alluring hint of bitterness. Andy Nusser, the chef at Casa Mono, provided the recipe, enough to feed the entire town of Peñafiel. I made drastic cuts (4 quarts of stock down to 2 cups, for example), but still had enough for a party. My freezer now holds the bonus. Though time consuming, the meat cooks mostly unattended.

Oxtail Stuffed Peppers

TIME: 4½ HOURS

2 oxtails, about 3 pounds each, cut into 4- to 5-inch sections

Salt and freshly ground black pepper

3 medium onions, diced

2 garlic cloves, 1 sliced

4 ounces serrano ham in one slice, diced

1 small green bell pepper, cored, seeded, and diced

2 tablespoons fresh flat-leaf parsley

1 plum tomato, finely chopped

1 bay leaf

Pinch of red chile flakes

1 cup dry red wine

2 cups beef stock

Two 7.8-ounce jars whole piquillo peppers, drained and patted dry (about 24 peppers)

1. Discard the narrow end section of each oxtail. Season the rest with salt and black pepper. Place the meat over high heat in a 6-quart casserole or braising pan and sear until browned. Remove from the casserole. Reduce the heat to low and add 2 of the diced onions, the sliced garlic clove, and the ham. Sauté until the onions are soft. Remove from the heat.

2. By hand or in a food processor, finely chop the remaining diced onion and the whole garlic clove with the bell pepper and parsley. Mix with the tomato and add to the casserole. Cook, stirring, over medium heat until the vegetables are soft. Stir in the bay leaf, red chile flakes, wine, and stock. Bring to a simmer.

3. Return the oxtails to the casserole, baste with the stock, cover, and reduce the heat to very low. Cook, turning once, until the meat is fork-tender, about 3 hours. Remove the oxtails and finely chop or shred the meat. Strain the liquid and discard the solids. Mix ⅔ cup of the liquid with the meat.

4. Stuff the peppers with the meat. Pour 1 cup of the liquid into a shallow baking dish. Arrange the peppers in the dish. Save the yummy leftover liquid for another use; it can be frozen for up to 2 months. To serve the peppers, heat the oven to 350°F. Place the room-temperature stuffed peppers in the oven and bake until heated through, about 15 minutes. Serve.

YIELD: 8 TO 12 SERVINGS

COOK'S NOTES: Piquillo peppers, quintessentially Spanish, are not sold fresh in the United States. But purveyors of Spanish products, both in shops and online, always have them. They are worth keeping in the pantry because they can also be stuffed with seafood for a quick hors d'oeuvre. 🥫

LOIRE VALLEY REDS

Among the many wonderful, distinctive red wines in the world, those from the Loire Valley may well get the least respect in proportion to their superb quality. It does little good to wonder why. That this has been true for many years, despite the occasional ravings of committed Loire lovers, breeds a certain fatalistic acceptance. So let's concede that although we may speak warmly and openly here about the many reasons to love Loire reds, they will nonetheless remain our little secret. Regardless of the pleasure they offer, and the fact that they are relatively inexpensive, we need not worry that they will suddenly be in great demand. Not even the most curious newcomers are likely to cross the moat of public indifference to see what all the bargains are about.

Their loss. Personally, I believe Loire reds are always a top choice regardless of the occasion. For large gatherings, I can think of no better combination of quality and value than gamays from the Touraine region. These wines, made from the same grape as Beaujolais, are lively and fresh, yet with a mineral earthiness that makes them interesting.

Wines made from côt, as malbec is called along the Loire, are another good choice—my favorite malbecs all seem to come from the Loire, rather than from the regions that claim malbec as their own: Cahors, in southwestern France, and Argentina.

I haven't even mentioned the odds and ends that sometimes wash up on these shores, a Loire pinot noir, say; or a pineau d'Aunis, an ancient grape that can be exceptional; or the wonderful whites; or even the most significant red grape in the Loire, cabernet franc.

The Loire's most widely available reds are made from cabernet franc, including the best, most expensive, and perhaps the longest-lived Loire reds, the Saumur-Champignys from Clos Rougeard. The Clos Rougeards are hard to find, though not impossible. But wines from Chinon and Bourgueil, the two biggest red wine appellations in the Touraine region of the Loire? No problem—unless you're looking for them on a restaurant wine list. Then they become scarce.

I've often thought that I could gauge certain wine lists by whether they include some good Loire reds. The wines are versatile with all sorts of foods, including, surprisingly, Asian cuisines. The key, of course, is whether they are good. As with every other region, the Loire produces plenty of wines that are harmless, incompetent, or just plain cynical, which is what happens when winemakers who know better settle for harmless or incompetent. But the best are lively, balanced, nuanced, and complex, with the sort of lithe agility that makes them great with food.

All the praise in the world is unlikely to win much of a new audience for these wines. They seem to rebuff attention inherently. For people who already know and love them, and who revel in their easy availability, that's good news. Even better, the Loire is just the leading edge of a vast array of wines that are delicious and moderately priced, yet will always be considered marginal, idiosyncratic, or exotic. 🍷

RED WINE WITH OYSTERS? There's controversy for you. And it was a challenge that Eric put at my doorstep. That's about as controversial as it gets. The pairing becomes a trifle easier when the bivalves are cooked, not served raw. I broiled them with a simple, creamy glaze that I bolstered with just a dollop of red miso paste. With oysters done this way, the earthy, spicy wines of the Loire, many soft and open on the palate, come through as lovely partners.

Oysters with Miso Glaze

TIME: 30 MINUTES

24 oysters on the half shell, juices reserved

Clam juice or fish stock, as needed

1½ tablespoons unsalted butter

½ cup minced shallots

4 teaspoons all-purpose flour

1 tablespoon fresh lemon juice

1 tablespoon red miso paste

1 cup heavy cream

Salt and freshly ground white pepper

½ cup fine dry bread crumbs

1. Arrange the oysters on a baking sheet, using crumpled foil or a layer of rock salt to keep them steady. A large madeleine pan covered in foil is an excellent alternative. Measure the oyster juices and, if needed, add enough clam juice to make ½ cup. Heat the broiler.

2. Melt the butter in a saucepan over low heat. Add the shallots and sauté until soft. Whisk in the flour, cook briefly, and add the oyster juice and lemon juice, whisking until blended. Whisk in the miso, then gradually whisk in the cream. Cook for 3 to 4 minutes until well blended. Season with salt and white pepper. Mix in the bread crumbs.

3. Spoon the bread crumb mixture onto the oysters, covering them completely. Broil until glazed and bubbling, 5 minutes. Serve.

YIELD: 4 TO 6 SERVINGS

COOK'S NOTES: Try to find oysters that have some character, brininess, even metallic hints. They will improve this dish and have their say against the wine. 🍶

POMEROL AND SAINT-ÉMILION

Several centuries ago, when the wines of the Médoc achieved reknown across the wine-drinking world, the areas to the east of Bordeaux, often called the Right Bank, were largely anonymous backwaters. Today, Pomerol and Saint-Émilion, the two leading Right Bank regions, are as justly celebrated as any of the Left Bank communes, while lesser-known areas like Côtes de Castillon and Canon-Fronsac are being discovered for the potential bargains they offer.

Nobody would label Pomerol a bargain, however. This small, unprepossessing region is the home of Pétrus, one of the most coveted and expensive wines in the world, along with a small collection of other jewellike estates like Trotanoy, Le Pin, and Vieux Château Certan. Unlike in the Médoc, the chief grape of Pomerol is merlot, and nowhere else on earth does merlot achieve wines of such finesse and complexity, at a price, naturally. Cabernet franc, too, plays a crucial role in the Pomerol blend.

Saint-Émilion is an altogether bigger, more variable region. Both merlot and cabernet franc play leading roles here, too, and Saint-Émilion has served as something of a laboratory over the past twenty-five years for many of the more rich, voluptuous, concentrated expressions of Bordeaux that have achieved great popularity.

Both Pomerol and Saint-Émilion generally produce wines that are less austere and more accessible than those of the Médoc, but where Pomerol seems to maintain its dignified, if sumptuous, sometimes mysterious, reserve, Saint-Émilion can positively drip with welcoming warmth, at least in some of its more modern manifestations. At the same time, it's home to such elegant classics as Cheval Blanc, Figeac, and Ausone.

Because Saint-Émilion is so much bigger, with terrain that can vary tremendously, the wines are far less consistent in style than Pomerol's. Figeac, for example, which has an unusually high proportion of cabernet sauvignon in its blend, leans to an almost Médoc-like dry leanness, while other producers, like Pavie, to name one, are altogether more ripe, intense, and powerful. You also find a far greater range of prices in Saint-Émilion.

This is not to say that Pomerol's wines are uniform. Styles there differ as well, but on a more concise spectrum.

Meanwhile, the satellite regions, with less-celebrated names and, theoretically, at least, terroirs of less potential, are fertile grounds for investigating what all the fuss is about in the first place. They may give only a taste of the possible grandeur that awaits, but the prices are far more friendly. ♆

FISH IN RED WINE SAUCE IS A WINNING PARTNER for a bottle of Saint-Émilion. There are many traditional French preparations that accomplish this with panache. In the Bordeaux region a matelote, often made with eel, is typical. A riff on the dish comes from the repertory of Gordon Ramsay, a brash, talented chef. His line-caught turbot in Saint-Émilion sauce does require the full attention of the cook the whole time, with nothing suitable for advance preparation. I try to avoid this kind of intensive cooking; here I gave in for the delectable result. Though you do not have to use a Saint-Émilion for the sauce, a Bordeaux-style wine, especially one with a generous component of merlot, is particularly appropriate. The same goes for the wine to sip in the kitchen as you taste the sauce for seasoning, and especially, your choice to pour at the table.

Turbot Poached in Saint-Émilion

TIME: 1 HOUR

8 medium Yukon gold potatoes (about 1 pound)

7 tablespoons crème fraîche

8 tablespoons (1 stick) unsalted butter, preferably high-fat European style, diced

Salt and freshly ground black pepper

3 tablespoons extra virgin olive oil

16 cipollini onions, peeled

1 large shallot, finely chopped

2 cups Saint-Émilion or other dry red wine, preferably merlot

2 cups fish stock

1 pound turbot or sea bass fillets, skinned, in 4 uniform pieces

1 tablespoon chopped fresh flat-leaf parsley leaves

COOK'S NOTES: Turbot is the largest of the flatfishes, the flounder family. Other meaty, white-fleshed fillets, like sea bass, can be substituted. 🧂

1. Place the potatoes in a pan of well-salted boiling water and cook until tender, about 15 minutes. Drain, peel at once (wear rubber gloves), and mash in a ricer. Return the potatoes to the pan, heat briefly, and add 5 tablespoons of the crème fraîche and 1½ tablespoons of the butter. Season with salt and pepper and set aside in the pan, covered.

2. Heat 2 tablespoons of the oil in a small skillet. Add the onions and sauté over medium heat until lightly browned and tender. Set aside, covered, to keep warm.

3. Heat the remaining 1 tablespoon oil in a wide saucepan or sauté pan that can hold the fish in a single layer. Add the shallot and sauté over low heat for 5 minutes. Add the wine and stock and bring to a simmer. Slip the fish pieces into the pan. Poach until just firm, 3 to 4 minutes. Remove the fish, draining it well. Place it on a warm plate and cover to keep warm.

4. Boil the cooking liquid until reduced to about 1 cup. Whisk in the remaining 2 tablespoons crème fraîche and season with salt and pepper. Over low heat, add the remaining 6½ tablespoons butter, bit by bit, whisking it in. The sauce will thicken somewhat and turn glossy.

5. Reheat the potato puree and spoon it into the center of each of four dinner plates. Place a piece of fish on top and place the onions around. Gently reheat the sauce and spoon it over each portion. Sprinkle with parsley and serve.

YIELD: 4 SERVINGS

MÉDOC, PESSAC-LÉOGNAN, AND GRAVES

Even eternal truths need to be repeated: Bordeaux is one of the world's greatest wines. In terms of complexity, longevity, soulful sense of place, and sheer refreshment, Bordeaux remains not merely a great example but a benchmark.

Why does this even need to be said? The reasons are complex, but one important factor is that the prices of fine Bordeaux have risen well beyond the means of many wine lovers, so the tendency outside the realm of collectors and the wealthy has become to forget about the region. Yet, with the focus of the wine trade and the wine media largely on top Bordeaux names, the less-expensive side of Bordeaux is ripe for rediscovery, both by the trade, which has largely been indifferent to it but now has a prime opportunity to sell it, and consumers, who simply have not had access to very much good, cheap Bordeaux.

The truth is, good, moderately priced Bordeaux is out there, wines that convey if not the grandeur of the region's best wines at least a sense of what's so good about them. Many of those wines will come from the well-drained, gravelly soils of the Médoc and Graves, classic Left Bank Bordeaux from the areas west of the Gironde and Garonne rivers, where cabernet sauvignon is king.

Even these wines will show a variety of styles. Some are heavily influenced by modern blends of Bordeaux grapes from around the world. These tend to be lush, dense, and concentrated, with perhaps a higher proportion of the softer merlot grape in the blend than the more austere cabernet sauvignon. Others show more finesse and refinement, with good acidity, which helps keep wines fresh and invigorating, and good structure, the skeleton of tannins and acidity that transports the flesh of flavors through the mouth and helps wine age.

The Médoc, north of the city of Bordeaux, includes prestigious communes like Pauillac, Saint-Julien, Margaux, and Saint-Estèphe, along with a host of satellite regions. To the south of the city is the historic Graves region, the best of which is now designated Pessac-Léognan.

The organization of Bordeaux is far simpler than that of Burgundy, and most estates are far larger. The hundred-acre vineyard that would be subject to fine divisions of quality and price in Burgundy is one large entity in Bordeaux, which leaves it to each individual producer to decide how to price and market the grapes.

Decades ago, the influential Bordeaux enologist Émile Peynaud urged producers to create secondary, cheaper labels for grapes of lesser quality, reserving their best grapes for their top wines. At the time, many producers were aghast at making less wine by diverting grapes to a second label, but now all of Bordeaux seems to have embraced the idea of second labels. I have mixed feelings. They can obviously be good, but emotionally I'd like to feel I'm getting the best a producer has to offer. Also, they're not always great values as they trade on their illustrious siblings.

Even in accessible vintages, good Bordeaux requires time before it shows its best. Lower-end wines may need only two or three years, or maybe five or seven for the more structured ones. You might bemoan the fact that they demand patience. Or you could be thankful that even moderately priced Bordeaux improve with age. 🍷

RACK OF LAMB. FILLET OF BEEF. ROASTED SQUAB. DUCK. There you have the obvious choices for main courses to serve with the complex, often tannic but well-balanced and eminently food-friendly classified Bordeaux. But that very food-friendliness can welcome other, more demanding ingredients to pair with these classic, prestigious wines. Their pedigree suggested a fish of aristocratic breeding, wild Alaskan king salmon. The kings are the largest and most muscular of the western salmon family. Though the salmon could be simply grilled to complement fine Bordeaux, a red wine sauce provides an added guarantee that it will do justice to the wines. The seared, medium-rare fish rests on a bed of lentils, which contributes a nutty earthiness that plays off extremely well against the sturdy tannins of youthful grand cru princelings.

Grand Cru Salmon with Lentils in Red Wine

TIME: 1 HOUR

2 tablespoons extra virgin olive oil

1½ ounces pancetta, diced

2 shallots, minced

1⅓ cups French lentils, rinsed and drained

8 fresh thyme sprigs

3½ cups chicken stock

1¼ cups dry red wine

2 pounds Alaskan king salmon fillets, preferably Copper River, in 4 portions, with skin and pinbones removed (see page 87)

Salt and freshly ground black pepper

1 tablespoon all-purpose flour

1 tablespoon unsalted butter, softened

1. Heat 1 tablespoon of the oil in a heavy 3-quart saucepan. Add the pancetta and shallots and sauté over medium heat until they are starting to color. Stir in the lentils, 4 of the thyme sprigs, and the stock. Bring to a simmer, partly cover, and cook until the lentils are tender, about 30 minutes. Add the wine and simmer for 10 minutes more. Remove from the heat.

2. Drain the liquid from the lentils into a small saucepan. Place the drained lentils over very low heat. Remove the thyme.

3. Heat the oven to 450°F. Season the salmon with salt and pepper. Dust the skin with the flour. Heat the remaining 1 tablespoon oil in a heavy ovenproof skillet. Add the salmon, skin side down, and sear on high heat until the skin is browned, 2 to 3 minutes. Turn the salmon, place the skillet in the oven, and cook for 5 minutes for medium-rare, or longer, to your desired doneness.

5. Divide the lentils among four warm dinner plates and top each with a piece of salmon, skin side up. Heat the liquid from the lentils and whisk in the butter. Season to taste. Spoon the sauce over and around the salmon and lentils. Garnish with the remaining 4 thyme sprigs and serve.

YIELD: 4 SERVINGS

COOK'S NOTES: For the best texture and flavor, it's important to use small French lentils, either the green variety from Le Puy or brown Champagne lentils. Soaking is not necessary, so the entire dish can be on the table in just an hour.

BORDEAUX AT THE TABLE usually means what's in the glass, not on a plate. Though in Bordeaux the lamb might also be local. And if the contrarian in me will often seek the unexpected, like fish with these wines, there is actually no finer partner for a good wine from the region than some sort of lamb dish, even if the meat was not pastured in Pauillac. Here you have plump loin chops masquerading as steak au poivre with other whole spices along with black pepper, the sorts of seasonings that lamb might welcome in India.

Lamb Chops au Poivre

TIME: 40 MINUTES, PLUS 1½ TO 3½ HOURS SEASONING

1 tablespoon whole black peppercorns

½ tablespoon coriander seeds

1 teaspoon brown mustard seeds

½ teaspoon fennel seeds

4 loin lamb chops, 1½ inches thick (about 2 pounds), fat well trimmed

2 tablespoons grape seed oil

1 tablespoon unsalted butter

1½ tablespoons finely chopped shallots

5 tablespoons beef stock

1 tablespoon Cognac

3 tablespoons crème fraîche

Salt

1 teaspoon minced fresh flat-leaf parsley

1. Use a mortar and pestle or a spice grinder to coarsely crush the peppercorns, coriander seeds, mustard seeds, and fennel seeds. Coat the lamb chops top and bottom with this mixture, pressing it into the meat. Place the chops on a platter, cover, and refrigerate for 1 to 3 hours. Remove from the refrigerator 30 minutes before cooking.

2. Heat the oil in a cast-iron skillet on medium. Add the chops and cook for 7 minutes. Turn the chops, cover the pan, and cook for 7 minutes more for medium-rare, or until done to taste. Remove to a warm serving platter and cover loosely with foil.

3. Pour off the excess fat from the pan. Add the butter and cook on low until melted. Add the shallots and cook on low until soft. Add the stock, Cognac, and crème fraîche and cook on medium, stirring, until the sauce has thickened somewhat, about 1 minute. Season with salt.

4. Place 2 chops on each of two dinner plates. Spoon the sauce over and around. Scatter parsley on top and serve.

YIELD: 2 SERVINGS

COOK'S NOTES: You'll want to crush the spices but not pulverize them, so if you use an electric grinder, take care not to overdo it. And it's best to remove the fatty little tails from the chops and trim off as much of the exterior fat as you can. 🝊

THESE BORDEAUX CAN BE FOR EVERYDAY DRINKING OR FOR SPECIAL OCCASIONS. At their finest they offer a balance of food-friendly elements, driven by elegant fruit and acidity. Hints of spice, earth, herbs, and minerality also weigh in. And how much a bottle costs depends on the prestige of the château and also the vintage. I opted for a special-occasion dish for two lucky diners who have chosen to share one of the better bottles.

Fettuccine with Foie Gras and Truffles

TIME: 30 MINUTES

4 ounces prepared duck foie gras, canned or fresh *en torchon*

½ cup dry red wine

½ tablespoon unsalted butter or duck fat

2 tablespoons minced shallots

½ cup chicken stock

Salt and freshly ground black pepper

½ teaspoon dried thyme

½ ounce, or more, tinned black truffle, sliced thin, juice reserved

4 ounces fresh fettuccine

1. Reserve 1 ounce of the foie gras and slice it in half. Set aside. Dice the rest and place it in a bowl. Gradually add the wine to the diced foie gras and use a small whisk or a fork to blend the foie gras and wine together until smooth. Set aside.

2. Heat the butter in a 12-inch skillet. Add the shallots and sauté on medium until soft and barely tinged with brown. Add the stock and cook until the stock has reduced by half. Remove from the heat.

3. Stir the foie gras mixture into the pan. Heat gently for a couple of minutes at a very low simmer. Season with salt and pepper. Add the thyme and truffle juice. Remove from the heat, cover, and keep warm.

4. Bring a pot of salted water to a boil, add the pasta, and cook until al dente, about 5 minutes. Drain well. Transfer the pasta to the skillet. Place over very low heat. Add the truffles. Using tongs, turn the pasta to reheat it and coat it with the sauce. Check the seasoning. Divide the pasta into two warm soup plates and serve, with a slice of the reserved foie gras topping each portion.

YIELD: 2 SERVINGS

COOK'S NOTES: Convenience and elegance meet in this recipe. Tinned foie gras, mousse of foie gras from a fancy food shop, or, as some markets now sell, a slab of prepared cooked foie gras (called *en torchon* because the liver is usually poached wrapped in cloth) all work well. As for the truffles, fresh black ones are not necessary. In fact the less costly tinned ones, which also provide truffle juice, are best. 🗑

CALIFORNIA CABERNET SAUVIGNONS AND BLENDS

Between the 1970s and '80s, when Napa Valley established itself as cabernet sauvignon country, and the modern era beginning in the mid-1990s, the prevailing style of Napa Valley cabernets changed dramatically. The wines, which used to follow the Bordeaux paradigm of austere, fresh, structured wines, turned into something completely different. They became bigger, richer, more concentrated, softer, oakier, and more powerful, sometimes bordering on sweet, with little acidity or structure.

From around 2010, the pendulum in Napa began to swing back just a bit, to the point where, even if blockbuster cabernet remains the leading style, enough producers have embraced restraint that consumers now have a fair amount of choice. If you want a classic Napa cabernet that emphasizes flowers, red fruits, and a touch of the herbal, instead of a rich, plush cabernet of high alcohol and oaky sweetness, most likely you can find one. Not only is this great for consumers, it proves that Napa can produce wonderful cabernets in more than one style, and it underlines the point that, while style is due in part to where the grapes are grown, it is also very much a function of a winemaker's intent.

As good as Napa cabernets can be, though, they sometimes display a disappointing uniformity, as if whatever distinctive qualities the wines possessed were ironed out of them for fear of not fitting the expected profile that many consumers might have. This is not to diminish the quality of individual bottles, just to recognize the power of the Napa brand, both in marketing and in persuading wineries to toe a particular stylistic line.

Napa Valley, of course, is not the sole source for California cabernet. In fact, one of the world's greatest cabernet sauvignon–based wines, Ridge Monte Bello, comes not from Napa but from the Santa Cruz Mountains, which happens also to be a wonderful source for several good cabernets. And don't underestimate the cabernets of Sonoma County, which can often be superb. They may typically be a bit leaner and less plush than the standard Napa cabernet, but such generalizations can be dangerous, keeping in mind the importance of winemaker's intent. 🍷

RED MEAT, PLEASE. These wines demand the rich, lush taste of tender steak to balance the best of the lot, exhibiting well-knit, softly tannic complexity. High-alcohol, jammy examples would overpower almost anything but beef. Well, not quite. Bison, or buffalo, another meat that has forceful beefiness, would reinforce the Americanness of this pairing. Because bison has a slightly sweeter finish than beef, I combined a little tart pomegranate molasses with red wine as the deglazing medium. A few dollops of rich butter compensated for the leanness of the meat and turned the reduced, wine-enriched pan juices into a dark, syrupy finishing sauce. A wild rice pilaf infused with double-smoked bacon, rendered fragrant with the spice of ground cloves, and steeped in beef stock that had been sharpened with a little of the pomegranate molasses, completed the satisfying plate of food.

Bison Steaks with Smoky Wild Rice

TIME: 1 HOUR 15 MINUTES

1 tablespoon extra virgin olive oil

3 ounces double-smoked slab bacon, diced

½ cup finely diced red onion

½ teaspoon ground cloves

1 cup raw wild rice

2½ tablespoons pomegranate molasses (sold in Middle Eastern shops)

2½ cups beef stock

Salt and freshly ground black pepper

4 boneless bison strip loin steaks, each about 10 ounces, fat well trimmed

¾ cup dry red wine

1 tablespoon unsalted butter, preferably high-fat European style

1. Heat ½ tablespoon of the oil in a 3-quart saucepan. Add the bacon and sauté until lightly browned. Remove the bacon, leaving the fat in the pan. Add the red onion and sauté until just beginning to brown. Stir in the cloves. Add the wild rice and stir. Add 1½ tablespoons of the pomegranate molasses and the beef stock. Stir to blend. Season with salt and pepper.

2. Cover and cook at a slow simmer until the rice is tender and the liquid has been absorbed, about 45 minutes. Remove from the heat and set aside, covered.

3. Slick the remaining ½ tablespoon oil in a large heavy skillet. Place over high heat. Season the steaks with salt and pepper. Place in the pan and sear to medium-rare, about 3 minutes on each side. Remove the steaks to a warm platter and tent with foil. If all the steaks do not fit in the pan, cook just 2 at a time.

4. Add the wine to the skillet and cook over medium heat, scraping the bottom of the pan, until the wine has reduced by half. Whisk in the remaining 1 tablespoon pomegranate molasses, then, off the heat, whisk in the butter bit by bit, until the pan sauce turns syrupy. Taste and season with salt and pepper.

5. Mound the rice on each of four warm dinner plates. Slice the steaks and arrange the slices alongside the rice. Spoon the sauce onto the meat and serve.

YIELD: 4 SERVINGS

COOK'S NOTES: Bison is lean and less marbled with fat than a prime rib roast, a rib eye, fillet, or strip loin, so it should be cooked no more than medium-rare. The fillet is leaner still, but it's another cut that would be worth serving. 🥄

THESE ARE WINES THAT TASTING NOTES OFTEN DESCRIBE AS EARTHY AND PLUMMY. Add good acidity in the best of them and you have cabernets from a winemaker who is not aiming for a skyscraper if ten stories would do. Alongside? Hearty lamb shanks braised with ingredients suggested by the flavors in the glass, including dried plums, a touch of citrus, and spice. The bold richness of the meat and its sauce should be gracefully tamed by the structure and acidic balance of the wines.

Lamb Shanks in Red Wine with Prunes

TIME: 2¼ HOURS

1 cup pitted prunes

1 cup dry red wine

2 tablespoons extra virgin olive oil

4 lamb shanks, about 1 pound each, fat well trimmed

1 cup finely chopped onions

8 garlic cloves, minced

1 red bell pepper, cored, seeded, and slivered

1 teaspoon ground cumin

½ teaspoon Spanish smoked paprika

Salt and freshly ground black pepper

4 fresh thyme sprigs

2 teaspoons grated orange zest

Cayenne

Cooked couscous, for serving

1. Place the prunes in a bowl, add the wine, and set aside.

2. Heat the oil in a 6-quart casserole or sauté pan. Add the lamb and brown on all sides over medium heat. Remove from the casserole. Stir in the onions and garlic. Sauté on low until soft. Stir in the bell pepper, cumin, and paprika. Sauté a few minutes more. Return the lamb to the pan, and season with salt and black pepper. Add the thyme, prunes, and wine. Cover and simmer for 1 hour.

3. Turn the lamb shanks in the casserole and baste. Add the orange zest and cayenne to taste. Cover and cook on low until the lamb is tender when pierced with a fork, about 45 minutes more. Check the seasoning. Serve with couscous.

YIELD: 4 SERVINGS

COOK'S NOTES: You have to figure one shank per person; there's no other way. So try to buy smallish ones, about a pound each. 🧂 Lamb with prunes and cumin suggests North Africa, making couscous the appropriate partner alongside. 🧂

DECANTING

The reasons for decanting, or not decanting, are hotly debated and little understood, even among experts. Proponents generally cite two benefits: pouring wine off the sediment that develops as some wines age, and exposing younger wines to air to bring out their aromas and flavors.

Many good red wines produce sediment as they age, so once they reach middle age decanting these wines, very carefully, is advisable. Why carefully? The idea is to pour wine, not sediment. Assuming the bottle rested horizontally, possibly for years, sediment has settled to the bottom side. Stand the bottle upright at this point and what happens? Motion agitates the sediment so that decanting can't help.

The situation can be remedied in two ways. If you're at home and can plan ahead, set the bottle upright several days before you plan to open it. This lets the sediment resettle at the bottom of the bottle, though it squelches spontaneity. At restaurants, if you know you'll want a particular wine and can call a few days ahead of time, do it. Otherwise, a good restaurant will have a decanting cradle, which permits an older bottle to be kept on its side without stirring up sediment as it is removed from storage, transported briefly, opened, and poured.

Wines that age gracefully may eventually reach a point where even careful decanting is too violent. With advanced age, fragile aromas and flavors can shrivel like dried flowers when exposed to air, leaving behind the husk of the wine. In such cases, you can keep the wine in the decanting cradle and pour directly into glasses, taking care not to stir up the sediment. When does a wine reach that point? It's a judgment call: Pour a tiny sip to tell whether it is fragile, or vibrant and healthy.

While most experts agree on decanting wines to eliminate sediment, no such consensus exists on the question of decanting to give the wine air. Some say it does nothing, but I like to decant young reds that might be tannic or mute, and even young whites, which can likewise be reticent and will often benefit from aeration. —EA

CABERNET INTERNATIONALLY

Cabernet sauvignon stands as Exhibit A in any discussion of international grapes. It proved so popular and successful in Bordeaux, California, and elsewhere that wine producers and regions all over the world now grow it and make wines with varying degrees of distinctiveness. You name a place; no doubt, it grows cabernet.

Washington, Long Island, and Virginia are just a few of the other American regions that make wines of cabernet sauvignon, and around the world, Tuscany, South Africa, South America, and Australia have all produced acclaimed cabernets. Most famous are the so-called super Tuscans like the elegant Sassicaia, the lusher Ornellaia, and the powerful but precise Solaia. While these wines inspired a host of fancifully named lesser imitations, the best are superb in their own right.

South African cabernets have been highly successful, wines that ably combine power and finesse, and are often great deals as well. Australia offers some excellent cabernets, too, as well as a great deal of palatable bottles of little interest. Both Australia and Italy also blend cabernet unconventionally, as in Solaia's combination with sangiovese and the numerous variations on cabernet and shiraz in Australia. South America, too, particularly Chile, makes a lot of routine cabernet, with a few standouts, like Concha y Toro's Don Melchor.

It's impossible to generalize about such a varied collection of wines. While they may start out from the same grape, they achieve a wide range of styles. Partly this is because of where the grapes are grown. Sometimes, though, because it is so often a grape of choice for mass-market wineries, the spicy, tannic, herbal character of cabernet is manipulated to achieve a softer, easier-going profile. The result, often, is a sound, palatable, but ultimately insipid wine. 🍷

ANOTHER WAY TO ADDRESS CABERNET SAUVIGNON is the way it's done at a château in the Médoc, with a well-bred, rather classic main dish. Consider fillet of beef in thick tournedos slices seared and dressed with a wine-enriched sauce, and simple pot vegetables finished with a gloss of butter alongside. If you have a platter of silver or fine porcelain, this is the occasion for which to dust it off.

Tournedos of Beef with Pot-au-Feu Vegetables

TIME: 50 MINUTES

1 carrot, peeled

1 celery stalk

1 leek (white part only)

1 medium white turnip, peeled

1½ pounds fillet of beef, cut into 4 slices

Salt and freshly ground black pepper

1 tablespoon extra virgin olive oil

3 cups beef stock

1 cup dry red wine

4 fresh thyme sprigs

1 teaspoon Dijon mustard

3 tablespoons unsalted butter, softened

1 tablespoon minced fresh chives

1. Cut the carrot, celery, leek, and turnip into ¼-inch-thick matchsticks 2 inches long.

2. Season the beef with salt and pepper. Heat the oil in a 12-inch sauté pan. Add the beef and sear over high heat until browned but still almost raw inside. Remove from the pan. Add the carrot, celery, leek, and turnip to the pan. Add the stock and simmer over low heat until the vegetables are tender, about 10 minutes. Using a slotted spoon, remove the vegetables to a saucepan, draining well to reserve the stock in the sauté pan. Cover the vegetables.

3. Add the wine and thyme to the stock in the sauté pan and reduce to about 1 cup over high heat. Remove the thyme. Whisk in the mustard. Over low heat, whisk in 2 tablespoons of the butter, bit by bit, to thicken the sauce. Season with salt and pepper. Add the beef and cook over low heat, basting with the sauce until done, 4 to 5 minutes for medium-rare. Remove from the heat and transfer the beef and sauce to a warm platter. Tent with foil.

4. Reheat the vegetables in the saucepan with the remaining 1 tablespoon butter. Fold in the chives. Arrange the vegetables around the beef on the platter and serve.

YIELD: 4 SERVINGS

COOK'S NOTES: Butter to finish a sauce should be European style, meaning a higher fat content than the government standard of 80 percent. But it does not have to be an import. There are companies making butter in the United States at 84 and 86 percent. The lower water content yields a silkier sauce. These butters are also best for pastry, and if they are labeled "cultured," they will be more flavorful.

MERLOT

It wasn't all that long ago when merlot was one of the most popular grapes on the planet. Then, in 2004 the movie *Sideways* landed, with its unforgettably caustic disparagement of merlot, and merlot's status has never been the same since.

Well, let me amend that. In Pomerol and Saint-Émilion, where merlot is the leading grape, the wines are more highly valued than ever. And even in the Médoc, merlot has been gaining on cabernet sauvignon, which has historically been the leading grape. It's still planted all over the world, where it often contributes its lush, soft qualities to wines in ways both desirable and undesirable. But in the United States, at least, varietally labeled merlot has never regained its pre-*Sideways* currency.

Is that fair? Frankly, the movie spoke the truth in sneering terms, namely, that much of the merlot produced in the United States was not very good. Obviously, though, that does not mean that all American merlot is not good.

Long Island, for one, produces some excellent merlots—balanced, elegant, and earthy with aromas of violets and plummy flavors. The best Washington merlots reveal a structure that you rarely see in the typically plusher, softer California versions. They are not huge fruit bombs or oak monsters by any means, but surprisingly balanced, smaller-scale wines that belong on the dinner table.

Even California merlot, the prime target of *Sideways*, can be quite good: juicy and velvety. Nonetheless, most of the merlot produced in North America is generic stuff, grown in the hot Central Valley of California, mild and inoffensive to those who don't really like wine, but insufferable to those who do.

It may be that merlot is at its best in California as part of a blend, but if so, California law works against it. The law requires a wine to be at least 75 percent of a particular grape if it is to be labeled varietally—by the name of that grape—and grape names are what many consumers have gotten used to and what they expect. So many winemakers may make the commercial decision to, say, use at least 75 percent merlot or 75 percent cabernet sauvignon, even if the best wine is a 50-50 blend.

Consumers often express surprise at this, having expected wines like merlot or cabernet sauvignon to be 100 percent merlot or cabernet. But in France, Bordeaux varietals like merlot and cabernet are almost always blended, and seldom does merlot meet that 75 percent threshold. For every Pomerol like Pétrus, which is 95 percent merlot, you have great wines like Lafleur (50 percent merlot) and Vieux Château Certan (60 percent merlot).

Many people have pointed out the irony in the scene in *Sideways* in which the merlot-hating character, Miles, opens his treasured bottle of 1961 Cheval Blanc, which, they gleefully note, is 50 percent merlot and 50 percent cabernet franc. The moral, they say, is that Miles really does like merlot. Not likely. The moral, I think, is that merlot would often be better if it were blended with cabernet franc. 🍷

THIS BREAD SALAD WAS INSPIRED BY A SUMMERTIME TUSCAN PANZANELLA, but is more suited to the post-tomato season. (See page 111 for another panzanella.) It is cloaked in autumn tones and flavors, with cubes of butternut squash, pieces of cauliflower, and the earthy, hearty flavor of whole-grain bread. The panzanella could be a first course for a red wine dinner. It could be a side dish with chicken or meat, and could even be a salad course with a craggy slab of cheese like cheddar alongside.

Autumn Panzanella

TIME: 45 MINUTES, PLUS 4 HOURS MARINATING

3 cups peeled and seeded butternut squash in ¾-inch cubes

2 cups small cauliflower florets

8 soft sun-dried tomatoes, slivered

1 large Asian pear, peeled, cored, and diced

2 tablespoons chopped sweet onion

2 tablespoons drained capers

¾ cup extra virgin olive oil

¼ cup cider vinegar

3 cups cubed country-style whole grain bread

1 teaspoon ground cumin

Salt and freshly ground black pepper

2 tablespoons minced fresh dill

1. Bring 2 quarts water to a boil in a saucepan. Add the squash and cauliflower, cook for 2 minutes, drain, and place in a bowl of ice water to chill. When cooled, drain and place in a large bowl. Fold in the sun-dried tomatoes and Asian pear. Add the onion and capers and mix gently. Add ½ cup of the olive oil and the vinegar. Mix again.

2. Place the bread in a bowl of warm water, soak for 5 minutes, then squeeze dry. Heat 3 tablespoons of the remaining oil in a large skillet, add the bread, and sauté over medium heat until the bread dries out and is starting to brown. Season with the cumin, salt, and pepper. Fold into the squash mixture in the bowl.

3. Allow the ingredients to marinate for at least 4 hours at room temperature. Check the seasoning and fold in the dill. Add a little more oil if needed. Transfer to a serving bowl or to individual plates and serve.

YIELD: 6 TO 8 SERVINGS

COOK'S NOTES: Consider the vegetables and fruit in this recipe as a rough guide. Depending on what's available in the market, there are plenty of other possible candidates: broccoli, Brussels sprouts, mango, kale, and grapes come to mind. 🥄

RUSTIC, EARTHY NOODLES LIKE BUCKWHEAT SOBA might just be the ticket to tame a big, fruit-forward merlot. But not served cold, as they often are, and certainly not with the usual dashi, soy sauce, and mirin dressing. Here they are treated like pasta, and indeed, farro or whole wheat spaghetti can be substituted. They are dressed with diced mushrooms and chicken livers well moistened with stock. Each plate is finished with toasted panko, crunchy bread crumbs that speak the same language as the soba.

Soba with Mushrooms and Chicken Livers

TIME: 45 MINUTES

5 tablespoons extra virgin olive oil

½ cup panko bread crumbs

4 ounces speck or smoky bacon, diced

¼ cup minced shallots

8 ounces shiitake mushrooms, stems discarded, caps diced

Salt and freshly ground black pepper

½ pound well-trimmed chicken livers, cut into 1-inch pieces

2 tablespoons all-purpose flour

1 cup chicken stock, plus more as needed

1 teaspoon balsamic vinegar

12 ounces soba noodles

2 tablespoons minced fresh cilantro leaves

1. Heat 2 tablespoons of the oil in a large skillet, add the panko, and cook until golden. Remove from the pan and set aside. Wipe out the pan. Add 2 tablespoons of the oil, heat, and add the speck. Cook over medium heat until starting to brown. Remove to a bowl, leaving as much fat as possible in the pan.

2. Add the shallots and sauté until soft. Add the mushrooms and cook until wilted and starting to brown. Season with salt and pepper. Transfer to the bowl with the speck. Toss the livers with the flour. Add the remaining 1 tablespoon oil to the pan, add the livers, and cook, stirring gently, over medium heat, until firmed up and lightly browned but still pink inside. Transfer the livers to a cutting board and dice them.

3. Add the stock to the pan. Cook, stirring, until reduced by half, and then stir in the vinegar. Return the speck, mushrooms, and livers to the pan. Heat briefly and season with salt and pepper. Remove from the heat.

4. Bring a large pot of salted water to a boil. Cook the noodles for about 6 minutes and drain, but not too thoroughly. Fold the moist noodles into the chicken liver mixture and heat gently, adding a little more stock if needed. Serve, topping each portion with the panko and cilantro.

YIELD: 4 SERVINGS

COOK'S NOTES: Take a sharp knife to the mushrooms and livers, not a machine. The texture of the end result will be more uniform and far superior. 🧂

THE MUSCULAR SEAR AND SMOKY, CRISP BURNISH OF GRILLED FOOD HAS IMMENSE APPEAL. But achieving it takes more than a carefree encounter with hot coals (or gas) and a grate. The guy with an apron might scoff but I have increasingly come to rely on my oven to seal the deal with a slow bake after a quick sizzle. That's how I made these pork chops with their lusty Neapolitan topping to accompany an all-purpose merlot that delivers just a bit of spice on the palate. The slow cooking brings the meat gently to tender doneness, guarding the juices. It also grants the cook nearly an hour to assemble the rest of the dinner, and what does the guy with the apron know about that? Penne or other modest macaroni dressed just with olive oil and chile flakes is excellent alongside, to share the sauce with the meat.

Pork Chops Puttanesca

TIME: 1 HOUR 15 MINUTES

3 garlic cloves

½ teaspoon dried oregano

½ teaspoon crushed red chile flakes

¼ teaspoon salt

2 tablespoons extra virgin olive oil

1 tablespoon red wine vinegar

Four 12-ounce rib pork chops, preferably heritage pork, about 1¼ inches thick

1 small red onion, finely chopped

8 ounces ripe tomatoes, finely chopped

4 anchovy fillets in oil, drained and mashed

2 tablespoons pitted oil-cured black olives, chopped

½ tablespoon capers in vinegar, drained

1½ tablespoons golden raisins

½ cup dry red wine

1 teaspoon fresh oregano leaves, minced

1. Mash 1 clove of the garlic with the dried oregano, ¼ teaspoon of the chile flakes, and the salt to a paste in a mortar. Stir in 1 tablespoon of the olive oil and the vinegar. Spread this mixture on both sides of the pork. Set aside. Heat your grill. Heat the oven to 225°F.

2. Heat the remaining 1 tablespoon oil in a small skillet, add the onion, and sauté until translucent. Mince the remaining 2 cloves garlic and stir in. Add the tomatoes, remaining ¼ teaspoon chile flakes, anchovy, olives, capers, and raisins. Stir in the wine and cook on low until the mixture is thick, about 15 minutes. Set aside.

3. Grill the pork close to the source of the heat, turning once, until nicely browned but not cooked through, about 2 minutes per side. Transfer the pork to a baking dish, slather with the tomato mixture and place in the oven for 45 minutes for medium, longer for more well done. Arrange the pork on a serving platter, spoon any pan juices over it, scatter with oregano, and serve.

YIELD: 4 SERVINGS

COOK'S NOTES: For this recipe to produce the proper results it's important that the pork chops all be the same thickness. Do not take chances; shop at a reliable butcher. 🧂

CÔTES DU RHÔNE

Once upon a time, you knew what you were getting when you opened a Côtes du Rhône. More than likely it would be a light-bodied red with flavors of spicy fruit and Provençal herbs. While these Côtes du Rhônes of old might have varied from undistinguished to highly pleasing, you knew that you could order a carafe, a bottle, maybe even two, and expect a wine that would go down easily. Indeed, Côtes du Rhône became something of a synonym for blithe, gulpable bistro wines.

For better or sometimes for worse, those days are largely gone. On the plus side, the quality of grapegrowing and wine making in the Côtes du Rhône areas has greatly improved in the last thirty years. Rather than selling grapes to cooperatives, more growers are making their own wines and making them seriously, with reduced yields and greater care. Far fewer Côtes du Rhônes are thin and dilute, while far more are wines of character.

What could be wrong? Well, when improved methods aimed at making wines of greater concentration collide with the sort of very warm vintages that have become more frequent in the era of climate change, then you may well have something unanticipated in the glass. Nowadays, a surprising number of wines tend to be plush and polished, so jammy, sleek, and modern that they show little trace of identity. Others may be fruity and well made but are not particularly distinctive. But even in the warmest vintages, you can still find wines that show earthy mineral and herbal touches amid the fruit.

Theoretically, ordinary Côtes du Rhônes can come from any designated area in the Rhône region, north or south. Practically speaking, however, the vast majority of Côtes du Rhônes come from the southern Rhône region. With the exception of those few Côtes du Rhône from the syrah-centric northern Rhône, the wines are mandated to be at least 40 percent grenache. Certain wines receive the elevated appellation of Côtes du Rhône–Villages if they come from seventeen designated villages. These wines have the name of one of those villages appended to the appellation, and they must be at least 50 percent grenache.

As an illustration of how the appellations have evolved, the minimum required alcohol for a Côtes du Rhône is 11 percent, and for a Côtes du Rhône–Villages it is 12.5 percent. The minimum requirements in most appellations were set in another era, however, when the world was cooler and grapes were habitually picked when less ripe, and at higher yields, resulting in lower alcohol levels. It's the rare Côtes du Rhone these days that clocks in at less than 13.5 percent. Most are 14 percent or higher.

The bottom line is that what was once a bistro tipple is now often an innocuously fruity modern wine. Here's a rule of thumb that—fair warning—comes with numerous exceptions: As the price of Côtes du Rhône rises, the wine tends to become more generic. The less expensive the bottle, the more character it tends to show. 🍷

THE EYE CAN INFLUENCE WINE CHOICES almost as easily as the nose or the palate. A plate of dusky gnocchi darkened with black olive paste demanded red wine. The earthy flavor of the olives also dictated a wine with rustic heft. Without the olives, or with green ones instead of black, the dish, which was a highlight at La Terrazza, the restaurant at the Splendido Hotel in Portofino, Italy, could have easily welcomed a rich white wine. But I opted for a local red, a Rossese di Dolceacqua, a wine that Joseph Bastianich and David Lynch, the authors of *Vino Italiano: The Regional Wines of Italy*, state "is likely to remind you of a light-styled Côtes-du-Rhône." Voilà! The preparation is simple and will be successful as long as you apply a light touch.

Black Olive Gnocchi with Tomatoes and Basil

TIME: 1 HOUR

1 pound Idaho potatoes

3 tablespoons extra virgin olive oil

1 large garlic clove, sliced

1 pound cherry tomatoes, quartered

4 ounces pitted black or Kalamata olives, coarsely chopped

Salt and freshly ground black pepper

1 cup all-purpose flour

1¼ cups freshly grated Parmigiano-Reggiano, plus more for serving

2 large egg yolks, beaten

2½ tablespoons black olive paste (tapenade)

20 fresh basil leaves, slivered

COOK'S NOTES: You can purchase plain potato gnocchi for this dish. But what about the olives? Add a tablespoon of olive paste (tapenade) and 1½ ounces of pitted olives, chopped, to the sauce. 🖅

1. Place the potatoes in a saucepan, cover with salted water, and boil until tender, about 25 minutes. Meanwhile, heat the oil in a skillet, add the garlic, and cook over medium heat until barely starting to color. Stir in the tomatoes. Add half of the olives to the skillet. Cook briefly, until the tomatoes collapse. Season with salt and pepper, and remove from the heat.

2. When the potatoes are tender, peel them and rice into a large bowl. Mix all but 3 tablespoons of the flour with the cheese, toss with the potatoes, and pile in a mound on a work surface. Make a well in the center. Mix the egg yolks and olive paste and place in the well. Finely chop the remaining olives and add to the well. Knead to blend the ingredients and form a soft dough. Shape into a ball and divide it into 8 portions. Roll each into a rope about 10 inches long and ½ inch in diameter. Cut into ½-inch dumplings (gnocchi). Dust with the remaining flour and lightly pile in a bowl.

3. Bring 4 quarts salted water to a boil. Reduce the heat to a fast simmer, add the gnocchi, and as they rise to the surface, use a slotted spoon or skimmer to remove them to a colander. Drain.

4. Reheat the sauce in the skillet, fold in the basil, and add the gnocchi. Heat, gently mixing, then check the seasoning and serve with extra cheese alongside, if desired.

YIELD: 4 SERVINGS

HERE YOU HAVE ONE OF MY FAVORITE RECIPES. The glowing peppers, shiny eggplants, sleek zucchini, ripe tomatoes and herbs speak the language of Provence. Elsewhere, when these vegetables beckon from farm stands, I routinely assemble a bright ratatouille. For years I have grilled most of the vegetables before combining them in the sauté pan. The ratatouille is best when each of the ingredients is cooked separately, à point, then combined at the end. Grilling—or broiling, which is a fine alternative—reduces the amount of oil needed, especially for the eggplant.

Grilled Ratatouillle

TIME: 1¾ HOURS, INCLUDING SALTING

1 medium eggplant (about 1 pound), cut into ½-inch-thick slices

2 medium zucchini, about 6 ounces each, trimmed

Salt

1 large red bell pepper, cut into eighths, seeds and ribs removed

1 large onion, cut into ½-inch-thick slices

4 to 5 tablespoons fruity extra virgin olive oil

4 large garlic cloves, sliced

1 pound ripe plum tomatoes, peeled and chopped fine

8 fresh thyme sprigs, leaves stripped off

3 tablespoons minced fresh basil

Grated zest of ½ lemon

Freshly ground black pepper

2 tablespoons pine nuts, toasted

1. Spread the eggplant slices on a large plastic cutting board. Cut the zucchini vertically into ½-inch-thick slices. Spread them on the cutting board. Dust the vegetables with salt. Set aside for 30 minutes, turn, dust with salt again and set aside 30 minutes. Rinse and pat dry.

2. Meanwhile, light a grill to very hot. (The vegetables can be cooked under a broiler instead of on a grill.) Place the bell pepper pieces, skin side down, on the grill and grill until the skin blackens. Place them in a paper bag. Place the onion slices on the grill and sear on both sides. Remove and chop into ½-inch pieces.

3. Brush the eggplant and zucchini slices with about 2 tablespoons of the oil. Grill until seared. Remove and chop into ½-inch pieces. Scrape the skin from the bell pepper and chop the pepper into ½-inch pieces.

4. Heat 2 tablespoons of the remaining oil in a large skillet or sauté pan. Add the garlic and sauté over medium heat until starting to color. Add the onion and bell pepper and sauté for 5 minutes, stirring. Add the eggplant and zucchini and sauté for 5 minutes. Add the tomatoes, thyme, half the basil, and the lemon zest. Sauté for 5 minutes, stirring. Season with salt and pepper.

5. Fold in the pine nuts, the remaining basil, and additional oil, if desired. Serve or set aside to serve at room temperature.

YIELD: 4 TO 6 SERVINGS

COOK'S NOTES: The final assembly is quick, but the dish does improve if it is allowed to sit for an hour or so, then tasted and reseasoned, perhaps with some additional fresh herbs, before serving. To me, ratatouille is always best at room temperature. 🗑

GLASSWARE

Here are the two most important things to know about wineglasses: Good glassware without a doubt will enhance good wines, but you most definitely do not need as many different sorts of glasses as glassware producers would like you to believe.

Any good wineglass will be capacious. It ought to allow a good-size pour that will fill the bowl no more than a third of the way up. This allows plenty of room for swirling the wine without fear of its flying out of the glass. Make sure the stem is long enough so that you can easily hold the glass without touching the bowl. The bowl itself should be tall, with the rim tapering inward to funnel aromas up toward your nose, and the rims should not be thick. Beyond that, it all depends on your budget. The more you spend, generally, the more elegant the glasses will be. Cheaper glasses will be less fine, while more expensive glasses may be more fragile but more beautiful. Clear glass is best. Decorative beading, cut glass, and colors interfere with examining the wine within.

The notion that you need a different glass for every type of wine is nonsense. I don't even think you need different glasses for white and red wines, although traditionally red-wine glasses are bigger and wider than glasses for white. Glasses for red wine generally fall into two categories: Bordeaux glasses, which are taller and narrower, and Burgundy glasses, which are wider. Does it make a difference? Only in terms of tradition.

Flutes for Champagne are elegant, but the shape doesn't do the wines any favors. Good Champagne should be consumed out of good wineglasses. Similarly, the small copita used for sherry is another tradition that you can profitably ignore. Just serve sherry out of ordinary wineglasses, too.

Occasionally, a restaurant will serve wine in tumblers. Unless the wine is young, fresh, and very simple, this strikes me as reverse snobbery. Sure you can drink wine from tumblers. You can also drink it from paper cups. But why would anybody want to do that?

You can easily get by with one set of good glasses, as long as you buy more than you think you'll need in order to accommodate unexpected guests and breakage, because they will break.

I like to keep one set of glasses for everyday use and one beautiful set for special occasions. The everyday glasses can easily be washed in the dishwasher, but the special set, made of finer glass, is a little more fragile, at least I think it is. I wash them without soap most of the time, just several applications of hot water. —EA

THE NORTHERN RHÔNE

The northern Rhône Valley of France is the ancestral home of the syrah grape. From the granite hillsides of this slender valley, syrah has traveled around the world, most notably to California and Washington State, and to Australia, where it is more commonly known as shiraz. But the northern Rhône is where it started and from where, to my taste at least, the greatest expressions of syrah all come.

Only recently, however, has the greatness of these wines been widely recognized. At the turn of the twentieth century, Hermitage might have been known to a wide audience, but Côte-Rôtie was still a backwater. Not until late in the twentieth century was Cornas considered anything other than a rustic, fierce wine. The reputations of Saint-Joseph and Crozes-Hermitage are still works in progress. Great northern Rhône reds are immediately distinctive with their haunting, savory flavors, reminiscent of the aromas of black olives, violets and bacon, pepper and herbs. No other wines are quite like them, and the best can last for thirty years or more.

Côte-Rôtie is at the northernmost tip of the valley. The name, Côte-Rôtie, famously translates as "roasted slope," implying hot weather. In fact, Côte-Rôtie may represent the northernmost cool-climate limit for growing the syrah grape. It is dominated by a network of ancient terraced granite vineyards on an impossibly steep slope facing south into the sun, which bathes the vines in light more than in heat.

Côte-Rôtie is naturally compared with Hermitage, to the south. In the gender-specific thinking of this Romance-language culture, the more burly, robust Hermitage was typically described as masculine, while the more aromatic, delicate Côte-Rôtie was called feminine. In fact, the classic Côte-Rôties of old often seemed closer in style to the grace and finesse of wines from Burgundy to the north rather than to the muscular Hermitages. Sadly, this traditional style has largely given way to a more powerful expression of Côte-Rôtie—big, fruity, and often oaky— although quite a few producers today land somewhere in the middle.

Hermitage is altogether the more imposing wine, robust and tannic in its youth before giving forth its perfumed glory. Together, Hermitage and Côte-Rôtie are tiny appellations, no bigger, really, than a couple of good-size Bordeaux vineyards.

Years after Hermitage and Côte-Rôtie achieved enviable status as objects of desire, Cornas, on the southern end of the northern Rhône, was regarded as their bumpkin cousin, powerful yet perhaps embarrassing to introduce in polite company. Yet in the last thirty years or so a new Cornas has emerged, not so much homespun as wild, with captivating aromas and flavors. If it hasn't quite risen in status and price to the level of Hermitage and Côte-Rôtie, it's on its way.

That leaves the economy end of the northern Rhône. Saint-Joseph, its boundaries greatly expanded in the last fifty years, is a long, spindly appellation covering the western bank of the Rhône from Condrieu to Cornas. From historic granite hillside sites, Saint-Joseph can be superb, expressing the character of the northern Rhône but accessible a little sooner than Hermitage, Côte-Rôtie, and Cornas. From the flatlands, Saint-Joseph is serviceable. From top producers, Crozes-Hermitage can likewise be a wine of character. Too often, though, it's a simple, pleasant wine coasting on the name of its big brother. 🍷

THE NORTHERN RHÔNE REGION, the source of Crozes-Hermitage and other terrific syrah wines, is the gateway to the south of France. It inspired a hint of Provence for this pairing. Grilled quail seasoned liberally with garlic, fresh thyme, and black pepper, in a sauce bolstered with niçoise olives and thickened with a dab of tapenade, suits these bold but balanced wines that often convey a hint of herbs and olives on the nose.

Grilled Quail with Olives and Polenta

TIME: 1 HOUR 15 MINUTES, PLUS MARINATING

8 whole quail

Salt and freshly ground black pepper

6 garlic cloves, thinly sliced

20 fresh thyme sprigs

½ cup hearty red wine

6 tablespoons extra virgin olive oil

1 cup yellow cornmeal for polenta, preferably stone-ground

1 ounce pancetta, minced

½ cup chicken stock

¼ cup niçoise olives

2 teaspoons black olive paste (tapenade)

COOK'S NOTES: Quail are sold either whole or semiboneless. Wholes ones should be butterflied for easy grilling. Be sure to pluck out any stray pinfeathers. Sometimes the birds, which are sold gutted and cleaned, still have their little hearts inside. Leave them to enhance any gamy flavor. As for the polenta, it must fall in a thin, steady stream into the pot of boiling water, as you stir all the while with a wooden spoon. 🗑

1. Butterfly the quail by using kitchen shears to cut them up the backbone. Flatten each slightly by pushing on the breast. Season with salt and pepper, scatter with half the garlic and 16 thyme sprigs, and place in a large bowl. Pour the wine and 4 tablespoons of the oil over the quail, cover, and refrigerate for 4 to 5 hours.

2. Place the cornmeal in a resealable plastic bag and seal. Bring 4 cups water to a boil in a 3-quart saucepan. Add 1½ teaspoons salt. Snip off one tiny corner of the bag and pour in the cornmeal in a thin stream from the opening in the bag, stirring constantly. Cook, stirring, for 25 minutes. Grease an 8-inch square baking dish with some of the remaining oil. Spread the cooked polenta evenly in the dish and set aside.

3. Shortly before serving, light a grill. Transfer the quail from the marinade to a platter, reserving the marinade. Leave the thyme sprigs and garlic bits clinging to the quail. Remove the polenta from the dish, cut it into 4 squares, then cut each square on the diagonal to make 8 triangles.

4. Heat the remaining oil in a skillet. Add the remaining garlic and the pancetta and sauté until barely golden. Add the stock and the reserved marinade and cook until sauce is slightly reduced, about 5 minutes. Add the olives, olive paste, and leaves from the remaining thyme. Season with pepper and, if desired, salt. Heat to a steady simmer, then remove from the heat.

5. Grill the polenta triangles until marked by the grill, about 3 minutes per side. Remove to a serving platter and cover loosely with foil to keep warm. Grill the quail, skin side down, until browned, about 3 minutes. Turn and continue grilling until the breast meat is medium, 5 to 8 minutes. Arrange the quail on a platter surrounded by polenta triangles. Briefly reheat the sauce and spoon it over the quail and polenta. Serve.

YIELD: 4 SERVINGS

THE WINES OF THE NORTHERN RHÔNE can also offer a worldview. Their balance makes them amenable to many dishes. Though steak, hamburgers, or burgers made from ground lamb would provide enough heft and richness for the wines, a more finely tuned response is welcome. A Thai-style beef salad, with slices of marinated skirt steak on a bed of greens that are dressed in a warm Asian vinaigrette, provides bite and sharp focus to this pairing.

Thai-Style Beef Salad

TIME: 1 HOUR, PLUS 3 HOURS MARINATING

5 tablespoons tamari soy sauce

1½ tablespoons Thai fish sauce (nam pla)

1 tablespoon toasted sesame oil

Juice of 2 limes

1 teaspoon grated peeled fresh ginger

1 bulb lemongrass, trimmed and minced

1 garlic clove, minced

1 teaspoon Sriracha (Thai red chili sauce), or to taste

1½ pounds skirt steak (about 2 steaks)

6 cups arugula, heavy stems removed

4 scallions, chopped

⅓ cup cilantro leaves

¼ cup grape seed or extra virgin olive oil

1 tablespoon Thai fried shallots (sold in Asian groceries; optional)

1. Combine the soy sauce, fish sauce, sesame oil, half the lime juice, the ginger, lemongrass, garlic, and Sriracha in a large bowl. Cut each steak in half, place in the bowl with the marinade, turn to coat, and allow to marinate at room temperature for 3 hours, turning from time to time.

2. Heat a grill or broiler to very hot. Place the arugula, scallions, and cilantro in a large bowl. Remove the steaks from the marinade. Pour the marinade into a small saucepan with the remaining lime juice and the grape seed oil. Bring to a simmer.

3. Grill or broil the steaks for about 2 minutes on each side, until medium-rare. Remove to a cutting board. Pour the hot marinade over the arugula mixture and toss. Arrange on a platter. Slice the steaks on the bias and place on top of the greens. Scatter with fried shallots, if using, and serve.

YIELD: 4 SERVINGS

COOK'S NOTES: The dish can be paired with Thai rice noodles—about 6 ounces is the proper amount. Boil, drain, cool, and dress them with sesame oil, a little soy sauce, and a generous handful of chopped scallions, and offer them alongside. 🧂

ONCE YOU ARE IN THE RHÔNE VALLEY HEADING TOWARD PROVENCE, North Africa is not far. So to serve with sleek northern Rhône wines, a chicken tagine, Moroccan-style, bolstered with prunes, olives, lemon, and mint, is appropriate. The wines themselves are herbaceous, a trifle spicy, hinting of olives, and often redolent of cooked dried fruit. There you have it all.

Chicken Tagine with Prunes and Olives

TIME: 1 HOUR 15 MINUTES

10 chicken thighs, with bone and skin

Salt and freshly ground black pepper

1 medium onion, finely chopped

1 tablespoon minced garlic

1 teaspoon smoked paprika, the hotter the better

1 teaspoon ground cumin

18 pitted prunes

36 pitted picholine or other small green olives

1 cup chicken stock

1 tablespoon unsalted butter

1 lemon, zest removed in thin strips

1 tablespoon finely chopped mint leaves

1. Dry the chicken pieces and season with salt and pepper. Heat a large, heavy skillet, preferably cast iron, to very hot. Add the chicken (in batches, if necessary) skin side down, and sear until the skin is golden brown. Remove chicken as it browns (do not turn it) and set it aside.

2. Discard all but a thin film of fat from the pan. Add the onion and garlic and sauté on low until soft. Stir in the paprika and cumin, cook for about a minute, and then add the prunes, olives, stock, and butter. Cook, stirring, for about 5 minutes. Season with salt and pepper. Transfer the contents of the pan to a 12- to 14-inch tagine, sauté pan, or casserole. Place the chicken on top, skin side up.

3. Cover and cook on medium-low heat for about 40 minutes, until the chicken is cooked through. Serve immediately or set aside to be reheated. To serve, scatter strips of lemon zest and mint on top, squeeze the lemon over the ingredients, and bring to the table, covered.

YIELD: 6 SERVINGS

COOK'S NOTES: A pottery tagine is a marvelous piece of equipment, designed to be self-basting as the steam rises into the conical lid and condenses back onto the food. At the same time the sauce reduces as some of the moisture is absorbed into the clay. The first time you use a clay tagine it should be soaked before heating. After that, you are home free. And it's meant to be used on top of the stove, not in the oven. In Morocco, you see tagines simmering on little charcoal burners at roadside cafes. With the chicken tagine? There is nothing better than some fluffy steamed couscous. 🥘

CHÂTEAUNEUF-DU-PAPE AND GIGONDAS

Nothing about Châteauneuf-du-Pape is sleek or polished. It's a rough-and-tumble wine, sometimes ungainly and fierce, but just as often warm, open, generous, and full of pleasure. It can be intense and complex—it's not at all simple. Yet it sometimes can be as friendly as a big, good-natured dog. Occasionally, it's too friendly.

Châteauneuf is always a big wine, but in the last twenty years, Châteauneuf has gotten decidedly bigger, and in particularly ripe vintages the wines can be huge—full of lush, opulent fruit with powerful, jammy flavors.

Personally, I prefer more focused and angular Châteauneufs, which balance spicy fruit flavors with earthiness, minerality, and whiffs of flowers and herbs. Few wines offer as visually clear a sense of place as these sorts of Châteauneuf. When you stick your nose into a glass and breathe in, you can actually feel transported to Provence, to perpetually windy slopes and rocky terrain redolent of garlic, lavender, and thyme.

While the wines that are lumped together in the Rhône region are bound by the Rhône river, northern and southern Rhônes are completely different characters. The reds of the northern Rhône, like those of Burgundy to the north, are based on a single grape. Syrah rules the north, even if the vignerons of Côte-Rôtie occasionally throw in a little viognier, and the fascination of these wines is in the various expressions of this one grape.

But Châteauneuf and the southern Rhône is a land of blends. Traditionally, the wines were field blends of many grapes grown side by side. While the appellation's rules permit the use of thirteen grapes in the blend, most wines nowadays, with occasional exceptions, are dominated by grenache, backed up by mourvèdre and syrah.

Grenache is also the basis for some of the lesser wines of the southern Rhône, like Gigondas, a close neighbor. Perhaps as a result of the increased popularity of Châteauneuf, or its rising cost, I've seen more Gigondas in the last few years, especially on restaurant wine lists, where they are often touted as less-expensive versions of Châteauneuf.

I find most Gigondas to be sound, fruity, generous wines. They can be extremely likable. Yet placing Gigondas on a level with Châteauneuf is mostly wishful thinking, or salesmanship. Good Châteauneuf offers a kind of crumbling magnificence and grandeur that mostly eludes these more straightforward wines. Only occasionally do I find the characteristic aromas of wild herbs and spices that can add an extra dimension and relieve the general fruitiness.

Let's be clear. I don't mean to criticize Gigondas; I simply want to adjust expectations. Every sort of wine has its place, and I especially value good everyday wines. Taken on that level most Gigondas are quite enjoyable and are often good values. But they rarely rise to the level of exalted. 🍷

AT AN OUTDOOR WEDDING RECEPTION SOME YEARS AGO in the south of France, it was an immense paella cooked over an open fire that stole the show. Lip-smacking memories of it come back from time to time, like when I have Châteauneuf-du-Pape in my glass. Talk about marriages: Paella's Mediterranean flavors are made for these earthy, meaty reds, where a tomato richness can sometimes peek through. For most cooks, paella is a complicated, time-consuming production number, best saved for that Saturday-evening dinner party. But it can easily be smaller and simpler, especially if you learn to keep the correct rice and a stash of saffron in the pantry. This paella, made just with a collection of sausages and no folderol, produces a satisfying one-pot dinner in hardly more time than it takes to babysit a risotto.

Mixed Sausage Paella

TIME: 50 MINUTES

4 cups chicken stock

½ teaspoon saffron threads

3 tablespoons extra virgin olive oil

6 ounces chorizo, sliced

6 ounces merguez (lamb sausage), sliced

6 ounces garlic sausage, sliced

1 large onion, finely chopped

½ cup finely chopped red bell pepper

3 garlic cloves, minced

1 teaspoon Spanish smoked paprika

1½ cups Spanish short-grain rice

½ cup tomato puree, fresh or canned

Salt and freshly ground black pepper

½ tablespoon chopped fresh flat-leaf parsley

1. Heat the stock in a saucepan. Add the saffron and set aside. Heat the oil in a 12- to 14-inch paella pan or cast-iron skillet. Add the chorizo, merguez, and garlic sausage, and sauté on medium until lightly browned. Remove from the pan.

2. Add the onion, bell pepper, and garlic to the pan and sauté until soft. Stir in the paprika and rice. Stir in the tomato puree. Strain the stock and add. Return the sausages to the pan. Stir once, season with salt and black pepper, and cook on medium until the liquid is absorbed and the rice is tender, about 25 minutes.

3. Remove the pan from the heat and place a sheet of parchment paper on the surface for 10 minutes. Remove the parchment, scatter the parsley on, and serve, making sure to include any crusty bits that cling to the pan with each portion.

YIELD: 4 TO 6 SERVINGS

COOK'S NOTES: Paella is always cooked on top of the stove or on a grill in Spain. And if some of the rice sticks to the bottom of the pan and browns, that's a good thing. Called *socarrat*, the crusty rice is prized by diners in the know. Letting the paella rest at the end, covered by a sheet of paper (newspaper is often used in Spain), improves the texture.

AS A COLD-WEATHER COMPLEMENT FOR CHÂTEAUNEUF-DU-PAPE or other wines from the southern Rhône, this thick, rib-sticking soup does the trick. The soup's whisper of meaty smoke and brambly fragrance of thyme clinch its ties to the land of the wine. The recipe, from Freemans Restaurant on the Lower East Side of New York, is easy. And copious. But leftovers freeze well.

Hearty Split Pea Soup

TIME: ABOUT 2 HOURS

1 pound slab bacon, cut into ¼-inch-thick slices

1 large onion, chopped

1 carrot, peeled and chopped

1 celery stalk, chopped

1 head garlic, cloves peeled and sliced thin

Salt and freshly ground black pepper

1 pound dried green split peas, rinsed and picked over

4 bay leaves

3 quarts chicken stock

½ bunch fresh thyme, leaves stripped from stems

1. Cut the bacon into ¼-inch dice. Place it in a heavy 6-quart pot over medium-low heat. Cook until the fat is rendered and translucent. Add the onion, carrot, celery, and garlic. Cook until the onion and garlic are soft and translucent. Season with salt and pepper.

2. Add the split peas, stir to coat with the fat, and add the bay leaves and stock. Increase the heat and bring to a boil. Reduce the heat so the soup simmers. Skim the foam that rises to the surface, continuing to do so for about 10 minutes, until no more foam appears. Add the thyme leaves. Simmer, uncovered, until the split peas are soft and starting to fall apart, 1 hour or longer.

3. Remove the soup from the heat. Discard the bay leaves. Add seasonings to taste. Puree the soup in a food processor in several batches—short of being perfectly smooth. You want to be able to spoon up some texture. Reheat the soup, skimming off any foam. Stir from the bottom to mix well, then ladle into bowls and serve.

YIELD: 10 TO 12 SERVINGS

COOK'S NOTES: Look for split peas that have a use-by date on the package and are relatively fresh; they will cook faster and better. This recipe can also be made with lentils.

THE REDS OF THE SOUTHERN RHÔNE can be high-end, serious stuff, or suitable for a picnic. This seafood salad, with all its components seared on the grill, would be an elegant first course or the main course for a more casual occasion. The edge of char picks up the smoke in some of the wines, as does the bitterness contributed by the radicchio. As for olives, you can't say Southern Rhône without them.

Grilled Seafood Salad

TIME: 1 HOUR

12 large shrimp, peeled

½ pound sea scallops, hard tendon removed

2 small to medium calamari, cleaned

½ pound swordfish, skinless

6 tablespoons extra virgin olive oil

3 tablespoons sherry vinegar

Salt and freshly ground black pepper

1 small head radicchio, quartered

2 large slices sourdough bread from a round loaf

3 scallions, chopped

1 tablespoon chopped pitted picholine olives

1 garlic clove

1 tablespoon minced fresh flat-leaf parsley

1. Combine the shrimp, scallops, calamari, and swordfish in a bowl. Toss with 2 tablespoons of the oil and 1 tablespoon of the vinegar. Season with salt and pepper. Plan to use a perforated grilling pan or eight or more thin bamboo skewers, soaked.

2. Light a grill. When the grill is hot, heat the grilling pan, and brush with a little of the oil. Or thread the seafood on the skewers, using 2 skewers side by side about ½ inch apart so the food will be secure. It doesn't matter in what order you skewer the seafood. Sear the seafood, turning it to cook both sides, about 5 minutes per side. Remove to a bowl as it is done. Sear the radicchio quarters on the grill and also toast the bread on the grill.

3. Remove the seafood from the skewers if you used them. Cut the shrimp in thirds, the scallops and swordfish in half, and slice the calamari. Pile the seafood in a bowl with the remaining olive oil, vinegar, the scallions, and olives. Coarsely chop the grilled radicchio. Add to the bowl. Rub the toasted bread with the garlic, dice it, and add it to the bowl. Season with salt and pepper, add the parsley, and serve the salad while still a bit warm.

YIELD: 4 TO 6 SERVINGS

COOK'S NOTES:
Threading food to be grilled on a double skewer stabilizes it, making the kebab easily turned for even searing.

AUSTRALIAN SHIRAZ
Shiraz has been Australia's wine ambassador, sounding its own friendly "G'day" to the world. Sometimes, the greeting has come with a powerfully fruity sip. Other times, it's in the form of a cute, unthreatening label, like the so-called critter wines that earned popularity on the winning appeal of a winsome kangaroo or koala. To a significant portion of the wine-drinking public, however, Australian shiraz came to be thought of as heavy, jammy, oaky, and high alcohol, and not in a good way.

Stereotypes are always troubling, and wine stereotypes are no different. I bristle when I hear some European winemaker assert that Americans make only big, powerful, alcoholic wines. Of course, many Americans say the same thing about Australian wines: The reds are all heavy bodied and high octane, overwhelming combinations of thick fruit flavors, oak, and alcohol. Or, in their inexpensive, mass-market manifestations, they taste like artificial confections.

I know this is not true. Good shiraz ripples with big, bold fruit flavors, but it's also harmonious. Try an old standby like Penfolds St. Henri, a sibling shiraz to the far more famous and expensive Grange. Where Grange demonstrates that power and balance together can achieve a dense but lovely wine, St. Henri epitomizes elegance and purity. Unfortunately, many Australian wines have bolstered the bad stereotypes, of both the cheap confections and the over-the-top powerhouses.

Australia also makes another style of shiraz, a style rarely seen outside of Australia. These cool-climate shirazes are fresh, restrained, and savory, with finesse and moderate levels of alcohol. They are surprisingly subtle, very much owing their allegiance to the northern Rhône Valley but with a healthy dollop of some sunny Aussie flavors. Yet, because Australian producers also have a stereotyped view of American wine drinkers as wanting only the cheap stuff or the powerful, flamboyant styles, they exported very few of these wines to the United States. Nonetheless, as Americans prove themselves to be a far more diverse group, I think more and more of these wines will be coming to the United States.

These more restrained wines tend not to come from the better-known regions like the Barossa Valley and the Hunter Valley. Instead they hail from the Yarra Valley east of Melbourne, or northeast Victoria. Even so, you can occasionally find a lovely, harmonious, restrained Barossa Valley shiraz. Another stereotype shattered. 🍷

THIS BRAISED DISH, similar to what the French call a daube or estouffade, can handle a shiraz from any vineyard on the planet. It is certainly in total harmony with the complex, deeply fruited, sometimes herbaceous flavors these wines deliver. The splash of orange does link it to the south of France, land of syrah. I used chunks of short ribs, a cut I love for its succulence and one that takes beautifully to long, slow cooking. I own a stove-top earthenware casserole, which is my choice for both braising and serving. But an enameled cast-iron pot would work as well.

Short Ribs Provençal

TIME: 3½ HOURS, PLUS OVERNIGHT MARINATING

6 tablespoons extra virgin olive oil

2 cups dry red wine

2 onions, cut into 1-inch chunks

3 carrots, cut into 2-inch lengths

4 garlic cloves, crushed

6 fresh thyme sprigs

1 blood orange or regular juice orange

Salt and freshly ground black pepper

4 pounds short ribs, cut into 2-inch chunks

1 teaspoon dried herbes de Provence

1 tablespoon tomato paste

1. Combine 4 tablespoons of the olive oil, the wine, onions, carrots, garlic, and thyme in a large bowl. Use a vegetable peeler to cut three 3-inch strips of orange zest and add them, along with the juice of the orange. Season with salt and pepper. Add the short ribs, cover, and refrigerate overnight.

2. The next day, remove the meat from the marinade and pat dry on paper towels. Strain the marinade into a large measuring cup. Reserve the vegetables.

3. Heat the remaining 2 tablespoons oil in a 4-quart casserole. Add the meat, a few pieces at a time, and lightly brown. Remove to a bowl.

4. Add the onions and garlic to the casserole, lower the heat, and cook until starting to brown. Add the herbes de Provence. Return the meat to the casserole with the reserved thyme, carrots, and orange zest. Pour in 1¼ cups marinade. Bring to a simmer, season with salt and pepper, lower the heat, cover, and cook for 3 hours. Moisten with more marinade, if needed.

5. Skim the excess fat from the surface, check the seasoning, stir in the tomato paste, and serve from the casserole.

YIELD: 6 TO 8 SERVINGS

COOK'S NOTES: Skim off excess fat and the short ribs can be served as soon as the cooking is complete. But if the schedule permits, the dish will be best if refrigerated overnight after it finishes cooking. Reheat the next day, perhaps with a little of the reserved marinade added back to bolster the sauce. Small pasta to help to sop up the sauce would be my choice alongside. But couscous, rice, or even luscious white beans could also make excellent partners. 🫙

CRU BEAUJOLAIS Wines classically must meet certain criteria
to be called great. They need to have the capacity to age, evolve, and improve, to show complexity
and to inspire contemplation while satisfying the soul through sheer deliciousness. They ought
to have a distinctive sense of place—that is, express the character, conditions, and culture of a
particular region. Recent years have seen the rise of other, if less convincing, standards for "greatness," like high ratings and high prices.

By whatever scale you use, Beaujolais has rarely been included in anybody's pantheon of
great wines. It has been considered an archetypal joyous wine, pleasant and thirst quenching.
But consequential? Hardly. It lacks, to use a ponderous word, "gravitas." I've said as much myself,
but I have reconsidered. I've had so many really good, complex Beaujolais wines that I can't help
thinking, these wines are great.

Now, "Beaujolais" itself is an awfully vague term, so let me be clear about which wines
I'm calling great. Beaujolais is often used to refer to all the wines of the region, but technically,
what is called, simply, Beaujolais is the region's most basic wine. These bottles are often the least
expensive, from vineyard sites considered to have the least potential. Plain Beaujolais from a
good producer, like Pierre-Marie Chermette's Cuvée Traditionnelle or Jean-Paul Brun's L'Ancien,
epitomizes the lip-smacking pleasure for which the region is known.

A step up in the hierarchy is Beaujolais-Villages, wines that can be extremely pleasant and
great values. At the top are the ten Beaujolais crus, villages thought to be so distinctive that their
names are appellations. They are—deep breath—Brouilly, Chénas, Chiroubles, Côte de Brouilly,
Fleurie, Juliénas, Morgon, Moulin-à-Vent, Régnié, and Saint-Amour.

These are the wines that I have come to believe are capable of greatness, especially in good
vintages in which the wines show all the delicious drinkability for which Beaujolais is known,
yet are structured and balanced as well. Wines like these can show layers of complex flavors with
added dimensions of depth, purity, and nuance, and they make me feel grateful that, unlike so
many great wines, they are affordable as well.

I haven't mentioned Beaujolais nouveau, the reason for so many of the recent woes of
the Beaujolais region. What began as a quaint local custom of celebrating the harvest each
fall by making a fruity young wine with some of the new grapes became a worldwide marketing phenomenon that changed the way many in the region grew their grapes and made their
wines. The result, when the fun wore off, was an oversupply of poor wine and a region in such
economic trouble that for some growers it was less expensive to let grapes rot on the vines than
to harvest them.

The nouveau fad created an image problem as well. Many consumers think only of nouveau,
and of harmless fruity wine, when they think of Beaujolais. The recent past is a difficult obstacle
to overcome.

Even as the nouveau phenomenon grew, some Beaujolais vignerons made serious wines
regardless of fashion. These wines went beyond the pre-nouveau ideal of Beaujolais as a gulpable joy. Indeed, their goal was to show what could be accomplished when the gamay grape was

grown with painstaking care in the best granite soils, with yields kept low and manipulation in the winery kept to a minimum.

These are the wines that demonstrate the future of Beaujolais and make the case that great wines need not be only deep and brooding, or beautiful and multifaceted. The combination of serious, expressive, and joyous works pretty well, too. 🍷

OPEN BOTTLES

Once a bottle of red wine is opened and served, leftovers can be enjoyed but the bottle should be recorked or sealed with a good stopper and refrigerated. Most gadgets that are designed to pump out the air and so forth do not make a huge difference. In fact, the best approach is to keep a couple of clean, spare half bottles on hand and decant your reds into those so as little of the remaining wine as possible is in contact with air.

In recent years the proliferation of boxed wines, often in three-liter sizes, has benefitted those who like to have a glass of everyday wine ready to drink no matter what. The wines in these boxes are not the finest and they are not meant for aging, just for consuming on the spot, But the way they are packaged prevents any contact with oxygen since the wine is usually in a plastic bladder that collapses as the liquid is dispensed through the spigot. When the box is not being used I find it best to keep it on its side to avoid any dripping from the spigot.   —FF

GAMAY GRAPES TURNED INTO BRIGHT, VIGOROUS WINES need some verve alongside. You can slice some forcefully seasoned terrine of pork or game, some unctuous rillettes, or ruddy slices of cured meat. With Beaujolais, fish also makes the cut. The shad and shad roe that betoken spring along the East Coast can benefit from some Beaujolais-friendly pork. Here the pork is a prosciutto wrapping, with sage, for an oceanic interpretation of the classic Roman saltimbocca. The acidity, offhand herbs, and sly fruit in these wines are in tune with rich but delicate shad and shad roe. If you prefer one to the other, you can fix the recipe as you wish, though you will need about 28 ounces of fish.

Saltimbocca of Shad and Shad Roe

TIME: 30 MINUTES

50 fresh sage leaves, 30 of them chopped

1 medium shallot, finely chopped

4 tablespoons (½ stick) unsalted butter, softened

1 teaspoon fresh lemon juice

Sea salt and freshly ground black pepper

1 pair shad roe, cleaned

1 shad fillet (about ¾ pound)

6 ounces prosciutto di Parma, sliced thin

3 tablespoons extra virgin olive oil

½ cup dry white wine

Lemon wedges, for serving

1. Combine the chopped sage leaves, shallot, and butter in a food processor or a mortar and process or pulverize to make a smooth mixture. Season with the lemon juice and salt and pepper.

2. Pat the shad roe dry, separate into 2 lobes and cut each in 4 pieces. Use a sharp knife to cut the skin off the shad fillet. Cut the fillet into 10 to 12 equal pieces. Cut the prosciutto into 2-inch-wide strips. Spread the sage butter on one side of each piece of roe and fillet. Wrap each in a wide strip of proscuitto. Arrange on a platter, cover, and refrigerate until shortly before serving.

3. Heat the oil in a large heavy skillet on medium-low. Place the pieces of shad and shad roe in the skillet and sauté, turning once, until lightly browned, 2 to 3 minutes per side. Place a whole sage leaf on each piece and arrange on a serving platter or divide among individual dinner plates. Pour the wine into the skillet, and cook on medium-high for about 1 minute, stirring, until slightly reduced. Spoon the sauce over the saltimbocca and serve with lemon alongside.

YIELD: 4 SERVINGS

COOK'S NOTES: Lacking shad, because of the season or your geography, you can use slices of other meaty, firm-fleshed fish like monkfish, or even large shrimp. 🗑

HERE IS ANOTHER OPTION: pappa al pomodoro, the Tuscan bread soup. I will not let a summer slip by without whipping up this lusty treasure. But in my latest rendition, taking its cue from the Catalan bread rubbed with tomato, or pan con tomate, Italy meets Spain. With a touch of saffron, some spicy chorizo, and smoky paprika, my thick soup acquired a rich Spanish accent. So what if the wine at hand is French? You can count on the delicious wines from Beaujolais to welcome the world.

Thick Tomato-Bread Soup, Catalan Style

TIME: 30 MINUTES, PLUS 30 MINUTES COOLING

¼ cup extra virgin olive oil

4 garlic cloves, slivered

4 ounces chorizo, casing removed, crumbled

½ teaspoon smoked paprika

3 pounds ripe beefsteak tomatoes, peeled

Generous pinch of saffron threads

2 cups finely diced crustless country bread

Salt and freshly ground black pepper

2 tablespoons minced fresh flat-leaf parsley

Grated aged Manchego (optional)

1. Heat the oil in a large sauté pan. Add the garlic and cook over low heat until soft. Add the chorizo, increase the heat, and cook until just starting to brown. Stir in the paprika. Remove the pan from the heat.

2. Place a sieve over the pan, halve the tomatoes horizontally, and squeeze them into the sieve to remove the seeds and allow the juices to fall into the pan. Remove the sieve and reserve the pulp. Heat the juices in the pan until warm, add the saffron, and set aside off the heat for 10 minutes.

3. Finely chop the tomato pulp by hand or in a food processor and add it to the pan. Bring to a simmer. Stir in the bread. Cook, stirring, for 5 minutes. Season with salt and pepper. Allow to come to room temperature, stirring from time to time, about 30 minutes. Fold in the parsley and serve. Pass some grated aged Manchego alongside, if desired.

YIELD: 4 SERVINGS

COOK'S NOTES: The traditional method for peeling tomatoes is to plunge them for about a minute in boiling water, then rinse them with cold water. But there are now serrated vegetable peelers that are convenient to use as an alternative. 🥫

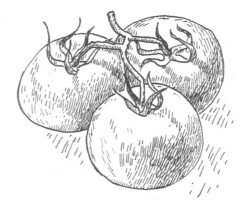

BARBERA

Oh, me. Oh, barbera. Are we growing old together? My once-youthful scruff now comes in gray, while you, Giacomo Conterno Barbera d'Alba, who sustained me in my graduate-school days at eight dollars a bottle, cost more than fifty dollars now! Inevitable, of course—I mean the graying. But fifty dollars for barbera, what can this signify?

Partly, I suppose, the price indicates that more people appreciate this once-humble wine. More important, though, it demonstrates how the estimation of Giacomo Conterno as a great producer has risen spectacularly over the decades, as has the worldwide thirst for Barolo, Conterno's primary stock in trade. Just as an unassuming little Bourgogne rouge made by an exalted vigneron costs as much as another Burgundy producer's premier cru, so have the prices risen for barberas from top Barolo and Barbaresco producers, who often make the best versions.

In the Langhe region of the Piedmont, in northwestern Italy, barbera largely remains the little brother to nebbiolo, the grape of Barolo and Barbaresco. Around Alba, prime Barolo country, nebbiolo hogs most of the best vineyard sites. Barbera must settle for leftovers, some choicer than others. This was the natural order of things. Barolos sold for big bucks and were socked away to age. Barberas were bottled for immediate pleasure, were sold cheap, and were opened at dinner.

That's how it was when I was first developing a taste for wine. Those memorable, and inexpensive, bottles of Conterno captured me with their gorgeous, juicy, yet bitter red fruit that danced a tightrope between sweet and savory, propelled along by an energetic, vivacious acidity. For me, it was an easy-to-swallow lesson in how wine could be both joyous and thought provoking, while performing its basic function of making food taste better.

Barberas from the hilly Asti region to the northeast of the Langhe would seem to have it a little easier than their Alba siblings. Nebbiolo is not grown so much around Asti, so barbera gets the best vineyard sites. Indeed, in the 1980s, Braida di Giacomo Bologna, a producer of Barbera d'Asti, pioneered the aging of single-vineyard barberas in barrels of new French oak, winning critical acclaim and raising prices accordingly.

Braida's success inspired other producers to age their wines in new oak, often with unfortunate results. The lively immediacy of this honest wine often ended up buried beneath vanilla and chocolate cheesecake, wiping away any trace of regional identity.

Nowadays, at least, barbera seems to have settled into a more confident period. The over-indulgence in oak is no longer so evident. The key issue is of balance. The structure in barbera comes from its buzz-saw acidity, which keeps it fresh and cuts through rich fatty foods. If the acidity is out of whack, barbera can be unpleasantly aggressive, like heartburn in a glass. But when the balance is correct, the wine seems poised on a knife's edge between sweet fruit and mouthwatering acidity, the tension keeping the wine lively.

Are differences between the Asti and Alba barberas discernible? Many producers will say that the Barberas d'Alba tend to be plusher and fruitier, while the Barberas d'Asti are tauter in texture. Honestly, with so many variables in the vineyard and cellar, it's very hard for anybody else to tell the difference. 🍷

WHETHER THEY HAIL FROM ALBA OR ASTI, barberas tend to share a warmly rustic, earthy profile, striking dark, fruity chords, sometimes with notes of black truffle. Mushrooms, I thought, as I tasted. And pasta. Perhaps even a beefy red sauce. But mushrooms can also masquerade as that beefy red sauce, almost making a classic ragù a meatless one. Chopped cremini mushrooms, an unfancy variety that is a small step up in price from plain white mushrooms but a big one in terms of flavor, are the basis for the sauce. Tomato paste and black olive paste (tapenade) add some heft and complexity.

Fettuccine with Mushroom Ragù

TIME: 40 MINUTES

3 tablespoons extra virgin olive oil

3 garlic cloves, slivered

½ cup chopped onion

1 pound cremini mushrooms, very finely chopped

2 tablespoons tomato paste

1 tablespoon black olive paste (tapenade)

⅓ cup dry red wine

1 tablespoon finely minced fresh oregano, or 1 teaspoon dried

Salt and freshly ground black pepper

12 ounces fresh fettuccine

Grated pecorino, preferably Tuscan, for serving

1. Heat 2 tablespoons of the oil in a large skillet. Add the garlic and onion and sauté until soft. Add the mushrooms and cook over medium heat until they wilt and give up their juices. Do not let the juices evaporate. Stir in the tomato paste and tapenade. Add the wine, cook briefly, then season with the oregano, salt, and, generously, pepper. Remove from the heat.

2. Bring a large pot of salted water to a boil. Add the fettuccine, stir to separate the strands, and cook for about 3 minutes. Drain. Transfer the pasta to the skillet. Add the remaining 1 tablespoon oil. Cook, gently folding the ingredients together, until the mushroom mixture has reheated and is evenly blended with the pasta. Add additional salt and pepper, if needed.

3. Serve with cheese on the side.

YIELD: 4 TO 6 SERVINGS

COOK'S NOTES: Alongside the pasta offer grated pecorino, Tuscan if possible. Why pecorino? The hard sheep's milk cheese is piquant and acidic, not as sweet as Parmigiano-Reggiano, so it adds a stronger dimension to the rich egg pasta and its "meaty" mushroom sauce. Why Tuscan, since there are pecorinos from practically every region in Italy? It's the variety I prefer. 🧂

LAGREIN AND TEROLDEGO

People often complain to me that wine confuses them. They don't want to memorize the myriad names and places. They want it to be effortless and easy.

I understand the feeling. Most people don't want to spend an inordinate amount of time thinking about what they eat or drink. That's why franchise restaurants were invented. And mass-market pinot grigio. And wine bureaucracies, which are often more concerned with increasing the sales of big commercial brands than with promoting the little-known appellations and grapes, visionary producers, and distinctive styles that give many wine cultures their depth, mystique, grace, and beauty.

No doubt, for example, many people will not want to burden themselves with learning about obscure red grapes like teroldego, from Trentino in northern Italy, and lagrein, from Alto Adige, to the north near Austria and Switzerland. They're not easy to pronounce—tehr-AWL-deh-go and lah-GRAH'EEN—and are hardly mellifluous. Only a handful of producers outside northeastern Italy have them in their repertories, and very few examples make it to American shores. Nonetheless, they are well worth seeking out.

Teroldego in the hands of a leading producer like Elisabetta Foradori can be enchanting, almost purple but not inky, with the aroma of dark fruit layered with smoke and earth. On the palate it is fresh and lively, with just the right amount of cleansing bitterness to leave the mouth ready for more. Unusually, when you swallow, the lingering effect is of texture rather than flavor. You feel the pleasant reminder of its light tannic grip. And lagrein produces congenial, straightforward wines that can be deliciously plummy, earthy, and chewy, dark and full-bodied but not heavy, with a pronounced minerally edge. It can combine richness and delicacy, and is enjoyable both young and with five or more years of aging.

Esoteric, wonderful wines and grapes like these can be found all over Italy, and indeed, around many historically wine-producing regions. For drinkers, they add richness and context at the meager price of modest exertion. Sure, we could live simply on pinot grigio and sangiovese, and never risk the tinge of fear and confusion that comes from trying something new and different. But then we'd miss out on frappato and aglianico, fumin and romorantin, mencía and trousseau, and countless other individualized pleasures.

Not to treasure wines like teroldego and lagrein is like asking why anyone cares about *culatello* or *guanciale* when we already have boiled ham and bacon. Most people won't care, and that's fine. But for people who've savored the creamy, smooth, delicately porky flavor of a rosy swatch of culatello, the great ham of Emilia-Romagna, it's a silly question. Of course we need teroldego and lagrein. 🍷

MOST OF THESE WINES EXHIBIT BRACING, FOOD-FRIENDLY ACIDITY. They often deliver a pleasing funkiness as well, and that feature suggested a match with chicken livers. Why not chicken liver tacos? And then, fresh rhubarb in the market inspired a springtime salsa, the tartness mellowed with a bit of honey in the mix. I included some sweet onions to layer in the tacos. The lagreins handle these flavors with aplomb. Though this dish has nothing to say about northern Italy and especially the Veneto, it illustrates just how open minded a good wine can be.

Chicken Liver Tacos with Rhubarb Salsa

TIME: 1 HOUR

2 medium rhubarb stalks, cut into ¼-inch dice (about 1½ cups)

⅓ cup finely minced scallions

1 jalapeño, seeded and minced

½ cup pickled cocktail onions, halved

2 teaspoons honey

3 tablespoons cider vinegar

Salt

Chipotle powder or cayenne

¼ cup yellow cornmeal

1 pound chicken livers, trimmed, cut into 1-inch pieces

5 tablespoons olive oil

1 large sweet onion, sliced thin

Eight 7-inch soft corn tortillas

2 tablespoons chopped fresh cilantro leaves

1. Have a bowl of ice and water ready. Bring 2 quarts water to a boil in a saucepan. Add the rhubarb, blanch for 20 seconds, then scoop out with a slotted spoon into the ice water. Leave the rhubarb in the ice water for a minute, then drain well, remove any ice, and transfer to a medium bowl. Fold in the scallions, jalapeño, and cocktail onions. Dissolve the honey in 1 tablespoon of the vinegar in a small dish and add it to the rhubarb mixture. Season with about ¼ teaspoon salt and chipotle powder to taste. Set aside.

2. Heat the oven to 200°F. Place the cornmeal in a bowl and season with salt and chipotle powder. Dredge the chicken livers in the mixture. Heat 4 tablespoons of the oil in a large skillet. Add the chicken livers and sauté on medium, turning, until lightly browned but still pink inside. Remove to a heatproof dish, cover with foil, and place in the oven. Heat the remaining 1 tablespoon oil in the skillet. Add the sweet onion and cook over medium heat, stirring, until golden. Add the remaining 2 tablespoons vinegar, stir to deglaze the pan, and remove from the heat.

3. Wrap the tortillas in a clean dish towel and place in a steamer over simmering water. Add the cilantro to the rhubarb salsa. Remove a tortilla from the steamer. Spoon some of the sweet onion in a line down the center, top with 2 or 3 pieces of the chicken livers, then about 1 tablespoon of the salsa. Roll the tortilla around the filling and place on a platter, seam side down. Repeat with the remaining tortillas. Serve any remaining salsa alongside.

YIELD: 4 SERVINGS

COOK'S NOTES: Lacking rhubarb, you can use celery, but another salsa will also do, especially a tart green one made with tomatillos. 🥫

VALPOLICELLA

The world is full of mystifying wines, and few are as familiar yet as little known as valpolicella. Where does valpolicella come from? Well, that we can answer: the Veneto region of northeastern Italy. And we know it is red. What grapes are used? How is it made? Is it any good? For those questions, the answers I'm afraid are pretty murky.

Back when I was a child in the 1960s and '70s, valpolicella meant the cartoon Italian accent of countless radio commercials for a mass-produced wine that achieved great popularity. Succeeding generations knew valpolicella mostly through hearing it disparaged as a thin, insipid wine, generally an apt description. Commercial producers had taken the easy way, abandoning difficult-to-farm hillsides for vineyards on the flats, where high yields of dilute grapes were easy. Meanwhile, as people began to prefer bigger, richer red wines like valpolicella's brawnier sibling, amarone, producers began to reserve their best grapes and vineyards for more profitable amarone production.

Still, the winemaking renaissance that has occurred throughout Italy has also come to valpolicella. Grapes from the original valpolicella zone are designated valpolicella *classico*, while those that have a higher level of alcohol and that receive an additional year of aging are designated *superiore*.

With new seriousness of purpose, many producers have rededicated themselves to valpolicella. It has not replaced amarone at the top of most winemakers' production charts, not even close. But it is clear today that many valpolicellas are delicious and wonderful values, though all over the map stylistically.

Let's start with the murkiness. Valpolicella is a blended wine. The corvina grape must make up to 40 to 70 percent of the mix, with rondinella 20 to 40 percent and molinara 5 to 25 percent. Up to 15 percent of the blend can include barbera, sangiovese, negrara, or rossignola, while up to 5 percent can come from other red grapes. Got that?

Clearly winemakers have a lot of room for variation, but that's only the beginning. As consumer tastes changed, valpolicella producers began to use techniques of concentrating and darkening the wines. Some added semi-dried grapes that might have been used for amarone. Others took valpolicella and refermented it with the skins and sediment of the semi-dried grapes used for amarone. The results were bigger, richer wines, somewhere between classic valpolicellas and amarones. Many producers call these wines *ripasso*, or *ripassa*, which means "passed through again." They can be quite good, though I personally prefer the light texture and delicacy of a valpolicella made the traditional way.

The best valpolicellas offer floral aromas and flavors of tart cherry and occasionally chocolate, turning refreshingly bitter as you swallow. Some are a bit herbal, and others spicy. The most noticeable differences will be texture, density, and focus—that is, the better wines will have flavors that are more precise and sharply defined.

The biggest problem for consumers is that producers are under no obligation to label their wines ripasso, or to indicate what methods they've used to make the wines. Without research, it is hard to know what you're getting. And even then, some producers vary their methods from year to year, depending on the vintage. Sound confusing? Ah, well, that's Italy for you. 🍷

THE GRACEFULNESS EXHIBITED BY MOST VALPOLICELLAS is a perfect match for rich and silken arctic char, a fish in the trout family with flesh that suggests salmon. Some prosciutto and tarragon give the fish an edgy complexity that is in harmony with these wines.

Arctic Char with Prosciutto

TIME: 1 HOUR 15 MINUTES

3 tablespoons extra virgin olive oil

2 medium red onions

3 tablespoons red wine vinegar

½ cup dry red wine

1 arctic char (about 3 pounds) boned and butterflied, or 2 fillets with skin, each about 1 pound

Salt and freshly ground black pepper

1 small bunch fresh tarragon, heavy stems removed

5 thin slices prosciutto di Parma, coarsely chopped

1 tablespoon unsalted butter, softened

1. Heat 2 tablespoons of the oil in a large skillet. Add the red onions and sauté over low heat until very tender, about 20 minutes. Add the vinegar and 3 tablespoons of the wine, reduce slightly, and remove from heat.

2. Preheat oven to 425°F. Place the fish, skin side down, on a work surface. Use needle-nose pliers or tweezers to pull out any pinbones. Season with salt and pepper. Spread about two thirds of the onions on one fillet. Place tarragon on the onions and cover with prosciutto. Close up the fish or place the second fillet on top, flesh side down. Rub the skin with the remaining 1 tablespoon oil. Place the fish in a baking dish, place in the oven, and bake for about 20 minutes. The fish should be somewhat underdone in the middle.

3. Meanwhile, add the remaining wine to the onions left in the skillet. Bring to a simmer. Swirl in the butter, bit by bit, to thicken the sauce slightly. Set aside. When the fish is done, transfer to a serving platter and spoon the remaining onions and sauce around it. Serve by cutting it into sections that include both the top and bottom fillets and the filling.

YIELD: 6 SERVINGS

COOK'S NOTES: A 3-pound arctic char is the perfect size for this recipe. In its place, a whole red snapper or New Zealand pink snapper would work.

AMARONE

Contrary to a widely held belief, big, powerful, almost monstrously concentrated wines are not a recent New World invention. No, before the first New World wines sent the alcohol meter reeling toward 17 percent, amarone from Italy was setting the standard for dense, lush red wines that were routinely 15 to 16 percent alcohol.

But unlike some of those New World wines, which have the comic, pumped-up character of professional wrestlers, a good amarone has the more refined muscularity of a naturally robust athlete. It's a wine that you can't imagine any other way.

Amarone, or Amarone della Valpolicella to give it its more formal name, is the flagbearer of a special class of wines that are made from dried grapes. Amarone uses the same blend of grapes as valpolicella, its lighter red sibling in the Veneto region: mainly corvina and corvinone, along with some other grapes like rondinella. But while most valpolicellas are made conventionally, the grapes picked for amarone are left to dry for several months, either in airy open barns, the traditional method, or in special temperature- and humidity-controlled rooms. As the grapes shrivel, the juice becomes concentrated and richly sweet. Fermenting all this sugary grape juice into dry wine ensures that it will be high in alcohol.

While the method of making wine from dried grapes dates perhaps as far back as Roman times, the typical practice was to stop the fermentation before all the sugar was consumed by yeast, leaving a sweet wine, Recioto della Valpolicella. Only in the last century did winemakers begin producing a dry wine, noticing its pleasantly bitter flavor reminiscent of almonds or walnuts. At first it was called *recioto amaro* ("amaro" meaning bitter), now known as amarone.

The extraordinary power of amarone and its potent complex flavors make it a kind of specialty wine. It's not something you'd gulp down with dinner under the summer stars, nor would you pair it with any food not typically described as sturdy or brawny. But on days when the weather turns truly cold, when you have to summon up the crackle of an imaginary fire to feel warm, and when the menu selection turns to haunches of stag, pungent cheeses, and other earthy, gamy foods, then it's the perfect time for amarone.

Amarone has become highly popular, and, perhaps not surprisingly, a lot of bad amarone is on the market. The reason for this is fairly simple. Amarone, the most prestigious and expensive wine in the Veneto, was long made in small quantities. So the wine producers in the valpolicella zone did what winemakers all over the world like to do when rules inhibit potential profits: They changed the rules, greatly expanding the legal limits of the region in which valpolicella and Amarone della Valpolicella could be made. As a result, a lot more amarone was produced from grapes grown on lesser sites. On the whole, the wine's production has more than tripled since 1990.

Nowadays, amarones from the original production zone are labeled "classico." But even that is not a clear signal of higher quality. When amarone is good, it is very good, leaving only the challenge of finding the right time to drink it. That is particularly hard if gamy meats and powerful cheeses are not often on your table. But I think I have a solution. Few things are as frustrating to wine lovers as the common cold. Stuffed noses make it nearly impossible to smell and taste most wines. But amarone? Take two glasses and call me in the morning. 🍷

AMARONES TAKE NO PRISONERS. You want subtlety and grace? Talk to the folks who make red wine in the Alto Adige and find yourself a veal roast to cook. Amarones are all about depth, tannins, earth, tar, and black truffles. And if you plan to open one of these wines for dinner, you might as well go into the woods and bag a wild boar. Another, simpler option would be to consider sausage. Dice wild boar sausage—or your favorite pork sausage—and toss it with sturdy shredded kale, a winter vegetable that offers almost tannic complexity, and you will have a fine partner for your amarone.

Pasta with Wild Boar Sausage and Kale

TIME: 1 HOUR

1 pound wild boar sausages

1½ pounds fresh kale

4 tablespoons extra virgin olive oil

1 cup chopped red onions

3 garlic cloves, sliced

2 cups tomato puree, fresh or canned

½ cup dry red wine

Salt and freshly ground black pepper

1 pound orecchiette, strozzapreti, or other small macaroni

Red chile flakes

1. Quarter the sausages lengthwise and peel off the casings. Dice the sausages.

2. Trim the heavy stems from the kale and discard. Rinse, then chop the kale leaves medium fine.

3. Heat 3 tablespoons of the oil in a 4- to 5-quart heavy skillet, sauté pan, or casserole. Add the red onions and garlic and cook, stirring, over medium heat until softened. Add the sausages and cook, stirring, until they begin to brown. Add about a third of the kale and when it has wilted, continue adding it until all has wilted. Stir in the tomato puree and wine. Simmer over low heat for about 10 minutes, season with salt and pepper, cover the pan, and continue simmering.

4. Bring a large pot of salted water to a boil. Add the pasta and cook until al dente, about 8 minutes. Drain well and add to the kale mixture. Add the remaining 1 tablespoon oil and fold the ingredients together. Add red chile flakes to taste and more salt, if needed. Stir a few more times, then serve.

YIELD: 6 SERVINGS

COOK'S NOTES: Cook the kale, from which you have sliced off the heavy stems, gradually as it wilts. And take the time to heat the cooked pasta in the sauce mixture so all the ingredients are amalgamated. Though this is a dish that is easily reheated, it is at its most enjoyable if the pasta is added to the kale and sausages shortly before serving, making the reheat a brief one. 🥫

DOLCETTO

With food, most people recognize that all sorts of meals can satisfy and delight. A magnificent feast at a culinary temple does not cloud the ability to appreciate the pleasure of a perfect hamburger. A great novel does not diminish the enjoyment of a well-turned historical romance. While we acknowledge a hierarchy of genres, excellence is excellence.

Yet with wine, we sometimes overlook a mountain of potential pleasures for the peak experience. I know more than a few people who believe that if a wine is not a benchmark bottle, it's not worth drinking. It's a kind of blindness reserved for those who have never felt moved by the everyday joy that wine can offer, and who consequently measure all wines on a single scale rather than adjust their scales according to context.

The dolcetto wines of the Langhe region of northwestern Italy are a perfect case in point. There, a hierarchy is clear. The nebbiolo grape rules. A good, well-aged Barolo or Barbaresco—the major nebbiolo wines—is a transcendent pleasure. But these wines are expensive and getting more so.

Naturally, it would not occur to most people in the Langhe to drink nebbiolo daily. It's not affordable, for one thing. But more important, great bottles speak in a complex way that demands more attention, more focus, and more time than is appropriate at most nightly family meals. These wines are rightly reserved for occasions that warrant them.

Everyday wines tend to be simpler, though nonetheless satisfying. In the Langhe they are mostly barberas and dolcettos, with a smattering of fringe wines like freisa, ruché, pelaverga, and grignolino. Of barbera and dolcetto, it's always seemed to me that dolcetto was the less appreciated. For better or worse, barbera producers have taken their stabs at transformation, trying to make age-worthy wines reared in oak barrels, and charging prices that reflect their ambitions. But dolcetto, thankfully, has not been favored with similar efforts at improvement. Instead, it is almost always free of the blemishing of new oak flavors. Left to its own devices, dolcetto offers what naturally makes it so winning: an object lesson in the very Italian push-pull of blending bitter and sweet flavors, along with an earthiness and a rounded, lightly tannic texture.

Most dolcettos come from the Alba region, and the wines can be inconsistent. Perhaps this is because in Alba, the dolcetto grape often plays third fiddle behind nebbiolo and barbera, and does not always receive top vineyard sites or the loving care it warrants. On the other hand, dolcetto is the pride of Dogliani, which may be why many experts believe the best dolcettos are from Dogliani.

It's fascinating how well the various wines of the Piedmont dovetail. In a sense, the great nebbiolo wines represent the ultimate achievements, with a complete balance of tannins, acidity, and complex flavors. Each of the other wines encompasses a portion of the nebbiolo spectrum. Barbera offers buzz-saw acidity and vibrant fruit, while dolcetto is more tannic, less acid, with softly bitter fruit. It's a well-ordered universe in which each wine has its place and its role. A great Barolo is a rare and wonderful pleasure. A great dolcetto can be a nightly one. ♟

SOMETIMES A FINE PAIRING COMES FROM CONTRAST. Red sling backs, not black, with the gray tweed. Or a wine rich in berried fruitiness tamed by the surprise of a bitter salad alongside. Treviso, an oblong variety of radicchio, in a stuffing for squid and for a wilted salad on which to bed it, is the bitter component to stand up to a young, bright dolcetto. The Treviso brings out structure and pleasantly tannic nuances in the wine and makes the fruit fight a bit to reach the head of the line.

Stuffed Squid with Wilted Salad

TIME: 1 HOUR

12 whole squid with tentacles (about 1½ pounds), cleaned

2 heads Treviso or radicchio, quartered and cored

½ cup extra virgin olive oil

2½ ounces pancetta, finely diced

2 garlic cloves, minced

1 tablespoon minced peeled fresh ginger

3 scallions, minced

⅔ cup dry bread crumbs

3 tablespoons Thai fish sauce

2 tablespoons red wine vinegar

Salt and freshly ground black pepper

1. Remove the squid tentacles and chop finely. Rinse and dry the squid bodies. Finely chop 1 Treviso head. You should have about 1 cup. Shred the second head of Treviso into strips ½ inch wide and keep separate.

2. Heat 1 tablespoon of the oil in a large skillet. Add the pancetta and cook over medium heat until starting to brown. Add the garlic, ginger, and chopped tentacles and sauté for about 1 minute. Add the chopped Treviso and scallions and cook until softened. Stir in the bread crumbs and fish sauce. Stir for about a minute, add a tablespoon or two of water to release the crumbs clinging to the pan, and transfer to a bowl.

3. Stuff the squid bodies with the mixture, not packing them too tightly and leaving ½ inch headroom. Secure with toothpicks. Rub with 1 tablespoon of the remaining oil. Place on a foil-lined baking sheet. Heat the broiler to very hot.

4. Meanwhile, heat the remaining oil in a skillet. Add the shredded Treviso and cook until wilted. Stir in the vinegar, toss, season lightly with salt and pepper, and transfer to a platter.

5. Broil the squid close to the source of heat until barely browned, 1½ to 2 minutes on each side. Place on the bed of wilted salad and serve.

YIELD: 4 TO 6 SERVINGS

COOK'S NOTES: Round heads of radicchio can be used instead of Treviso. And when it comes to cooking squid, there are two choices: fast or long and slow. For this recipe the stuffed squid should be broiled as quickly as possible. That will keep them tender. 🗒

LAMBRUSCO

I don't think I've been any place where drinking sparkling wine is as ritualistic as in Italy. Meals with even the slightest claim to ceremony must begin with spumante, even if it is pushed aside after a few sips. They often end with something sparkling and sweet as well, like a bright moscato d'Asti, likewise ignored after a couple of tastes.

Italy also has its tradition of vivace reds: fresh, effervescent wines that are consumed throughout a meal. These wines, unlike the prelude and finale, are gulped with gusto. Many are regional curiosities, like Gragnano, a fizzy red from Campania, but one of these red sparklers is more widely known, and deservedly so: Lambrusco.

Yes, Lambrusco. Hey, relax! I don't mean the candied, fizzy wine that sold so many millions of cases annually in the United States in the 1970s and '80s, consigning the term "Lambrusco" to that special place of contempt otherwise reserved for wine coolers and fortified street wines. I mean real Lambrusco secco, dry, earthy, and slightly bitter yet joyous and exhilarating, beloved by millions in Emilia-Romagna.

I have been on a genuine Lambrusco kick for some years now and I've been delighted to see delicious evidence of its rebirth where I live in New York. Restaurants dedicated to the hearty, rich cuisine of Emilia-Romagna, like Via Emilia and Osteria Morini, offer extensive lists of Lambruscos and an opportunity to drink it in a reasonable approximation of authentic conditions. Where not so many years ago I would have been hard pressed to find a handful of Lambruscos in stores, now I can easily put my hands on a few dozen different bottles.

The best of these frothy, low-alcohol, relatively undemanding wines are energetic and exuberant, offering the sort of blithe refreshment that people used to associate with Beaujolais. These are not complex wines—nobody will mistake them for Barolo or Brunello di Montalcino. They tend to be fruity and simple, with a dry, earthy, pleasantly bitter edge that shapes and channels the fruitiness. And while they can be rustic, many have more finesse than might be expected. By the way, they take beautifully to a chill, making them wonderful summer reds.

Lambrusco is both the name of the grape and the name of the official zones in which it is made. Myriad strains of the Lambrusco grape can be used, but the major selections are grasparossa, salamino, and sorbara. Those called Lambrusco Grasparossa di Castelvetro are thought to be the most tannic and fullest bodied, while Lambrusco di Sorbara tends to be more fragrant. I am partial to Lambrusco Salamino di Santa Croce for the sole reason that the salamino grape got its name because its bunches resemble small salamis.

Most Lambruscos are made to sparkle efficiently and inexpensively in big pressurized steel tanks. But a few are still made by the traditional method, as with Champagne: The wine is bottled with yeast and sugar to induce a second fermentation, producing the bubbles.

Bottom line: Lambrusco is a super value that goes great with food, particularly simple grilled meats, fatty *salumi*, rich pasta sauces, and cheeses. In return, it demands very little except to be understood for what it is. That sounds like a pretty good deal all around. ♟

LAMBRUSCO MAY BE ONE OF THE BEST EXAMPLES of a wine that demands the food of a region. Rich meats like prosciutto, rimmed or studded with creamy fat, clamor for the Lambrusco's fizz and dark fruit. On a warm day this wine is fun to drink, chilled, with pizza, for example; BLTs; or to my thinking, ribs. You won't find baby back ribs on menus in Modena, but their succulence and fat suit the wine. You might detect echoes of fine aceto balsamico, the intense aged vinegar of Modena, in this wine. I will not insist you spend more on vinegar than the wine because cheaper balsamicos have become a joke. So, instead of balsamico, this marinade and mopping sauce calls for saba, a syrupy concentrated grape must that's a cousin of the vinegars. Good balsamic vinegar.

Baby Back Ribs with Saba Slather

TIME: 1 HOUR, PLUS OVERNIGHT MARINATING AND 2 HOURS ROASTING

½ cup fresh sage leaves, plus more for garnish

1 head garlic (about 12 cloves), roasted, cooled, and cloves peeled

3 tablespoons Dijon mustard

Freshly ground black pepper

½ cup saba (Italian grape must syrup)

½ cup dry red wine

¼ cup extra virgin olive oil

1 tablespoon red wine vinegar

2 racks baby back ribs (about 24 ribs)

1. Place the sage and garlic in a food processor or mortar. Process to a paste. Place in a 1-quart bowl and add the mustard, a generous grinding of the pepper, and the saba. Transfer half of this mixture to a container, cover, and refrigerate. Add the wine, oil, and vinegar to the rest for a marinade.

2. Cut the racks in half. Place on a work surface, meaty side down. Work the point of a sharp knife under the thin membrane on the bone side of the ribs, enough so you can use a dish towel to grab the membrane and peel it off. Place the ribs in a shallow dish in one or two layers. Pour the marinade over, turn the racks to coat, cover, and refrigerate overnight.

3. Heat the oven to 275°F. Place the ribs in a roasting pan. Pour the marinade into a saucepan and add the reserved saba mixture. Bring to a boil, reduce the heat, and simmer for about 10 minutes, until thickened. Set aside. Cover the rib pan with foil. Bake for 2 hours. Add any pan juices to the cooked marinade mixture.

4. Light a grill. Brush the ribs with the reduced marinade mixture. Grill about 6 inches from medium-hot coals or gas, basting and turning the ribs frequently, until nicely browned and glazed, 15 to 20 minutes. The ribs can also be cooked under a broiler. Cut them apart between the bones, pile on a platter, garnish with sage, and serve.

YIELD: 8 APPETIZER OR 4 MAIN-COURSE SERVINGS

COOK'S NOTES: Pulling the membrane off the bone side of the rack of ribs will make it easier for the marinade to do its work and facilitate slicing when the ribs are done. The two-step cooking process, first a slow bake, then a fast grill, guarantees tender meat and a flavorful, lightly charred end result. 🥫

MONTEPULCIANO D'ABRUZZO

Cheap wines are always in fashion, but merely cheap is no bargain. When times are hard, what's needed are wines that obey the dictates of the dwindling bank account while satisfying the craving for reliable refreshment and restoration, and even piquing the interest a bit. That's where Montepulciano d'Abruzzo comes in.

This lively, juicy red wine comes from the rugged Abruzzi hills above the Adriatic coast of central Italy, a region long known for its tidal wave of mass-produced reds. Abruzzi is dominated by giant cooperatives pumping out adequately palatable wine, but it is evolving and improving, like much of southern Italy, with more and more serious producers taking the lead in seeking higher quality. And these serious producers have raised the bar for everybody.

Good Montepulcianos are solid and enjoyable, bursting with tart cherry and earth flavors, sometimes augmented by herbal and floral aromas and, in the best, a minerally complexity.

Allow me to pause momentarily to offer the obligatory distinction between montepulciano, the grape, which is grown in the Abruzzi region and northward into Le Marche, and Montepulciano, a town in Tuscany and the source of a very different wine known as Vino Nobile di Montepulciano, made from the sangiovese grape. Furthermore, neither montepulciano nor Montepulciano should be confused with Montalcino, another Tuscan town famous for its Brunello di Montalcino.

Montepulciano d'Abruzzo is the kind of wine that I'm happy to find shoring up the bottom of any decent wine list, and not just Italian lists. It is resolutely dry, with enough soft fruit to be drinkable when young, yet tannic enough to keep it trim and energetic. While it pairs naturally with any dish that has tomato sauce, it's as versatile as Barbera d'Alba or good Beaujolais. What you won't find with Montepulciano d'Abruzzo is much variation in flavors.

You will find some variation in price among the wines, and the best wines are often found in the middle ground. What makes these wines worth more? It's hard to say for sure, but when growers commit themselves to quality, among the first things they do is to reduce their vines' yield. This requires work, but generally produces grapes with more interesting and intense flavors. It also means less wine and thus, higher prices.

Winemakers can go too far, as well. They can invest in small barrels of new French oak and all sorts of technology to produce powerful, concentrated flavors. But often, the more expensive and ambitious a bottle is, the more it sacrifices the character of its region.

Does this mean that Montepulciano d'Abruzzo is destined to be only an inexpensive guzzling wine? Not that there's anything wrong with that, of course, but the answer is no, emphatically. Two idiosyncratic Abruzzi producers, Edoardo Valentini and Emidio Pepe, have demonstrated that with singular vision, meticulous care, and spare-no-expense viticulture and wine making, Montepulciano d'Abruzzo can be magnificently deep and complex. Their bottles are also extremely expensive, difficult to find, and require long aging.

Nonetheless, they prove that montepulciano can make world-class wines. For the most part, though, consider Montepulciano d'Abruzzo a world-class bargain. 🍷

EGGPLANT ALLA PARMIGIANA HAS A LOT IN COMMON with Montepulciano d'Abruzzo. Both the dish and the wine are everyday staples in low- to middle-tier Italian restaurants, at the budget end of the menu. They are rarely worth raves. Usually, there is more to recommend about the wine than the dish. There are times when a glass or a bottle of Montepulciano would be welcome. Eggplant alla parmigiana (or eggplant Parmesan, as it is often rendered) all too often amounts to punishing the handsome and versatile vegetable by armoring it with a welter of breading, tomato sauce, and oozing cheese. But there are exceptions. A complex wine with a balance of fruit and earthiness sits apart from the pack. Similarly, eggplant alla parmigiana that is flavorful yet light and fresh tasting, like the one served at Il Pellicano on Italy's Tuscan coast, is a great match for a good Montepulciano d'Abruzzo, or a better wine.

Eggplant alla Parmigiana

TIME: 1¾ HOURS

4 small eggplants,
each 6 to 8 ounces

Salt

1 cup extra virgin olive oil

1 large garlic clove, chopped

Freshly ground
black pepper

2 pounds plum tomatoes,
peeled and diced

1 cup freshly grated
Parmigiano-Reggiano

Leaves from 8 fresh basil
sprigs or ½ bunch fresh
oregano, plus more for
garnish

1. Trim the eggplants and cut crosswise into ¼-inch-thick slices. Sprinkle with salt and place on one or more racks (cooling racks for baking) on a rimmed baking sheet. Set aside for 30 minutes.

2. Heat 2 tablespoons of the oil in a skillet on medium. Add the garlic and a sprinkling of salt and pepper, and cook until golden. Add the tomatoes and cook down a few minutes until they lose some of their liquid. Season to taste. Transfer to a food processor and pulse briefly until the mixture is nearly pureed.

3. Rinse and dry the eggplant slices. Heat half of the remaining oil in a skillet on medium-high. Fry as many eggplant slices as fit comfortably until golden, adding more oil and eggplant in batches. Transfer the fried eggplant to paper towels to drain.

4. Heat the oven to 350°F. Spread a little of the tomato sauce in a 9-inch square or round baking dish. Add a third of the eggplant, then half the cheese, half the basil, and half the remaining sauce. Repeat the layers. Top with a layer of eggplant. Bake for 20 minutes. Remove from the oven and allow to sit for 5 minutes. Garnish with fresh basil and serve hot or at room temperature.

YIELD: 6 TO 8 FIRST-COURSE OR 4 MAIN-COURSE SERVINGS

COOK'S NOTES:
Unlike most eggplant alla parmigiana, this is made without mozzarella, and it is even delicious when not piping hot.

MOUNT ETNA
I can't imagine what it's like to live next to a volcano, much less situate my family and my hopes for its future within spewing distance of one.

I've not yet been to Mount Etna. I did spend a couple of days in Naples a few years back. I remember staring transfixed across the gulf at Mount Vesuvius, imposing and pregnant with lava and fire. I did not have to dwell upon Pompeii to feel uneasy. The gaping cone of the volcano unnerved me, even as my friend, a Neapolitan, waved away the danger, assuring me that the city had elaborate, detailed, well-organized evacuation plans. Having honked my way through the chaos of Neapolitan traffic, I had my doubts.

Yet vineyards have been cultivated on the foothills and slopes surrounding Mount Etna since Pompeii was still a thriving den of depravity. Despite regular smolderings, belching of ash, and flows of lava, Etna is today one of the most exciting and remarkable wine regions in Italy.

That is because a legacy of eruptions has left copious deposits of rocky volcanic soils, the sort of easily draining, nutrient-poor earth that can be so conducive to good wine. And because the variety of micro-terroirs at elevations ranging mostly from 1,000 to 3,200 feet offer so many possible articulations of the indigenous Etna grapes: mostly the sleek, graceful nerello mascalese, with a small assist from its pudgier sibling, nerello cappuccio, which together generally make up the blends for Etna Rosso, the officially approved term for Etna red wines.

But I like to think it's the edginess of a precarious existence that gives these wines their nervous energy. Prosaically, it's a freshness that comes from lively acidity. The combination of energy and the lightness and elegance of the nerello mascalese grape makes the evolution of Etna red wines in the last few decades one of wine's most welcome trends. The whites, too, are worth exploring.

If you haven't already guessed, I love these wines—the lightness of their textures, the purity of the red-fruit and mineral flavors, their refreshing nature, their elegance, and their subtlety. They have the weightlessness of good Burgundy, though not the complexity and the tradition (at least, not yet). Despite the fact that Etna is an ancient source of wine, many of the leading producers today are newcomers, drawn there by the conviction that wines from Etna will be like no others. Marc de Grazia, an American importer of wines from Piedmont and Tuscany, decided Etna was where he wanted to settle down and make his own wine. He founded Tenuta delle Terre Nere, and since 2002 has been issuing multiple cuvées.

Andrea Franchetti of Passopisciaro made wine in Tuscany before adding vineyards on Etna to his holdings. Alberto Graci abandoned his career as a banker to make wine on Etna. And Frank Cornelissen came from Belgium to Etna, where he makes extreme wines unlike almost any others on earth, which people tend to love or hate. Not everybody is a newcomer, however. Ciro Biondi's family has made wine on Etna for generations, as have the Calabrettas. Others like Murgo and Fattorie Romeo del Castello measure their time on Etna in decades.

With so many backgrounds, the wines come in an assortment of styles, from determinedly old school to frankly modern to quirky and idiosyncratic. Yet the wines are also bound together by the taut, graceful texture that speaks of the combination of Etna and the nerello grapes. ☐

WINES THAT ARE LEAN AND LIGHT, with good acidity and some earthy tannins, like Etna rossos, are among the most versatile. But this recipe stays fairly close to home, featuring thick strands of bucatini tossed with canned tuna, a robust mix of olives and capers, a liberal showering of herbs, and some meaty chickpeas. Zapped with chiles and moistened with only olive oil and pasta cooking water, the dish, from Barbuto, a casual New York restaurant that's a Californian-Italian hybrid, is finished with the crunch of bread crumbs. The textures and flavors provide complexity to spare. Like the wines.

Bucatini with Tuna

TIME: 30 MINUTES

1 pound bucatini or penne

5 tablespoons extra virgin olive oil

1 garlic clove, smashed

1 small shallot, minced

2 large pinches of red chile flakes, or to taste

½ cup pitted oil-cured black olives, sliced

¼ cup large salt-cured capers, well rinsed and drained

½ cup cooked chickpeas

12 ounces imported canned solid tuna, preferably in olive oil, drained

¼ cup chopped fresh flat-leaf parsley leaves

¼ cup chopped fresh mint leaves

Salt and freshly ground black pepper

½ cup lightly toasted coarse bread crumbs

1. Bring a large pot of salted water to a boil. Add the bucatini and cook until al dente, about 8 minutes.

2. Meanwhile, heat 2 tablespoons of the oil in a very large skillet if using bucatini, or a large skillet if using penne. Add the garlic and shallot and sauté until soft. Add the red chile flakes, olives, capers, and chickpeas and cook for another minute or so. Break up the tuna into thick flakes and add. Cook until warm. Remove from the heat.

3. Drain the pasta, reserving about 1 cup of the pasta water. Add the pasta, parsley, and mint to the skillet. Return to low heat and toss well. Add the remaining 3 tablespoons oil and the pasta water to moisten the ingredients. Season with salt, pepper, and more chile flakes, if desired. Transfer to a warm serving bowl, top with the bread crumbs, and serve.

YIELD: 6 SERVINGS

COOK'S NOTES: The water in which pasta is cooked is an invaluable finishing agent for a dish. It will moisten one that is too dry, put a complex array of ingredients on speaking terms, and even help to reheat a sauce. Rescue a cup or so before the pasta has finished cooking and set it aside, covered. If you do not wind up using it, you have lost nothing.

AGLIANICO

The vast ocean of wine that is Italy is fed by many rivers. Sangiovese and nebbiolo, universally considered to be among the world's great grapes, pour in to acclaim. They are joined by floods of crowd-pleasers like pinot grigio and workhorses like montepulciano and trebbiano, which account for many serviceable but indistinct wines. Lesser-known varieties trickle in from all directions, adding wonderful flavors and nuances. One of my favorites is a red grape that seems largely taken for granted, when it's thought of at all. It stirs little excitement. I'm not sure why, because I find the wines delicious, structured, and ageworthy.

I'm talking about aglianico, the primary red grape of Campania, which encompasses Naples and Salerno on the western coast of southern Italy, and of Basilicata, the arch and instep of the boot. Aglianico has been termed the Barolo of the South, a seemingly admiring phrase made hollow by a patronizing note. Yes, the tannins, acidity, and dark flavors in aglianico bear a resemblance to the great Piemontese wine. But aglianico has much to offer of its own. Perhaps it's time to shed the notion that aglianico's value comes from what it resembles rather than from what it is.

Aglianico comes in several different styles, some accessible and easy to drink young, and some that, like Barolo (sorry about that), require significant aging to soften their tannic intensity. Not that aglianico is heavy by any means. Regardless of differences in texture and density, most aglianicos will be distinctively structured and earthy, with flavors of red fruit, licorice, and menthol. As is true in many parts of the world, aglianico producers have largely backed off from their earlier use of small barrels of new French oak, leaving natural grape tannins with little in the way of vanilla and chocolate flavors imposed by the barrels.

Most aglianicos come from Campania, which has a range of appellations. Taurasi is the most famous and prestigious, while others include Aglianico del Taburno and Irpinia. The best appellation from Basilicata is generally Aglianico del Vulture. As one might guess from this land of extinct volcanoes like Mount Vulture and decidedly active ones like Mount Vesuvius, aglianico thrives in volcanic soil, especially on sunny hillsides where the ripening season can stretch well into the fall. While the Campania appellations are generally better known than those of Basilicata, I would not sell the Basilicata wines short. I've had fascinating wines from the region, and I believe it has great potential.

Though aglianicos may seem instinctively to be cold weather wines, it's just as easy to imagine their accompanying steaks and sausages sizzling on the outdoor grill. Even in the summer, aglianicos can be just right—savory and robust enough to stand up to such dishes, while lively and intriguing enough to invigorate the palate. That sounds like a great combination to me. 🍷

THESE WINES, WHETHER ROUGH HEWN OR MORE REFINED, can handle with grace a lusty plate of rustic "farrotto," a dish that paraphrases risotto using farro, a kind of wheat, instead of rice. Here, to channel the sunny south of Italy, it is seasoned with sun-dried tomatoes, saffron, fennel, pecorino, and a dollop of butter.

Farrotto with Sun-Dried Tomatoes and Saffron

TIME: 2½ HOURS

1½ cups farro
(about 10 ounces)

¾ cup boiling water

5 cups vegetable stock

½ teaspoon saffron threads

2 tablespoons extra virgin olive oil

1 medium red onion, finely chopped

3 large garlic cloves, sliced

½ cup chopped red bell pepper

1 teaspoon fennel seeds

8 soft sun-dried tomatoes, not in oil, slivered

½ cup dry red wine

Salt and freshly ground black pepper

1 tablespoon unsalted butter

1½ ounces pecorino, grated

1. Place the farro in a bowl, add the boiling water, and set aside until the water is absorbed, about 1 hour. Place the stock in a saucepan, bring to a simmer, add the saffron, and remove from the heat.

2. Heat the oil in a 3-quart saucepan. Add the red onion, garlic, and bell pepper, and sauté on low until the vegetables are soft. Stir in the fennel seeds and sun-dried tomatoes. Set aside.

3. When the farro has absorbed the water, add it to the vegetables. Cook, stirring, on medium, for about 2 minutes. Stir in the wine and cook until it evaporates. Season with salt and black pepper. Lower the heat to medium-low. Start adding the stock, about ¾ cup at a time, stirring, and adding more as the liquid is absorbed. You have to stir only from time to time, not constantly. After about 45 minutes, all the stock should be used and the farro should be al dente, with some of the grains just starting to break. The grains should be bound by a liquid that has a thickened, creamy consistency.

4. Check the seasoning. Add the butter and when it melts, remove the pan from the heat and stir in half of the cheese. Serve, dusted with the remaining cheese.

YIELD: 4 MAIN-COURSE OR 6 FIRST-COURSE OR SIDE DISH SERVINGS

COOK'S NOTES: Using the risotto method, farro takes longer to cook than rice. Presoaking helps speed things up a bit. The recipe works with Arborio rice, with no preliminary soak, if you prefer.

BIERZO AND RIBEIRA SACRA I have

often described the current era as a golden age for wine lovers, who have available to them an unprecedented diversity of wines that were practically unknown to the world a few short years before. A case in point: the red wines of northwestern Spain made from the enchanting, haunting mencía grape.

The best of these wines come from two nearly adjacent regions: Bierzo, in the northwest corner of Castilla y León, and Ribeira Sacra, on the eastern end of Galicia. Both of these regions offer unusual terrains and subtly different interpretations of their signature grape. Bierzo's wines tend to be darker and denser, and perhaps their winemakers are more likely to add a modern overlay of new-oak polish. Ribeira Sacra's wines are generally lighter-bodied with a silky balance of fruit and earthy minerality. Yet, in the best wines from both regions, the mencía grape shines through as well, offering exotic, almost wild fruit aromas and flavors that are unforgettable.

These are both ancient regions in which farmers tended animals, grew grain, and raised grapes, just another subsistence crop. Not until the late twentieth century for Bierzo and the early twenty-first for Ribeira Sacra did their wines go any farther afield than the nearest big city. For each, the potential for distinction comes from the combination of the indigenous grapes, the unusual soils, the peculiar microclimates, and the human determination to make singular wines.

But each region faces pressures against making such wines as well. Wine bureaucracies often prefer their producers to make squeaky clean, inexpensive wine for high-volume sales rather than distinctive or idiosyncratic wines. Some argue for planting grapes with proven international popularity, like cabernet sauvignon, merlot, or tempranillo, the grape of Rioja. Dedicated winemakers in Ribeira Sacra scoff at that view, calling it "Rioj-itis."

Ribeira Sacra in particular offers striking vineyards: stone terraces that rise up the face of impossibly steep hillsides from three different rivers. The Romans first carved these terraces to supply wine for their march to the Atlantic. Over the centuries the locals joined in, led by monks, who cut vineyards into canyons and precipitous gorges of the Sil and the two other rivers: the Miño and the Bibei.

By the middle of the twentieth century, many of these terraces had been abandoned, as young people left the countryside in droves in search of more lucrative jobs that required less backbreaking labor. The rejuvenation of these old vineyards is one of the most exciting wine stories of the early twenty-first century. How this region completes the transition from local to global promises to be one of the most interesting in the years to come. 🍷

A STRONG SPANISH ACCENT IS CONVEYED, in this dish, by the smoked paprika, white beans, garlic, bell peppers, and especially by the morcilla, Spanish blood sausage that is intensely rich and spicy. Chicken breasts rarely boast such vivacious accessories. These flavors will also show the rich, well-rounded mencías to advantage. And if your casserole is earthenware, all to the good. It will only improve the dish.

Chicken with Morcilla and Peppers

TIME: 1½ HOURS, PLUS TIME FOR OPTIONAL OVERNIGHT SOAKING AND COOKING BEANS

3 chicken breast halves, with wings, skin, and bones

6 chicken thighs, with skin and bones

2 tablespoons extra virgin olive oil

1 teaspoon Spanish smoked paprika

Salt and freshly ground black pepper

4 cups cooked cannellini beans, from 1½ cups dry beans, or 2 cans, rinsed

1 tablespoon sliced garlic

3 red bell peppers, cored, seeded, and cut into ½-inch-wide vertical strips

2 medium sweet onions, cut into eighths

12 ounces morcilla (Spanish blood sausage), cut into 1-inch-thick slices

1 cup dry red wine

2 fresh rosemary sprigs, leaves only

1. Separate the wings from the breasts. Cut each breast in half. Dry all the chicken pieces. Heat 1 tablespoon of the oil in a 12-inch skillet. Add the chicken, skin side down, and cook over medium-high heat, just until the skin is golden. Do not turn the pieces. You may not fit all the chicken in the pan at once; cook it in batches, if necessary.

2. Place the chicken in a bowl and rub with the paprika, salt, and pepper. Toss the beans with the garlic, season with salt and pepper, and spread in a large shallow casserole that can hold the chicken in a single layer. Place the chicken, skin side up, on the bed of beans. Heat the oven to 400°F.

3. Heat the remaining 1 tablespoon oil in the skillet. Add the bell peppers and onion chunks and sauté until starting to brown. Scatter around the chicken. Add the sausage to the skillet, sauté, stirring, for a couple of minutes until just starting to sizzle. Tuck the sausage pieces into the casserole. Pour the wine into the skillet, deglaze the pan, and pour the liquid over the ingredients in the casserole. Scatter the rosemary on top. Place in the oven and bake for 45 minutes, basting the chicken with the juices once or twice. Serve.

YIELD: 6 SERVINGS

COOK'S NOTES: If a Spanish food shop is not convenient, there are some excellent online sources for morcilla. Though other countries, including England, France, Germany, and Mexico, also make blood sausages, the Spanish variety tends to be spicier. 🧂

ARGENTINE MALBECS

Argentina is pumping out a river of malbec, and in the United States it has flown off the shelves at an astonishing rate. While Argentine malbecs can run to much more than a hundred dollars a bottle, those aren't the ones flowing out of the stores. Sales have been pushed upward by demand for inexpensive bottles.

At the lower end, the wines tend to be pleasing and amiable. What do you get when you spend a little more? Well-made wines with a little more polish and sleekness than the cheaper bottles, along with a little more richness and intensity. Altogether, the wines are juicy and straightforward, emphasizing fruit flavors with occasional nuances. They are consistent, generally unchallenging, and crowd-pleasing. What's not to like?

That really depends on your point of view. Malbecs' emphasis on soft, ripe fruitiness over more polarizing flavors and their velvety textures make them safe and reliable for people who may be unsure of their tastes. Some wines are a more ripe and jammy, while others are spicier and more linear. But these are small divergences in what is largely a uniform set of characteristics.

This leads to a paradoxical, underwhelming conclusion: Part of the reason malbecs are so popular is that they are not displeasing. In other words, their consistent profile is a virtue, especially for people who do not appreciate being surprised or challenged by a wine. The genre itself has become a brand.

Once outdoor cooking season gets under way in earnest, with its plethora of grilled and roasted meats, malbecs would make fine choices. I tend to think of them the way I did of zinfandels, before so many zinfandels became top heavy with alcohol. They are likable and powerful enough in their own right. And if you serve them slightly cool, well, then you have a fine summer party wine.

From a marketing perspective, Argentina has achieved an enviable position. These days, malbec sings out Argentina as clearly as do grass-fed beef and Eva Perón. Forget that malbec was brought over in the nineteenth century from France, where it's still grown, primarily in Cahors and in the Loire Valley. Argentina owns it now. 🍷

TERROR, OR SENSE OF PLACE, helps to define character and flavor. It applies to food as well as wine. To be tempted by Argentina is to dream of steak on a grill, and it's no accident that the meat echoes the density of the malbecs from Mendoza. Good beef delivers a tight package of sweetness, earthiness, and minerality, just like the wines. And what would beef in Argentina be without a slather of chimichurri, the iconic parsley-based green sauce? It is both sharply hot and herbaceously cool, especially with the addition of mint to intensify the whiff of eucalyptus in the wines. This chimichurri is not really a sauce because it is meant to play a more intimate role, seasoning the steak inside and out.

Chimichurri Hanger Steak

TIME: 45 MINUTES, PLUS 3 HOURS MARINATING

1 cup packed fresh flat-leaf parsley, minced

2 tablespoons minced mint leaves

½ jalapeño, seeded and minced

1 garlic clove, minced

6 tablespoons extra virgin olive oil

1 tablespoon red wine vinegar

¼ teaspoon red chile flakes

Salt and freshly ground black pepper

Cayenne

3 tablespoons panko bread crumbs

1 hanger steak (about 2 pounds)

1. Mix the parsley, mint, jalapeño, garlic, oil, and vinegar in a bowl. Season with salt, black pepper, and cayenne to taste. The chimichurri should have a kick. The ingredients, except for the oil and vinegar, can be chopped in a food processor, with the liquids drizzled in through the feed tube. But if those results are not finely textured, spread the mixture on a cutting board and finish chopping by hand. Reserve 3 tablespoons of the mixture and add the panko to the rest.

2. Butterfly the steak with a sharp knife, slicing it not quite through to open it like a book. Lightly pound any thicker areas to make the meat more uniform. Spread the chimichurri with panko on one side of the cut surfaces, fold the other side over, and use metal or wooden skewers to enclose the filling. Coat the outside of the steak with the reserved chimichurri (no panko). Set aside for 3 hours at room temperature if the kitchen is not warm, or in the refrigerator. Allow the steak to come to room temperature before cooking.

3. Heat a grill or the broiler. Grill or broil the steak for 6 to 8 minutes per side for medium-rare (depending on the heat). Allow to rest for 10 minutes, remove the skewers, cut the steak into thick slices, and serve.

YIELD: 4 SERVINGS

COOK'S NOTES: Hanger steak, which often delivers an appealing funkiness, is the best choice for this recipe, though flank steak is a good substitute. The recipe can even be accomplished with more luxury using a whole tenderloin, especially if you have eight or so guests. But regardless of the cut of beef, try to use grass-fed beef as they do in Argentina.

CHILEAN CARMENÈRE

Consumers tend to view countries like Chile as wine upstarts, with good reason. It's been only in the last few decades that Chile has been able to compete effectively in the modern global wine market. One reason for that, and perhaps a key to its future success, is carmenère, a little-known grape that requires a look back at Chile's surprisingly long wine history.

Wine has been produced in Chile for more than four centuries, since the first Spanish settlers brought vines with them in the mid-1500s. By the late nineteenth century, the Chilean wine industry had become especially successful, but not because the winemakers were particularly skilled or because the wine was very good. It was really a matter of luck.

In the late 1800s, European vineyards were devastated by phylloxera, a ravenous aphid that attacks the roots of vinifera vines, the species of all the great European grapes. Before the phylloxera epidemic, wealthy Chileans had brought home and planted cuttings of unaffected French vines. Even as phylloxera attacked vinifera plantings in North America and even in Argentina, Chile remained free of the bug. Possibly this was because of its geographic isolation, with the Andes to the east and the Pacific to the west. Or maybe it was because the combination of climate and soil was inhospitable, or because the government was vigilant in barring the import of vines carrying the bug.

Whatever the reason, the Chilean wine industry, virtually alone, was phylloxera free in the late nineteenth century, and to this day phylloxera has not been found there. Which brings us back to carmenère. The grape was widely planted in Bordeaux before phylloxera. It was reputed to produce excellent wine, but it ripened late and was susceptible to coulure, a natural condition that can produce extremely low yields. After phylloxera, it was not replanted; hardly any carmenère can be found today in Bordeaux.

That might have been the last word on carmenère had some French scientists visiting Chile in the early 1990s not been troubled by the appearance and character of Chilean merlot. Further studies revealed that much of the merlot planted in Chile was, in fact, carmenère, traceable most likely to cuttings brought over in the mid-nineteenth century.

While this might have been a blow in the merlot-happy 1990s, today it has the potential to be a great boon to Chile's wine industry, which, since the nation's political turmoil of the 1970s and '80s, has spent millions modernizing to compete worldwide.

Chile had developed a good reputation for reliable, low-priced sauvignon blancs and cabernet sauvignons, as well as for a few more expensive cabernets like Concha y Toro's Don Melchor. But nothing had emerged that made Chilean wine especially distinctive. Enter carmenère. Just as Argentina has achieved a reputation with a signature grape, malbec, it may well be that Chile's further emergence may depend on carmenère, which is produced virtually nowhere else in the world.

The wines tend to be all over the place stylistically, from simple and even rustic to polished and sophisticated. Some are characterized by dark, plummy flavors while others are more floral. Many wines have an attractive spicy quality as well. Often, though, these flavors are obsured by oak. One bit of advice to ambitious winemakers: Let carmenère be carmenère. ☙

FORTHRIGHT, ASSERTIVE, AND STURDY, Carmenères can also exhibit vegetal, cedary, herbaceous, roasted, and crushed fruit flavors. They are delicious with some kind of lusty eggplant dish. The repertory of Greek, Indian, Moroccan, Italian, and French eggplant dishes, some of which are elsewhere in this book, all offer possibilities. Another would be well-seasoned eggplant slices slipped into sandwiches and served with the distinctive wines. Not eggplant parm, but something with a little more class for a tailgate lunch, a brunch, or an informal supper. The eggplant is lightly fried, slathered with tapenade, and layered with Gruyère for a variation on the French croque monsieur. But now, with panini presses sold in every housewares store, they could just as well be Italian. Eggplant, cheese, and olives. You pick the country of origin. It might even be Chile, after all.

Eggplant Croques Monsieurs

TIME: 1 HOUR

1 eggplant (about 1½ pounds)

Kosher or fine sea salt

4 to 5 tablespoons extra virgin olive oil

Freshly ground black pepper

¼ cup black olive paste (tapenade)

1 tablespoon finely minced fresh flat-leaf parsley leaves

6 ounces Gruyère

½ round loaf country bread, cut into 12 thin slices, or 6 panini breads, split horizontally

1. Trim the bottom inch and top 2 inches off the eggplant. Using the wider portion that remains, cut the eggplant into 6 slices, each about ½ inch thick. Set aside the remainder for another use. Salt the eggplant slices on both sides and set aside for 30 minutes, then rinse and dry.

2. Heat 2 tablespoons of the oil to very hot in a large heavy skillet. Sauté the eggplant slices until lightly browned. Turn the slices, lower the heat to medium, and sauté until the eggplant is cooked and lightly browned on the second side. Place on paper towels to drain. Season with pepper. Mix the tapenade with the parsley. Spread on one side of each eggplant slice. Cut the cheese into thin slices.

3. Place the eggplant slices, tapenade side down, on 6 of the slices of bread. Top with the cheese, then the second slice of bread.

4. Heat the remaining 2 tablespoons oil in the skillet. Cook the sandwiches, cheese side up, over medium heat, pressing down with a spatula, until lightly browned. Turn over and cook the second side, adding a little more oil, if necessary. Alternatively, the sandwiches can be grilled in a panini press. Cut each sandwich in half and serve.

YIELD: 4 TO 6 SERVINGS

COOK'S NOTES: Salting the eggplant before cooking it draws out the moisture in the slices, making them less spongy and delivering a meatier end result. 🥫

DOURO REDS

The Douro Valley region of Portugal has so much going in its favor, it's almost ridiculous. It has looks. With its rows of terraced vines winding along steep, curvaceous hillsides that rise above the sinuous Douro river on the country's northern tier, it is one of the most beautiful wine regions in the world.

It has brains. Some of the brightest, most creative minds in the trade make wine in the Douro (pronounced DOH-roo). This is not surprising, given that the region is home to the port business, which, through long years of doldrums, has sent some of those minds scurrying in search of new and different products—namely, table wine.

It has history. Even though Douro is largely a newcomer to the commercial table-wine business—which really got going in the 1990s, and is still sorting itself out—the network of vineyards supplying the port trade goes back centuries, providing the fundamental material for making distinctive wines that speak of the region and nowhere else.

It has grapes, and because of all that history, many are from old, established vines. Portugal, isolated on the Atlantic edge of the Iberian Peninsula, has largely been immune from the pressures of conformity that have led so many historic wine regions to tear out their little-known indigenous red grapes in favor of those popular worldwide. Instead of cabernet sauvignon and pinot noir, it has port grapes, including touriga nacional, touriga franca, tinta barroca, and tinta roriz, which over in Rioja goes by the name tempranillo. Does that make the tinta roriz any less Portuguese? Well, Spain and Portugal share many things, including the Douro, which across the border is called the Duero, so no, the tinta roriz is no less Portuguese, though perhaps it's more familiar than the other grapes.

That leaves the wines.

Not surprisingly, the plummy fruit and spice flavors, the good acidity, and the occasionally rugged tannins are more than a little reminiscent of port. These distinctive qualities make these wines a welcome step up from, say, malbecs and others in the plush-and-fruity genre of international wines. At the same time, it's not hard to sense a sameness in the wines, a uniformity that seems to speak more of cautious wine making than of the characteristics of the region.

The process of discovery is going on right now in the Douro as many producers experiment with different methods and combinations of grapes. A cautious approach is understandable, particularly because many wineries are connected to the various port houses, where conservatism is part of the DNA.

The more expensive bottles are easy to single out. You can almost taste the investment: the new-oak barrels lending their woody, vanilla sheen; the density, richness, and power of the fruit flavors, which come from grapes that have been babied every step of the way. It can all be too much. On the cheaper end, the issues are different: out-of-control tannins or wines that lack verve.

Yet when the wines are well made and balanced, they can be juicy, earthy, and exotic, distinctive in the best sense of the word.

The still wines of the Douro may not have entirely arrived yet, but with so much going for the region, the potential is enormous. 🍷

THE RELATIVELY NEW BREED OF DRY RED WINES FROM PORT COUNTRY, Portugal's Douro Valley, are happy partners for meat. Though these wines can be sleek and polished, and can gracefully accommodate a refined plate of roast veal, the best of them have not shed the inherent earthiness of their origins and beg for hearty texture, bold flavor, and herbs. Think pork. I might sear garlicky linguiça sausages to serve with potatoes and greens, or simmer chunks of boneless pork with clams in a typical *cataplana*, a dish cooked in a copper pot that resembles a clam shell. This tender, juicy roast of rib chops in a sauce bolstered with port, honed with vinegar, and intensified with dark olives and herbs will also do the trick.

Braised Pork Roast with Olives

TIME: 1 HOUR 15 MINUTES

½ tablespoon extra virgin olive oil

One 3½-pound rack of pork, 6 ribs, boned, tied back onto the rack of bones

5 garlic cloves, minced

½ cup chopped red onion

3 bay leaves, preferably fresh

⅓ cup red wine vinegar

¾ cup ruby port

1 cup chicken stock, plus more as needed

Salt and freshly ground black pepper

¼ cup sliced pitted Kalamata olives

1 tablespoon chopped fresh flat-leaf parsley

1. Heat the oil in a 4- to 5-quart Dutch oven or stove-top casserole over medium-high heat. Add the pork and sear on all sides until lightly browned, about 20 minutes. Remove the meat from the pot.

2. Add the garlic and red onions and sauté over medium-low heat until soft. Add the bay leaves and deglaze the pan with the vinegar. Add the port and stock. Season the meat with salt and pepper and return to the pot.

3. Place over very low heat and cook, basting from time to time, for 40 to 45 minutes, until an instant-read thermometer registers 140°F. Add a little more stock if the liquid cooks down too fast. Remove the meat to a platter to rest for 15 to 20 minutes.

4. Reheat the sauce and add the olives and parsley. Adjust the seasoning as needed.

5. Slice the meat and separate the bones. Arrange on a platter, spoon the sauce over, and serve.

YIELD: 6 SERVINGS

COOK'S NOTES: Have your butcher separate the solid hunk of meat from the bones, then tie the roast back onto the rack so the bones contribute flavor and silky gelatin to the sauce and can be served with the meat. 🧂

PRIORAT

Spain is awash in ancient wine regions rejuvenating themselves for the modern age, but none of these historic lands has demonstrated its innate potential as well as Priorat. Thirty years ago, this isolated territory high in the hills of Catalonia was virtually unknown to most of the wine-drinking world. Today, Priorats command some of the highest prices of any Spanish wines.

This seems a remarkable journey in such a short time, especially given the calm, creeping, seasonal pace of viticulture. Yet the commercial end of the wine business speeds by so quickly that some consumers have already concluded Priorat is something of a has-been, another generic, international-style wine built largely on hype. Don't be fooled. The wines of Priorat are the real thing, distinctive and powerful expressions of a highly unusual terroir.

Ever since the twelfth century, when monks established the Priorato de Scala Dei, or the Priory of the Ladder of God, vines have been grown on the craggy hillsides of "Priorat," the Catalan term for Priorato. Indeed, the old stone terraces carved into treacherously steep hillsides testify to the indomitable human thirst for wine. Many of those terraces were left to crumble in the late nineteenth century after phylloxera ravaged Priorat, along with most European vineyards. And, while some of the vineyards were replanted, largely with garnacha and cariñena, or grenache and carignan, many were later abandoned as farmers left to find work in cities in the mid-twentieth century. Only when a group of intrepid Spanish producers arrived in Priorat in the 1970s, believing in the region's promise, did a recovery truly commence. Terraces were rebuilt, vineyards were revived or planted anew, and wine-making facilities were constructed. Recognition for the wines began to arrive in the late 1990s.

While old stands of garnacha and cariñena are still the most important grapes in Priorat, some internationalization was perhaps inevitable. Cabernet sauvignon, merlot, and syrah have also been planted, though they are largely added as blending grapes. French oak barrels are widely used for aging, further fueling suspicions of homogenization, and, to seal the deal, the wines are powerful and concentrated, leading to thoughts that they are made to appeal to American palates. This, I believe, is a thorough misunderstanding of Priorat.

Yes, these are big, dense wines, and the alcohol levels can be elevated, even if producers have pulled back after several years of seeking all-out power. That is the nature of garnacha. The wines of Châteauneuf-du-Pape, also dominated by grenache, offer a ready parallel in terms of size and power. Yet where the best Châteauneufs show indisputable evidence of Provence, with their dense, earthy, herbal wildness, the best Priorats are juicy, succulent, and full of distinctive mineral flavors not at all like Châteauneufs.

Priorat performs the rare feat of seeming to bridge the prevailing critical divide. Its wines are big, bold, sometimes jammy, and high in power and concentration, but also structured, balanced, and distinctively of a place. These huge wines are quite elegant as well.

I will be fascinated to see how things play out in Priorat. My guess is that the wines will continue to get better and better, particularly as the intricacies of the various terroirs become better understood. 🍷

MEMORABLE DISHES SOMETIMES COME OUT OF NOWHERE. During a visit to Catalonia, it was no surprise that there was plenty of breathtaking food, considering that the raison d'être for the trip was dinner at El Bulli, the famous restaurant, now closed, that was once considered to be the best in the world and El Celler de Can Roca, which later topped the list. But one evening in Tarragona, a city just south of Barcelona, we wandered into an old square with a number of cafés and tapas bars. Txantxangorri, a Basque place, was the only one that had seats. In addition to decent tapas, the menu listed rice dishes—not paellas. The rice with rabbit, served in a terra-cotta casserole, was simple and satisfying. Unlike the Michelin-starred dishes elsewhere, this, I thought, I could try at home.

Rice with Rabbit

TIME: 1 HOUR 15 MINUTES

1 rabbit, cut into 8 pieces

Salt and freshly ground black pepper

1 teaspoon ground Espelette pepper or Spanish hot paprika

1 cup dry white wine

5 tablespoons extra virgin olive oil

1 large onion, chopped

3 garlic cloves, finely slivered

1½ cups Spanish short-grain rice

1 tablespoon tomato paste

3½ cups chicken stock

1 tablespoon minced fresh flat-leaf parsley leaves

1. Use a cleaver to cut the rabbit pieces into about 24 small chunks, cutting through the bones as needed. Place in a bowl and massage with salt and pepper and ½ teaspoon of the Espelette. Pour in ½ cup of the wine and 2 tablespoons of the oil. Mix well, cover loosely, and marinate for 6 hours, refrigerated.

2. Dry the rabbit pieces and reserve the marinade. Heat 2 tablespoons of the remaining oil in a large skillet. Sauté the rabbit on medium-high until lightly browned but not cooked through. Remove the rabbit to a bowl. Lower the heat to medium and add the remaining 1 tablespoon oil to the skillet. Heat the oven to 375°F.

3. Sauté the onion and garlic in the skillet until just starting to color. Add the rice and stir. Add the reserved marinade, the tomato paste, the remaining ½ teaspoon Espelette, the remaining ½ cup wine, and the stock. Bring to a simmer. Taste and add salt, if needed.

4. Transfer to a 4-quart casserole, preferably earthenware. Tuck the rabbit pieces in, place in the oven, and cook, uncovered, until the rice has absorbed the liquid and is tender, about 40 minutes. Scatter the parsley on top and serve.

YIELD: 4 TO 6 SERVINGS

COOK'S NOTES: Though an earthenware casserole would be the vessel of choice for cooking this traditional dish, you can make the whole thing, from stove top to oven, in enameled cast iron. And if obtaining a rabbit is not in the cards, you can use a couple of Cornish hens instead. 🍶

LANGUEDOC-ROUSSILLON The perpetually

hyphenated regions of Languedoc and Roussillon seem always to be in states of transition. Let's begin by decoupling them and taking them one at a time.

Languedoc has sometimes been called the California of France. The grip of history, so powerful through most of France in the rules that govern its appellation system, is less evident in the Languedoc. If anything, the region's many years as a bulk-wine supplier for the rest of the country offer clear justification for the sort of experimentation that sometimes muddies the clarity of its identity.

Without the burden of past greatness, and lacking the clear delineation of rigorous appellations, many producers feel freer in the Languedoc to work with untraditional grapes in the region. Carignan, cinsault, grenache, syrah, and mourvèdre still predominate, though the proportion of syrah has risen as carignan has declined. But cabernet, merlot, and other international grapes are also part of the mix, especially in those wines labeled vin de pays.

As a result, wines can veer in style from bottle to bottle. Some evoke what I always imagine to be the wildness of the Mediterranean countryside: craggy, rocky hillsides redolent of lavender and wild thyme, the famous garrigue. Others are powerful modern wines, dominated by sweet fruit and oak. Some wines are stern, tannic, almost austere. Others are dense yet supple. And another style has emerged, incorporating the Beaujolais wine-making method of carbon maceration that can make spicy, easily accessible wines.

By far the most interesting wines are also the most distinct, those that could come from nowhere else but Mediterranean France. The smooth, fruity, oaky wines can no doubt compete on the global stage. Yet in the end, what will really set them apart from similar wines, whether from the United States, South America, Tuscany, or Australia? Price, perhaps? The wines most full of character still rely primarily on the traditional grapes, even the oft-despised carignan, which top Languedoc producers have proved can achieve great results if it's carefully farmed and the yields are kept relatively low.

As with its sibling, Roussillon is an exciting place, if only for seeing how efforts to adapt to a changing world will turn out. Dynamic winemakers have taken the challenge of this ancient Mediterranean land at the jagged foot of France. There, the Pyrenees form a physical and political border with Spain, but culturally and spiritually, Catalonia embraces both sides.

Roussillon begins with a lack of identity similar to that of Languedoc, and as an added handicap, it is even less familiar as a source of dry wines. Yet successful producers from outside the region, like Michel Chapoutier and Pierre Gaillard of the Rhône Valley, have set up operations there, while ambitious natives to Roussillon are making wines with painstaking attention to detail, hoping for the same sort of lightning-quick recognition that has buoyed Priorat, its Catalan sibling in Spain.

It's not necessarily a far-fetched notion. Dry reds from Roussillon are often said to have more in common with Spanish reds than with French. Both regions have stands of old-vine grenache and carignan, although in Roussillon these grapes are increasingly supplemented by mandated levels of syrah and mourvèdre, while in Priorat international grapes like cabernet sauvignon and merlot have made inroads.

Not surprisingly for such a sunny region, many of the wines are powerfully fruity, dense, and tannic, sometimes harshly so. Others are pleasantly robust and lusty.

While it tried to develop its reputation for dry wines, Roussillon has always been best known for its vins doux naturels, a misleading term for wines that are sweet because they are fortified, a natural process only by virtue of human intervention. While exploring what's new about Languedoc and Roussillon, it might also be worth revisiting such traditional honey-scented pleasures as Rivesaltes, Banyuls, and Maury. ♟

WINE STORAGE

Though it's possible to run to the wine shop and pick something up for dinner on a regular basis, having some wines on hand is a good idea. You might consider designating the bottles you especially like, if they're reasonably-priced, as your "house wine," purchased by the case and ready to open at a moment's notice. So you have a case or two—or more—of wine. Where and how do you best keep it? Though excessive heat is the enemy of fine wine, temperature fluctuations can also be damaging. Unless you have some kind of temperature-controlled storage unit, the first rule is not to keep wine in the kitchen, regardless of how convenient it might be. If you regularly drink white wine, having a bottle or two in the fridge is a good idea. But most of your wine will be much happier in a dark place in some other room, in a closed cabinet or a closet. And except for screw-cap bottles, place the wines on their sides to keep the corks moist. —FF

WHEN I THINK OF THE LANGUEDOC, I often think of duck, which is the basis for many regional dishes. The rich succulence of braised duck and rustic, slightly spicy turnips to soak up the cooking juices, are made to order for the rustic red wines of the sprawling region. I would not serve this duck dish with a jammy crowd-pleaser or a soft pinot noir. The Languedoc wines offer brash complexity, herbal notes, forthright acidity, and lingering, if somewhat reluctant fruit, all bespeaking terroir.

Duck Braised with Turnips and Shallots

TIME: 3 HOURS

One 5-pound duck, cut up, backbone and wing tips removed

Salt and freshly ground black pepper

8 shallots, peeled

6 medium white turnips (about 1 pound), trimmed, peeled, and quartered

½ cup dry red wine

8 garlic cloves

¾ cup well-seasoned duck, veal, or chicken stock

5 fresh thyme sprigs

1. Trim the excess fat from the duck. Season the flesh side with salt and pepper. Place a 4-quart ovenproof casserole over medium-high heat, put a 2-inch piece of the excess fat in the casserole, and, when the fat starts to render, remove it. Add the duck pieces, skin side down, and sear without turning until the skin is golden brown. Do not crowd the duck; add the pieces a few at a time. When the duck is seared, remove from the casserole and discard all but a thin film of fat from the pot.

2. Heat the oven to 325°F.

3. Place the shallots and turnips in the casserole and sear, turning gently, over medium heat until golden. Remove to a dish and season with salt and pepper. Pour the wine into the casserole and simmer briefly, scraping the bottom of the pot. Add the garlic and stock. Return the duck to the casserole, skin side up. Add the thyme, cover, and place in the oven for 45 minutes. Place the shallots and turnips in the casserole and cook until the duck and vegetables are tender, another 15 to 20 minutes. Serve.

YIELD: 4 SERVINGS

COOK'S NOTES: If you can find dried French Tarbais or coco beans to soak, then cook until tender, and serve alongside the duck, so much the better. White cannellini beans from Italy make a good substitute. 🗍

LANGUEDOC WINES, from the delightfully rustic to the more polished bottles, often share brambly, herbal notes. Alongside them I crave food showered with rosemary, that sturdy country herb. It could easily be carried by a lamb dish or seared tuna. But just vegetables? I cruised a Greenmarket where in late autumn, bright, glossy tomatoes and eggplants were giving way to roots, and I picked up some sunchokes. My guess was that Languedoc would be sturdy enough to accept their edge of sweetness, especially if cloaked in that essential rosemary. Simply scrubbed, sliced, and sautéed with shallots and garlic and finished with abundant herbs, the sunchokes were ready to be tossed with fresh pasta, preferably green. A generous splash of pasta water and shards of parmesan put everything on speaking terms, and some niçoise olives added the accent of the Pays d'Oc, as the south of France was once known.

Tagliatelle with Sunchokes and Herbs

TIME: 40 MINUTES

4 tablespoons extra virgin olive oil

⅓ cup thinly sliced shallots

2 garlic cloves, sliced thin

½ cup niçoise olives, pitted

1 pound sunchokes, scrubbed, sliced ¼-inch thick

Salt

10 ounces fresh green tagliatelle

Leaves from 3 branches fresh rosemary

2 teaspoons fresh thyme leaves

¼ cup coarsely chopped fresh flat-leaf parsley leaves

Freshly ground black pepper

1½ ounces firm Basque sheep's milk cheese, grated

1. Heat 2 tablespoons of the oil in a 12-inch skillet. Add the shallots and garlic and sauté on medium until they are soft but not brown. Add the remaining oil, olives, and sunchokes and sauté, stirring, for 5 minutes. Season with salt. Cover the pan and cook for about 15 minutes more, stirring once or twice, until the sunchokes are tender.

2. Meanwhile, bring a large pot of salted water to a boil for the pasta. Cook the pasta until al dente, about 4 minutes. Remove 1 cup of the pasta water. Drain the pasta.

3. Add ½ cup of the pasta water, the rosemary, and thyme to the skillet. Stir. Add the drained pasta to the skillet and using tongs or a large spoon, fold all the ingredients together. Add additional pasta water, if needed, to keep the mixture moist. Add parsley. Season with salt and pepper. Serve with the cheese.

YIELD: 4 SERVINGS

COOK'S NOTES: Recipes often call for knobby sunchokes to be peeled, a task more thankless than shelling fava beans. Count me out. Fortunately, I discovered that when sliced thin, still raw, sunchokes do not require peeling and make this recipe a breeze. 🔪

BANDOL

In the popular imagination, Provence calls to mind sunny, pastel images of hillside towns climbing up from the sea. For the wine lover, Provence mostly conjures up the tangy, lighthearted spirit of rosé, sipped within earshot of the water. It simply doesn't square that carefree Provence is also home to a superb red wine that practically epitomizes the word "brooding."

But then, anybody who has read the Marseilles-based novels of Jean-Claude Izzo knows that Provence has its dark side, too. As far as wine goes, that would be Bandol. There, in a pocket of terraced hills west of Toulon, within sniffing distance of the Mediterranean, surprisingly sturdy wines made largely from the mourvèdre grape can stun you with their haunting beauty.

When young, Bandol is deep, inky, and practically savage. As it ages, it emerges from the stranglehold of its tannic embrace. The best are decidedly dry and structured yet bewitching, with dark aromas like licorice, leather, and flowers, although with something wild and untamed as well. By its weight, tannins, aromas, and flavors, it can be reminiscent of nebbiolo, except for that wild element, which is very much mourvèdre's own.

Like many of Mr. Izzo's characters, mourvèdre is an immigrant. It is native to Spain, where it is called monastrell and dominates robust wines like Jumilla and Alicante. These wines are rich and highly aromatic. Mourvèdre is used to add structure in Châteauneuf-du-Pape, and is often a blending element in Australia, California, and Washington State. However, nowhere else are the conditions for mourvèdre as right as they are in Bandol, where the wines reach their apogee.

A century ago in Bandol mourvèdre was almost forgotten. It was the dominant red grape of Provence until phylloxera struck in the late nineteenth century, and it all but disappeared. Growers grafted their European vines onto American roots, which were resistant to the root-destroying phylloxera aphids, but the first rootstocks they chose were not hospitable to the persnickety mourvèdre vines. Many growers abandoned mourvèdre for more productive grapes.

The rebirth of mourvèdre in the region is largely credited to the efforts of the Peyraud family of Domaine Tempier, who fought in the 1930s to establish the Bandol appellation. When the appellation was officially granted in 1941—some life did go on in the war years—the rules required only that the red wine be 10 percent mourvèdre. That figure was slowly increased over the years until 1977, when it reached its current required level of 50 percent.

Today, a dozen or so producers in sunny Provence specialize in this excellent wine for winter. 🍷

HINTS OF ROSEMARY RISE IN THE BOUQUET OF THESE WINES, so why not let this herb carry the day? And with rosemary, you can't go wrong with lamb. Lamb of a boned leg, trimmed well and cut into big chunks as nearly uniform in size as possible would become kebabs. The lamb is treated to a simple marinade seasoned with rosemary, garlic, and sweet paprika, with a combination of lemon juice and olive oil as the medium to carry the flavors. The other component for the kebabs is mushrooms, to pick up the earthiness that emerges from some of the wines. I lightly sauté simple, inexpensive shiitake mushroom caps before seasoning them with more rosemary and garlic. This step, precooking them, guarantees that the mushrooms will be moist, not dry, as they clasp the meat on the skewers.

Grilled Lamb Kebabs with Rosemary

TIME: 40 MINUTES, PLUS MARINATING

2½ pounds boneless leg of lamb

4 tablespoons extra virgin olive oil

Juice of 1 lemon

1 teaspoon Spanish sweet paprika

3 tablespoons rosemary leaves

4 garlic cloves

Salt and freshly ground black pepper

32 medium shiitake mushrooms, stems discarded

1. Trim the lamb of silver skin, excess fat, and sinews. Cut it into 16 chunks about 2 inches square and place it in a bowl. Mix together 2 tablespoons of the oil; the lemon juice; paprika; 1 tablespoon of the rosemary; 2 of the garlic cloves, sliced; and salt and pepper. Pour over the lamb and turn to coat well. Cover, refrigerate, and marinate for about 6 hours.

2. Heat 2 tablespoons of the remaining oil in a large skillet. Add the mushrooms and cook briefly over medium-high heat, turning once, just until they start to soften. Set aside to cool.

3. Finely chop the remaining 2 tablespoons rosemary and 2 garlic cloves together and place on a small plate. When the mushrooms have cooled, dip the gill side of each cap into the rosemary and garlic mixture to coat lightly. Arrange, herbed side up, on a platter.

4. About 30 minutes before serving, heat a grill to very hot. Thread the lamb onto each of four skewers, using 4 pieces for each and sandwiching each piece of lamb between 2 mushroom caps, with the herbed side against the meat. Thus, cap-meat-cap, another cap-meat-cap, and so on.

5. When the grill is hot, grill the lamb to the desired degree of doneness, turning several times, about 15 minutes total cooking time for medium-rare.

YIELD: 4 SERVINGS

COOK'S NOTES: I prefer to buy the half leg, butt end, boned, and cut it into cubes myself. That way I can be sure the pieces will be uniform and will cook evenly. 🝙

BLAUFRÄNKISCH AND ZWEIGELT

If Austria is known at all for its wines, it's for whites. Its dry, minerally rieslings are fuller-bodied than Germany's, while its peppery grüner veltliners have achieved a vogue of their own. Yet as delicious as Austrian whites can be, the reds, most notably blaufränkisch and zweigelt, are themselves producing real excitement.

The two grapes are linked by geography and by heritage. The blaufränkisch grape is grown mostly in Austria, where it makes a spicy red wine that can be graceful yet intense, complex yet tangy. Blaufränkisch is made as well in Germany, where it is often called lemberger.

Zweigelt is a relatively new grape, developed in 1922 when an Austrian scientist, Fritz Zweigelt, crossed blaufränkisch with Saint Laurent. The grape was originally called rotburger, but mercifully, for English speakers at least, the name was changed to honor its creator. Zweigelts have a freshness and grace that allow them to go beautifully with a wide range of foods. The best bottles also have an exotic spice and floral character that makes them distinctive and unusual.

Blaufränkisch is an older grape, and it theoretically has the potential to make wines of greater depth and agreeability than zweigelt, but it is also more difficult to grow and make into wine. Not so long ago, blaufränkisch wines were hard to find in the United States. Those that were available often seemed as if they had been made with weight and power in mind rather than finesse. The results were heavy-handed, stolid wines of little grace and a lot of oak.

More recently, many producers have been taking greater care, seeking cooler sites for growing the grape and acting with more restraint in the cellar. As a result, the best blaufränkisches now are beautifully balanced, with smoky, spicy fruit flavors; winning textures; and a rippling acidity that make them seem juicy, savory, and refreshing. Nowadays, you can see a clear continuum from light-bodied, subtle wines to denser, richer wines that in the best examples betray no heaviness.

Zweigelts bring to mind such enjoyable everday wines as Côtes-du-Rhônes, lighter Bierzos, or maybe a spicy Beaujolais. They take well to a slight chill, making them fine reds for summer drinking. The lighter blaufränkisches are reminiscent of mildly peppery pinot noirs while the denser versions are a little closer in richness and texture to syrah.

The differences in texture can be partly explained by geography. Carnuntum, not far from Vienna, is generally a good source for graceful blaufränkisches, while the Burgenland to the east, abutting Hungary, tends to yield richer wines. 🍷

AUSTRIAN RED WINES, AMONG THEM ZWEIGELT AND BLAUFRÄNKISCH, are not the stuff of everyday drinking. That's mainly because they are not front and center in wine shops and on wine lists. But they should be because they are complex and balanced, offering aromas and tastes of mint, pepper, earth, and, especially in the blaufränkisch group, rich suggestions of sour cherries. They could provide harmonious drinking with plates of charcuterie, sautéed mushrooms, substantial fish like tuna and salmon, gamy birds like quail, and meats from veal stews to steak. Taking my inspiration from Austria, I prepared lamb schnitzel style. To pick up some of the herbal and pepper flavors in the wine, I devised a pesto sauce made with mint and horseradish to accompany the schnitzel. A dollop of sour cream enhances its Austrian accent.

Lamb Schnitzels with Mint-Horseradish Pesto

TIME: 40 MINUTES

½ cup all-purpose flour

Salt and freshly ground black pepper

¼ cup grated fresh horseradish

1 large egg

¾ cup dry bread crumbs

1½ pounds top round of lamb, in 4 pieces lightly pounded to ½ inch thick

½ cup packed fresh mint leaves

⅓ cup extra virgin olive oil

2 lemons

2 tablespoons sour cream

⅔ to 1 cup vegetable oil, preferably grape seed, for frying

1. Spread the flour on a dinner plate and season with salt and pepper and 2 teaspoons of the horseradish. Beat the egg with 1 tablespoon water in a shallow bowl. Spread the bread crumbs on a dinner plate. Dip the lamb pieces first in flour, shaking off the excess, then in the egg, then in the bread crumbs. Arrange on a platter and refrigerate.

2. Place the mint leaves and the remaining horseradish in a food processor and process until minced. Slowly drizzle the olive oil through the feed tube. Transfer to a serving bowl, stir in the juice of 1 lemon and the sour cream, season with salt and pepper, and set aside.

3. Heat vegetable oil to a depth of about ½ inch in a 12-inch skillet to very hot. Add 2 of the coated slices of lamb and cook over medium-high heat until browned, turning once, about 2 minutes per side. Try to keep the oil and the lamb moving in the pan by gently sliding the pan on the burner in a circular motion. When the lamb is done, place on several thicknesses of paper towels to drain. Repeat with the remaining lamb. The lamb will be medium-rare. If you want it more well done, reduce the heat to medium so it takes longer to cook.

4. Transfer to a platter and serve with the remaining lemon cut into wedges and the sauce.

YIELD: 4 SERVINGS

COOK'S NOTES: Coating thin slices of lamb in successive layers of seasoned flour, egg, and bread crumbs is classic schnitzel making. So is gently moving the pan of oil as the meat fries, a technique that lightens the breading. 🥫

GREEK REDS

Mavrotragano and mandilaria; limnio and vlachiko; and, of course, agiorgitiko and xinomavro. I know: It's all Greek. That's what is so exciting.

These indigenous red grapes represent a new wave of Greek wines now available in the United States. While whites remain the most familiar Greek wines (it's wonderful to see restaurants serving assyrtiko by the glass), Greece also offers a fascinating extension of the spectrum of world reds.

Not that these wines are radical departures from the familiar, as with retsina, the pungent, resinated Greek wine that is more often discussed than consumed, or the sad oxidized reds that years ago epitomized Greece's efforts to enter the global market. These are up-to-date reds, familiar yet subtly different from other modern reds, with an herbal inflection here, an earthiness there.

It's not just the names of the grapes that may seem daunting, but the geography. While the names of Greek islands have become more familiar on wine bottles as Greek whites have gained popularity, most of the reds come from northern and central Greece, even as you will also find a few reds from Santorini, Rhodes, and Crete. More likely are wines from regions of Macedonia in the northeast (like Naoussa, Kavala, Epanomi, and Côtes de Meliton), from Epirus in the northwest, and from Nemea on the Peloponnese peninsula.

Adding to the confusion is that many labels are in Greek and English, and the transliteration of Greek into English is, shall we say, not yet codified. You will find Greek words with multiple English renderings, like xinomavro or xynomavro, and mandelaria or mantilaria. Sometimes multiple spellings are on the same label.

Nonetheless, these wines promise adventure. The payoff is not merely the pleasure of discovery, but the affirmation that even jaded palates can find something new. It's the flip side of globalization: Yes, when little-known wines are taken from their home territory and sent around the world, a danger exists that they will end up homogenized, airbrushed of their distinctive characteristics. But the joy of diversity beckons, and if the wines retain their moorings, then you have something exciting.

Given the number of different grapes and regions, it's not surprising that these Greek reds range in style from light-bodied and fresh to dense and tannic. Some are sweetly fruity, though dry, while others are more savory. Some are lush and soft, others more focused. Happily, very few have the overly polished sheen that indeed signals a wine made with the international market in mind.

These intriguing wines include xinomavros, which can be lively and tannic, with aromas of red fruit and menthol reminiscent of nebbiolo. Grapes made from agiorgitiko may be easier going, with earthy, brightly fruity flavors. You may also find lush and savory blends of several different grapes.

The successes among these wines well warrant a spirit of adventure, yet it pays to be cautious when buying, especially with retail. With wines like these, which are gaining in popularity but haven't truly caught on, storage issues are a concern. By all means, investigate recent vintages. But dusty bottles that look as if they've been on a warm shelf for too long? They may recall the oxidized reds of yore. Steer clear. 🍷

AT LUNCHTIME BY THE POOL AT THE LAVISH, HISTORIC HOTEL LA MAMOUNIA in Marrakech, the buffet is global. The grilled lobsters are tempting to be sure, but fish boldly baked Moroccan style, with spices, herbs, tomatoes, and olives, was just as appealing. There is a Greek accent in this fish dish, with its garlic, lemon, parsley, peppers, tomatoes, olives, and olive oil. It's an easy, all-in-one recipe. Double or triple it and you have the anchor for a summer party menu, even on a buffet that's less copious than the one in Marrakech. Cool some Greek reds to pour alongside.

Baked Fish, Fez Style

TIME: 1 HOUR

2 large garlic cloves, minced

1 tablespoon minced fresh flat-leaf parsley leaves

1 tablespoon minced fresh cilantro leaves

1 teaspoon ground cumin

1 teaspoon paprika, preferably hot

Pinch of saffron threads, crushed

2 tablespoons white wine vinegar

Juice of 1 lemon

1 tablespoon tomato paste

4 fish fillets, each 6 ounces: fluke, black sea bass, or hake

1 pound large Yukon gold potatoes, peeled and cut into ½-inch-thick slices

3 tablespoons extra virgin olive oil

Salt and freshly ground black pepper

1 red bell pepper, cored, seeded, and slivered

1 pint (1 pound) cherry tomatoes, halved

½ cup pitted Kalamata olives

1. Combine the garlic, parsley, cilantro, cumin, paprika, and saffron in a dish big enough for the fillets. Mix the vinegar, lemon juice, and tomato paste in a small bowl. Add to the dish and mix. Place the fillets in the dish, turning to coat them. Cover and set aside to marinate for 2 hours at room temperature, 3 hours if refrigerated.

2. Place the potatoes in a saucepan and add water to cover. Bring to a boil, reduce the heat, and simmer for 15 minutes. Drain.

3. Heat the oven to 350°F. Brush a baking dish that can go to the table and will hold the fish in a single layer with a little of the oil. Spread the potatoes in the dish, season with salt and pepper, and place the fish on top. Scatter the bell peppers and tomatoes over the fish. Add a little more salt and pepper. Spoon any excess marinade over the fish, strew with olives, drizzle with the remaining oil, and cook for about 30 minutes, until the fillets are just cooked through.

YIELD: 4 SERVINGS

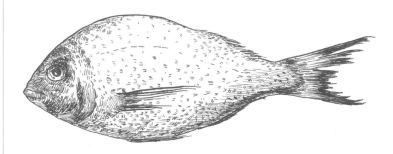

COOK'S NOTES: This dish is excellent served at room temperature instead of piping hot. 🖘

ZINFANDEL

No other wine is as entwined as zinfandel with all things American. When the experts recommend a wine for the Fourth of July, for Thanksgiving, or simply to dress up in red, white, and blue and march down Main Street, they pick zinfandel. It makes perfect sense, symbolically at least. Even if the grape is of European origin, almost all the zinfandel in the world is produced in California.

If anything, the zinfandel grape is an underdog thoroughly worthy of admiration. Grapes like cabernet sauvignon, pinot noir, and chardonnay are aristocrats by comparison, with regal European forebears. But zinfandel arrived, unheralded, by steerage, an advantage only in that it was never overshadowed by Old World antecedents like Bordeaux or Burgundy. Nobody even knew where zinfandel came from until genetic research in the 1990s revealed it to be of Croatian origin.

The geography of zinfandel is dominated by the Dry Creek Valley in Sonoma County. Its winding hillsides form a kind of promised land for gnarly old zinfandel vines, which produce wines that have a nobility seemingly at odds with the grape's brambly, outlier reputation.

Other regions, too, have staked a claim to zinfandel. The Russian River Valley produces lively, exuberant zins, while the Sierra Foothills offers an intense, jammier style. I've always liked the precise, jewellike zinfandels from Napa Valley, though truth be told, it's the rare Napa producer these days that chooses to make zinfandel in that style. Paso Robles, too, has developed a reputation for excellent zinfandel.

Zinfandel has regularly suffered from stylistic identify crises. In the last five decades it has gone through periods of monstrousness, full of alcoholic heat and almost portlike richness and intensity. I can't really envision a time when I'd seek out such a wine, unless I was stranded in an avalanche and the wine was ferried by a Saint Bernard.

It has also pulled back to points where some people have considered it overly meek. Right now it seems to be entering a sensible middle ground where fans of power can find wines that are nevertheless made with precision, while fans of restraint can find wines that show freshness and energy. Even these wines tend to be big, with the rare zinfandel under 14 percent alcohol. Hey, zinfandel is not Beaujolais; it naturally tends to be brawny.

The best zinfandels, to my taste, can be graceful, lively, and complex, even as they are full of peppery fruit. They can be juicy and exuberant, nuanced and structured. On the other side, plenty of zinfandels are still dispiritedly jammy and syrupy.

Certainly, lower alcohol levels by themselves are no guarantee that a wine will be fresh and energetic. Still, more zinfandel producers seem to be embracing the notion that wines can be both agile and intense rather than aiming simply for blockbuster power. That's a good thing. ♇

MY HUSBAND AND I WERE TO BE GUESTS AT A DINNER PARTY, and the host planned to open several bottles of zinfandel. I said I would bring the main course for eight to accompany them. I simmered short ribs and mushrooms in broth seasoned with soy sauce to play off the earthiness of the wines. An enrichment of sake and, eventually, Delicata squash, echoed their fruit. The steaming, soupy meat and vegetables were ladled over boiled soba noodles, and a Japanese pepper seasoning called *togarashi* contributed a finishing touch.

Short Ribs in Broth with Squash and Shiitakes

TIME: 3½ HOURS, PLUS OVERNIGHT CHILLING

6½ pounds short ribs of beef, cut into 2½-inch chunks with bone

1 cup finely chopped onions

1½ tablespoons sliced garlic

One 2-inch piece fresh ginger, peeled and minced

1 teaspoon ground cardamom

12 ounces shiitake mushrooms, stems discarded

½ cup sake

¼ cup soy sauce

6 cups beef stock

Freshly ground black pepper

2 tablespoons red wine vinegar

2 pounds Delicata squash, peeled, seeded, quartered lengthwise, and sliced 1 inch thick

2 bunches scallions, 4 inches of green left on

Boiled soba noodles and Japanese togarashi pepper blend, for serving

1. Place a big casserole, at least 8 quarts, over medium-high heat. Dry the meat and add as many pieces as will fit easily, fat side down. Brown on all sides, remove, and continue with the rest of the meat. Remove from the casserole. Lower the heat and add the onions, garlic, and ginger. Sauté until soft. Stir in the cardamom. Add the mushrooms and cook until wilted. Stir in the sake and soy sauce. Return the beef to the casserole. Add the stock, season with pepper, cover, and cook at a low simmer until the meat is tender, about 2 hours.

2. Remove from the heat, allow to cool, and, if possible, refrigerate overnight. The next day, discard the fat from the casserole. (If same day, skim off as much fat as possible.) Remove the meat. Discard the bones, trim off the gristle, and cut the chunks of meat in half. Return the meat to the casserole, bring to a slow simmer, and stir in the vinegar. Add the squash and scallions. Simmer, uncovered, until the squash is tender, about 10 minutes.

3. Place the noodles in big soup bowls. Spoon broth, meat, and vegetables over and serve togarashi for seasoning on the side.

YIELD: 8 SERVINGS

COOK'S NOTES: Simmering the meat on the bone guarantees the depth of flavor in the sauce. But preparing the dish a day in advance, so the bones can be removed and the fat can be skimmed off, refines the dish. 🖬

FORTIFIED AND SWEET WINES

It's impossible to generalize about sweet and fortified wines. They fall into several distinct categories, each offering splendid but distinct opportunities for enjoyment.

The majority of fortified wines are not very sweet. Except for Pedro Ximénez, sherries are not sweet at all. They are excellent partners for savory foods, especially charcuterie and cheeses. Madeira and port are sweeter and can be excellent with chocolate desserts, and tawny port is a particularly felicitous partner for many cheeses.

SHERRY

For years, enthusiasts have lamented the public's indifference to the manifest charms and complexities of sherry. Why doesn't everyone love sherry, they asked, celebrating it as the most undervalued, underappreciated wine in the world, as it languished in the back pages of wine lists and on the dustiest of retail shelves.

Finally, the drumbeat seems as if it is being heard. It may still occupy just a small niche among the wine-drinking public, but sherry has now incited excitement among a new generation of wine lovers who have learned that the place for sherry is not in the drawing room but on the dinner table.

Pale fino, served cool, is light and dry with a refreshing, saline tang that goes beautifully with seafood. Manzanilla, a fino made only in the seaport of Sanlúcar de Barrameda, is more delicate, yet with an intensity of salty flavor that belies its fragile texture. Amontillado, a long-aged fino, develops a complexity that can astound, especially when served with poultry.

Oloroso sherry doesn't get so much attention. Years of blending with cream sherry for the export market have led to the assumption that oloroso is sweet, but it's naturally dry and can be mindbending in its complexity, yet bright and harmonious as well. It's a wonderful combination with steak, venison, or, as people in Jerez like to suggest, wild boar.

Dry sherries, made from the palomino grape, evolve under the solera system, in which newer vintages are blended with older ones year after year, creating a family tree of blends that can stretch back decades. After the wine is fermented, it is fortified with neutral spirits to around 15 percent alcohol and placed in old barrels generally made of American oak.

Unlike most wine barrels, which are completely filled to prevent oxidation, a little headroom is left in sherry barrels, which offers a surface for a film of yeast to grow. This yeast, or flor, protects the wine from oxidation and contributes to the distinctively saline, nutlike flavor of fino sherries. In finos and manzanillas that receive even more aging, the flor dies out and the wines become amontillados. Some sherries never quite develop a vigorous flor. They may be fortified again to above 17 percent and become olorosos. These sherries develop paradoxically with an assist from exposure to air, and this oxidative quality gives them a richness and complexity. Another category, the rare palo cortado, are gender benders that start out as one sort of sherry yet become another, and vice versa.

What's made sherry particularly exciting is the gradual transformation of the business. For years the trade had been built on selling vast quantities of inexpensive, mediocre wine, but that model has been failing for decades. Now, small, like-minded shippers are bottling tiny quantities of extraordinary sherry that is challenging preconceptions.

For example, sherry companies have long advised consumers that fino and manzanilla must be drunk when young or they will lose vitality and wither. Why? Most sherries have been heavily filtered, which strips the life-sustaining force from the wine. But if you make a sherry with care and precision, and filter it only lightly, it can age and evolve beautifully for years.

The old sherries are still worth drinking. The new ones are worth cherishing. ♟

SHERRY AND TAPAS, LIKE DESI AND LUCY, are wedded together. First there is the supposed origin of tapas as small, complementary dishes of food placed on glasses of sherry or wine in a bar (*tapa* means "lid"). Flavor is what makes the match. The nuttiness of sherry, and especially the brininess of good manzanilla and fino, welcome the almonds, olives, cheese, sausage, clams, garlic, anchovies, and shrimp—the ingredients that enliven those mouthwatering tidbits. I assembled chorizo, garlic, capers, Spanish marcona almonds, and parsley; mixed them with bread crumbs; moistened them with olive oil; and used them as a topping for baked clam tapas.

Clams Baked with Chorizo

TIME: 45 MINUTES, INCLUDING OPENING CLAMS

1 garlic clove

¼ cup marcona almonds

1 tablespoon capers, rinsed and drained

2 tablespoons fresh flat-leaf parsley leaves

¼ cup extra virgin olive oil, preferably Spanish

3 ounces mild chorizo, casing removed, minced

½ cup dry bread crumbs

36 littleneck clams on the half shell

1. Turn on a food processor, drop in the garlic through the feed tube, and process until minced. Add the almonds, capers, and parsley and process until finely ground. (The garlic, almonds, capers, and parsley can also be finely chopped by hand in a mezzaluna.)

2. Heat 1 tablespoon of the oil in a medium skillet. Add the chorizo and cook over medium heat until it starts to sizzle. Add the almond mixture and the remaining 3 tablespoons oil and sauté briefly. Stir in the bread crumbs and cook, stirring, over low heat until the ingredients are well blended.

3. Heat oven to 500°F. Spoon the crumb topping onto the clams. Arrange the clams on a baking sheet. Bake until the topping is sizzling and lightly browned, about 10 minutes. Serve.

YIELD: 6 FIRST-COURSE SERVINGS, MORE AS TAPAS

COOK'S NOTES: As for the clams, because I like to open my own, I included that task in the overall timing. If you depend on your fishmonger to do the work, the recipe will take no more than 30 minutes. The clams can be passed as hors d'oeuvres to serve with sherry—or cocktails—but they also make a lively first course, with chilled glasses of manzanilla poured at the table. 🍶

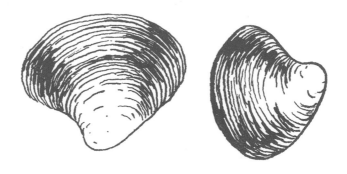

OLOROSO (AND AMONTILLADO) SHERRIES ARE NOT SWEET. They have toasty depth and richness, making them compatible with savory dishes, especially game and cheeses, and allowing them to be sipped until dinner winds down, with a dessert that delivers restrained sweetness. Dark, dried fruit poached in spiced lapsang souchong, a smoky black tea, and flamed with brandy, preferably Spanish, is perfect over ice cream. During the holiday season, it's almost liquid fruitcake.

Flamed Fruit Poached in Tea

TIME: 1 HOUR 15 MINUTES

3½ cups strong brewed lapsang souchong tea

2 cinnamon sticks

3 star anise

1 teaspoon whole allspice

1 tablespoon fresh lemon juice

3 tablespoons honey

6 ounces dried cherries

6 ounces pitted prunes

6 ounces dried black figs

1 pint vanilla ice cream

⅓ cup brandy, preferably Spanish

1. Place the tea in a 3-quart saucepan. Add the cinnamon sticks, star anise, allspice, lemon juice, and honey. Bring to a simmer. Add the cherries and prunes. Cut the stems off the figs and add the figs. Cook at a very slow simmer for about 30 minutes. Remove from the heat and set aside for 30 minutes or longer.

2. To serve, divide the ice cream among six bowls or large, stemmed wineglasses and bring them to the table. Return the fruit to a simmer and transfer all the fruit and sauce from the saucepan to a shallow serving dish.

3. Pour the brandy into the saucepan and heat briefly, until warmed. Light a match, hold it in a hand wearing an oven mitt, stand back, and ignite the brandy. Pour the flaming brandy from the saucepan over the fruit in the bowl, bring to the table and immediately spoon it over the ice cream, and serve.

YIELD: 6 SERVINGS

COOK'S NOTES: Though the compote steeped in smoky tea and flamed is designed for dessert, it could also be spooned alongside roast duck, goose, squab, venison, or pork. 🍶

KEEPING FORTIFIED WINES

The sugar content and the alcohol in most sweet and fortified wines make them a little less prone to oxidation and spoilage once they have been opened. You can keep an opened bottle of most sherries, ports, and Madeiras a good week, recorked, in a decanter or sealed with a good silicone stopper. Refrigerate them if possible. Manzanillas and finos are more delicate. They should be fresh when opened and are best kept for only a few days.

Also worth considering when purchasing sherries, ports, or Madeiras, is the size of the bottle. Though all these wines come in standard 750 milliliter sizes, which you might not finish at a single sitting, most are also sold in smaller quantities, 500 milliliter and 375 milliliter bottles. These are likely to be more practical—and economical— choices if a glass of fino before dinner or port after do not grace your regular routine. —FF

MADEIRA

Contrarians must love Madeira, the fortified wine produced on a jagged Portuguese island about three hundred miles off the Atlantic coast of Africa. It turns wine facts on their head. Everybody knows wines must be kept in cool, dark places free of excess vibrations. But Madeiras are purposely heated to more than one hundred degrees and were once considered best when subjected to the pitching and rolling of ships on long ocean voyages. In fact, it was in the era of colonization when Madeira's greatness was first recognized, by accident, as legend has it.

In the early seventeenth century the island of Madeira was a port for those sailing to Africa, the West Indies, and America. Ships would pick up casks of wine for the voyage. One time, the story goes, a cask was somehow misplaced and not discovered until the ship had returned to its home port. Amazingly, it was judged to be far better than when it had left. Producers began to send wine on voyages, just for the ride. The best were called vinhos da roda: round-trip wines.

Ocean voyages are no longer a part of Madeira production, but today barrels of the best wines are placed in the attics of warehouses to bake naturally under the island sun. The heat; the slow, controlled oxidation of long barrel aging; the high alcohol content, 17 or 18 percent, after fortification with grape spirits; and the searing acidity of the Madeira grapes render the wine practically invulnerable to the ravages of age. Even opened, a bottle can last months without noticeable deterioration.

Most Madeiras are blends of vintages and grapes. Some can be excellent and more affordable introductions to the pleasures of Madeira, particularly those aged for five, ten, or fifteen years and made with one of the leading noble grapes: sercial, verdelho, bual, and malvasia. Sercial is the driest and the lightest of the wines, and malvasia, or malmsey, the richest and the sweetest, though even a malmsey, with its beam of bracing acidity, can sometimes seem dry because it is so refreshing.

But it is the vintage Madeiras, made in minute quantities, that are the most exciting. By law, these wines must be aged for twenty years in barrels, although a new category, colheita, or harvest wines, can be released after five years in barrels. In practice, many vintage Madeiras are aged for many more than twenty years.

No other wines age as well as vintage Madeira. It's not uncommon to find bottles from the nineteenth century, or even the eighteenth. Not only are they still drinkable, they are in their prime. But very little vintage Madeira is produced, and even less leaves the island that gave the wine its name.

While it is great on its own at the end of a meal, Madeira, particularly the sercials and verdelhos from the drier end of the spectrum, also goes surprisingly well with savory foods. 🍷

THIS CAKE, WELL SOAKED WITH MADEIRA, is my version of Le Doris, from Simone Beck's cookbook *Simca's Cuisine*. Over the years, I have made changes in the recipe. First I have upgraded the quality of chocolate over the original supermarket sweet chocolate in the recipe. I switched to 70 percent bittersweet and slightly increased the amount. I also like the way brown sugar works with the Madeira. I use currants instead of raisins, and sometimes, as with the recipe that follows, I replace almond flour with all-purpose flour. The cake is delicious soon after it is baked; it can even be warmed just before serving. But if it is allowed to sit overnight, well wrapped, the flavor of the Madeira becomes more pronounced. Then it needs the whipped cream alongside, and to sip with it, a glass of Madeira.

Fortified Chocolate Cake

TIME: 1 HOUR, PLUS OPTIONAL OVERNIGHT RESTING

8 tablespoons (1 stick) unsalted butter, plus butter for the pan

⅓ cup dried currants

½ cup Madeira

8 ounces bittersweet chocolate (about 70 percent cacao), in pieces

Salt

3 large eggs, separated

1 cup packed light brown sugar

1 cup all-purpose flour, sifted

Confectioners' sugar

1 cup heavy cream

COOK'S NOTES: To serve with Madeira, it makes sense to use the same libation in the cake. But if you prefer to pour a port, a whiskey, or a brandy, do not hesitate to swap out the Madeira to match what will be in the glass. 🍸

1. Heat the oven to 375°F. Butter an 8-inch springform pan, line the bottom with parchment, and butter the parchment.

2. Place the currants and Madeira in a small saucepan, heat until warm, and set aside.

3. Place the chocolate and butter in a heavy saucepan over low heat. Add ½ teaspoon salt. Heat until the chocolate and butter are nearly melted, remove from the heat, and stir to completely melt the mixture. Set aside to cool a little.

4. Beat the egg yolks and brown sugar together until pale and creamy. Stir in the chocolate mixture, then the currants and Madeira. Fold in the flour.

5. With an electric mixer or by hand, beat the egg whites with a pinch of salt until they hold peaks. Stir about one quarter of the egg whites into the batter, then fold in the rest. Transfer to the baking pan, smooth the top, and bake for 20 to 25 minutes, until the surface is fairly firm, the top shows a little cracking near the edges, and a toothpick inserted into the center comes out almost clean. Place the pan on a rack to cool and unmold when cool. Peel off the paper. Wrap the cake in foil until ready to serve. The cake is best served the next day, but it can be served the day it is baked.

5. To serve, dust the top of the cake with sifted confectioners' sugar. Whip the cream with 3 tablespoons sifted confectioners' sugar and serve alongside.

YIELD: 6 TO 8 SERVINGS

TAWNY PORT
Society's urge for contemplative after-dinner drinks like port or Cognac seems largely to have faded. Other fortified wines like sherry, which is most often dry, and Madeira, which can be dry and, even when sweet, has the sort of searing acidity that can make it seem dry, are versatile enough to pair with savory foods. But short of becoming a cocktail ingredient, port, with its complex, sumptuous sweet and spicy flavors, remains a drink wonderfully suited for the postprandial role.

If you have the urge, only two things stand in the way of enjoying the glories of vintage port: time and money. Time, because port from good vintages can often require twenty years or more to soften its fiery, extravagantly fruity character. Money, because if you can find an older bottle that's ready to drink, it could cost several hundred dollars.

Luckily, alternatives exist. Late-bottled vintage ports are made from single vintages with grapes that are generally not as good as those used in traditional vintage ports. They are kept in wood for four to six years before they are bottled, a step that accelerates the aging process. This means they should be ready to drink within a couple of years after they are bottled.

These can be decent enough, but for me aged tawny port is a far better value. Tawnies are blends of wines from years that were not declared vintages. They do their aging in barrels or vats so that when they are finally bottled, they are ready for drinking.

Good tawnies generally come with an age statement, usually in ten-year increments, indicating the average age in the blend. For me, twenty-year tawny is ideal, showing the complexity of age at a still-affordable price. I find a ten-year tawny often to be too sharp and simple, while thirty- or forty-year tawnies are too expensive and can lack the vivacity that still enlivens the twenty-year-olds. The ten-year-olds are sweeter and more concentrated but less wily, giving you everything they have immediately instead of allowing flavors to unfold over time. 🍷

TAWNYS ARE THE ALL-PURPOSE PORTS, suitable to serve with cheese or a dessert. Dried apricots, which convey an element of nuttiness and tart sweetness, are particularly suited for a glass of tawny. Made with the dried fruit that has been soaked to soften it, then pureed and folded into beaten egg whites, no yolks, these individual apricot soufflés are light enough to follow an elaborate dinner. Like all soufflés, these are showstoppers. A bitter chocolate sauce is a garnish and will not overwhelm the port. Often, a vintage port would be the choice for chocolate, but the apricots are dominant here, so tawny it is.

Apricot Soufflés with Bitter Chocolate Sauce

TIME: 40 MINUTES, PLUS SOAKING

10 ounces dried apricots

4 tablespoons (½ stick) unsalted butter, melted

½ cup plus 3 tablespoons sugar

4 ounces high-quality unsweetened chocolate (99 percent cacao)

¼ cup light corn syrup

¼ cup tawny port or other sweet wine

1 teaspoon almond extract

10 large egg whites, at room temperature

1. Place the apricots in a bowl, pour in just enough hot water to cover them, and set aside to soak for 2 hours. Brush six 1-cup soufflé dishes or ramekins with butter and dust with 3 tablespoons of the sugar. Set aside on a baking sheet.

2. Melt the chocolate in a small saucepan over low heat. Stir in the corn syrup and ½ cup water. Cook briefly, until well combined. Transfer to a serving bowl and set aside.

3. When the apricots are soft and have absorbed most of the soaking water, puree in a food processor. Place in a very large bowl and stir in the port and almond extract. Heat the oven to 375°F.

4. Beat the egg whites in an electric mixer, using a whisk attachment, until very softly peaked. Gradually beat in the remaining ½ cup sugar until the whites are very glossy and hold their shape but are not rigid. Stir one quarter of the whites into the apricot mixture and fold in the rest. Divide the mixture among the soufflé dishes, place in the oven on a baking sheet, and bake for about 15 minutes, until lightly browned on top. Serve with room-temperature chocolate sauce on the side.

YIELD: 6 SERVINGS

COOK'S NOTES: The sauce requires fine unsweetened chocolate, labeled 99 percent, not the ordinary supermarket kind. 🍶 The only last-minute task is whipping the whites and finishing the soufflé mixture. Then the wait is a mere 15 minutes before the dessert can go on the table and the wine can be poured. 🍶

A DESSERT TO SERVE WITH TAWNY PORT at the end of a meal must have its sweetness in check lest it overwhelm the nutty, mellow wine. This cheese cake, made with fromage blanc, which is more delicate than the usual cream cheese used for such desserts, adds refreshing acid tang from fresh pineapple, a bit of earthy sweetness contributed by maple syrup, and a crust that depends on almonds, all of which welcome tawny port alongside. The strong alcohol in which the pineapple is cooked evaporates, leaving the whiff of golden rum.

Pineapple-Rum Cheese Cake

TIME: 2 HOURS

1 large pineapple, peeled, cored, and chopped

1 cup dark rum

5 tablespoons unsalted butter, melted

1½ cups ground almonds

5 tablespoons sugar

1¼ cups maple syrup

1¼ pounds fromage blanc

Juice of ½ lemon

3 eggs, separated

1. Finely chop the pineapple in a food processor. You should come away with about 4 cups. Place in a saucepan, mix with the rum, and set aside for 30 minutes.

2. Heat the oven to 350°F. Use a little of the butter to brush the bottom of a 9-inch springform pan. Mix the ground almonds with the remaining butter and 2 tablespoons of the sugar and press into the bottom of the pan. Bake 15 minutes, until lightly tanned. Set aside to cool.

3. Add ¼ cup of the syrup to the pineapple, bring to a boil, and simmer at a fast clip about 30 minutes, until the fruit turns jamlike and most of the liquid is gone. Set aside.

4. Beat or process the cheese and the remaining syrup until well blended. Add the lemon juice and egg yolks and beat or process until mixed. Whip the egg whites until softly peaked, dust with the remaining 3 tablespoons sugar, and beat until firm. Fold into the cheese mixture.

5. Spread the pineapple over the almond crust. Top with the cheese mixture. Bake for 35 to 40 minutes, until lightly browned and threatening to crack a bit around the edges. Allow to cool to room temperature before removing the sides of the pan and serving.

YIELD: 8 TO 12 SERVINGS

COOK'S NOTES: Though rum is called for, almost any other aged spirit, like bourbon, Cognac, or even añejo tequila can be sacrificed to cook the pineapple. 🍶

OFTEN, ON A DESSERT TABLE STATIONED AT THE FRONT OF A BISTRO or trattoria in Europe, and even on the elaborate dessert carts in high-end restaurants, there will be a big bowl of plump prunes poached in wine. It's a dessert that I love, but one that is rarely offered in the United States. Except for at my house. The prunes can be poached in everyday wines, like merlot or Chianti, or in fortified wines, especially port. Though I would sip a vintage port with this dessert, I would open a humbler bottle for the cooking. A whiff of orange adds an important flavor dimension. Some spices and a stingy amount of sugar are also needed. Allow the cooked, softened prunes to steep in the wine mixture as they cool. Then present them with panache, in generous stemmed wine goblets, with a soft cloud of whipped cream or crème fraîche on top.

Prunes in Port

TIME: 45 MINUTES, PLUS COOLING

2 cups ruby port

Two 3-inch strips orange zest

10 whole black peppercorns

6 cloves

2 cinnamon sticks

2 whole allspice

3 tablespoons sugar

1 pound prunes with pits, or 12 ounces pitted prunes

2 tablespoons triple sec

Softly whipped heavy cream or crème fraîche, for serving (optional)

1. Combine the port, orange zest, peppercorns, cloves, cinnamon sticks, and allspice in a 2-quart saucepan. Bring to a simmer. Stir in the sugar and simmer for 15 minutes. Add the prunes and simmer for 10 minutes more. Remove from the heat. Stir in the triple sec.

2. Transfer to a bowl, cover, and set aside for up to 3 hours before serving, turning the prunes in the wine syrup from time to time.

3. Serve, with a dollop of whipped cream, if desired, or refrigerate for up to 24 hours until ready to serve.

YIELD: 4 SERVINGS

COOK'S NOTES: For poached prunes I prefer not to use pitted fruit. The pits add succulence and nuttiness, in much the same way that fish is better cooked on the bone. And I look for large prunes, like those from Agen, in southwestern France, which are sold in many fancy food shops. 🍶

VERY SWEET WINES As with the first person to have

eaten a lobster, it took a brave soul to have first made wine from grapes infected with *Botrytis cinerea*, the noble rot. The fungus attacks the fruit, absorbing water and shriveling skins, and a metamorphosis takes place as ripe, healthy grapes shrink into a ghastly, desiccated mass.

That ancient plunge into seeming peril was telling. Almost always, making great sweet wines requires taking great risks. Whether it's encouraging botrytis, which intensifies the sweetness and adds a gorgeous honeyed aroma; or leaving certain grapes to hang long after others have been picked, hoping that they will become lusciously sweet, that it won't rain, and that animals won't eat them; or even allowing the grapes to freeze in order to concentrate the juice to nectarlike levels, the costs of time and labor are high, and the chances of failure are great.

For these reasons alone, elevated prices seem understandable for sweet wines that haven't been produced through technological shortcuts. They are not everyday wines by any means, which makes them ideal for special occasions like the holidays, when the sweetness of life is celebrated through cookies, cakes, and other desserts. The exquisite perfume and lush, rich flavors of a great sweet wine are a sublime counterpoint.

Sauternes, of course, is the best known of all sweet wines. Germany is renowned for its sweet wines as well, as are Vouvray, Alsace, certain parts of Italy, and even Australia. And one of the greatest and most unusual sweet wines is one of the least known, Tokaji aszu, which for centuries has been made in the Tokaj-Hegyalja region of Hungary.

Sweet wines are often called dessert wines, a term that I find too limiting, because the wines don't always have to be served after a meal. Admittedly, beyond a few exceptions, like Sauternes with foie gras, serving a sweet wine with a savory dish may strike many people as odd—unless they live in one of the great sweet-wine centers of the world. You might have to travel to Sauternes territory, southeast of Bordeaux, for a demonstration of how a good Sauternes can highlight and amplify the sweetness of, say, lobster.

I would never have thought to drink an auslese riesling with roasted leg of lamb, as was suggested to me once in the Mosel region of Germany. I didn't try it, but a good, sweet auslese, balanced by lively acidity, is a wonderful thing with lamb vindaloo—and, I imagine, with a mellow curried goat.

Chenin blanc is a grape that shares with riesling the remarkable ability to make wines ranging from bone dry to vibrantly sweet. I would drink a demi-sec Vouvray with richer sorts of seafood or poultry dishes. And in vintages where botrytis strikes the grapes, both chenins and rieslings become concentrated, making sweet, glowingly intense wines that can be gorgeous with strong cheeses. And Tokaji aszu would go well with apricots or cheeses, foie gras, and maybe a Thai coconut milk curry. But I'm also thinking of fried chicken, which goes with everything, or maybe I'd drink Tokaji aszu by itself. 🍷

VERY SWEET WINES like Tokay, Sauternes, beerenausleses, muscat de Beaumes-de-Venise, Banyuls, vin santo, and ice wines are called dessert wines. And that's what leads many people to think of them for sipping with dessert. Actually, they are best served in solitary glory, instead of dessert. You'd be surprised at how quickly they fade alongside a very sugary pastry or a crème brulée, which is quite a bit sweeter than most of these wines. They are fine alongside pungent cheeses; Roquefort and Sauternes is a classic pairing, and so is foie gras with Sauternes or Tokay. The recipe for foie gras with quince (page 29) could easily welcome a glass of Sauternes.

But at the end of a dinner, to nibble alongside a glass of one of these delectable wines, you cannot go wrong with truffles. The ones I devised are bolstered with brandy and nubbly with peanuts. They are also kissed with honey, to mellow the flavor. Nothing could be easier to prepare than chocolate truffles (you can make them just with chocolate and cream, no other embellishments). Homemade, they come in at a fraction of the price of storebought.

Brandy-Peanut Chocolate Truffles

TIME: 40 MINUTES, PLUS 4 HOURS CHILLING

1 pound 12 ounces semi-sweet chocolate, about 66 percent

⅔ cup heavy cream

1½ teaspoons floral honey, preferably lavender

3 tablespoons Cognac or Armagnac

6 tablespoons salted peanuts, coarsely chopped

½ teaspoon vanilla extract

1. Break 8 ounces of the chocolate in small pieces and place in a heatproof metal bowl. Heat the cream to a simmer and pour over the chocolate. Stir until the chocolate has melted and is smooth. If necessary, place the bowl briefly over low heat to finish melting.

2. Stir in the honey, Cognac, peanuts, and vanilla. Chill until firm, about 2 hours.

3. Scoop out small amounts of the chocolate mixture—a scant teaspoon each. Quickly roll the scoops into balls of about 1 inch in diameter. Place the balls on a platter or baking sheet lined with parchment paper. Place in the freezer to firm up, at least 30 minutes.

4. Break up the remaining chocolate and place 16 ounces (1 pound) in a microwave-safe bowl. Microwave for 3 minutes, stirring a few times, until melted. Stir in the remaining chocolate until melted. Skewer the truffles on a small fork, dip them in the melted chocolate to coat, and place them on a parchment-lined baking sheet at room temperature 15 minutes. Refrigerate until ready to serve.

YIELD: ABOUT 50 SMALL TRUFFLES

COOK'S NOTES: The first step in making these truffles—warm, melted chocolate and cream—is a classic mixture called ganache. It's used in many kinds of pastry and confectionary. 🍶

SUGGESTED MENUS

FORMAL DINNER:
Potted Shrimp (page 73)
Chilled Cauliflower Soup with Oyster Garnish
   (page 101)
Duck Breast with Quince Compote (page 127)
Snow Pea Salad (page 41)
cheese course
Fortified Chocolate Cake (page 221)

Champagne, Chablis, Pinot Noir,
Spätlese Riesling, Madeira

CELEBRATORY DINNER:
Spiced Chicken Liver Mousse (page 113)
Nearly Naked Fluke with Grapefruit
   (page 35)
Baby Pumpkins with Mushrooms (page 75)
Tournedos of Beef with Pot-au-Feu Vegetables
   (page 151)
Roquefort and Leek Tart (page 107)
Apricot Soufflés with Bitter Chocolate Sauce
   (page 223)

Champagne, Vouvray, Bordeaux-style red,
Auslese Riesling, or sweet white wine
such as Tokay

FAMILY DINNER:
Hearty Split Pea Soup (page 166) or
   Thick Tomato-Bread Soup, Catalan Style
   (page 173)
Thai-Style Beef Salad (page 162)
Prunes in Port (page 225)

Beaujolais Cru or Chianti Classico

NEW YEAR'S EVE:
Tarte Flambée with Caviar (page 25)
Seafood Choucroute (page 61)
Flamed Fruit Poached in Tea (page 218)

Rosé Champagne, Vintage Port

BUFFET SUPPER:
Crab and Asparagus Tart (page 49)
Jambon Persillé (page 119)
Mushroom Lasagna (page 123)
Baked Fish, Fez Style (page 211)
Autumn Panzanella (page 153)
Goat Cheese and Walnut Galette (page 55)

Mâcon white and Oregon Pinot Noir

DINNER AL FRESCO:

Taleggio and Mushroom Tart (page 20)
Lobster Spaghetti with Fresh Tomatoes
    (page 36)
A Mess of Pork Chops with Dijon Dressing
    (page 125)
Grilled Ratatouille (page 158)
Pain de Gênes (page 27)

Rosso di Montalcino or Barbera d'Asti

COCKTAIL RECEPTION:

Souffléed Crabmeat Canapés (page 17)
Mortadella Mousse (page 23)
Clams Baked with Chorizo (page 217)
Oysters with Miso Glaze (page 139)
Eggplant Croques Monsieurs (page 197)
Brandy-Peanut Chocolate Truffles (page 227)

Sparkling Wine

AUTUMN LUNCH:

Rillettes of Bluefish (page 28)
Mixed Sausage Paella (page 165)
Warm Deconstructed Caesar Salad (page 91)
Pineapple-Rum Cheese Cake (page 224)

Châteauneuf-du-Pape or Gigondas

CONVIVIAL BRUNCH:

White Clam Quesadillas (page 59)
Smoked Trout Frittatas (page 103)
Black Olive Gnocchi with Tomatoes and Basil
    (page 157)
Grilled Fennel Panzanella (page 111)

White Sangria, Côtes du Rhône

PICNIC:

Moroccan Carrot Soup (page 51)
Pan "Bagnat Sliders" (page 33)
Baby Back Ribs with Saba Slather (page 185)
Farrotto with Sun-Dried Tomatoes and Saffron
    (page 191)

Red Sangria, Rosé de Provence

ACKNOWLEDGMENTS

THIS BOOK COULD NOT EXIST without the dedication, enthusiasm, and good humor of Bernie Kirsch, our wine panel coordinator, who has organized and arranged every single panel that we've had since 2002. It's a thankless task, even if I am thanking him here. Bernie carries it off with consummate ease. He sets the tone for the friendly, welcoming atmosphere that is essential for the uninhibited exchange of thoughts and ideas that makes our panels so useful.

Nor could this book exist without my co-author, Florence Fabricant, who seamlessly integrates our wine panels into her very busy life. Her expertise in all matters of food and wine is clear in the fresh, endlessly creative recipes she contributes. Thank you, Florence, for all you do.

Crucial to the success of our wine panels, and to my own education, are the sommeliers and other members of the New York wine trade who so selflessly donate their time, thoughts, and energy to join our tastings. Their contributions go far beyond the brief mentions they may get in print. I am profoundly grateful to all of them.

I am humbled daily to work with writers and editors as talented, intelligent, skilled, and professional as my colleagues at the Dining section of *The New York Times*. They have saved me from countless errors while inspiring me with their great work. I would especially like to thank the publisher and top editors of the *Times* for their conviction that cultural coverage, including food and wine, is crucial to our journalistic mission.

Christopher Steighner, our deft, skilled, diplomatic editor at Rizzoli, has been patient with me beyond endurance. For that, I am much indebted.

Finally, I would like to thank my wife, Deborah, and sons, Jack and Peter, for their faith, tolerance, humor, and love.

—Eric Asimov

FIRST OF ALL, I CAN'T SAY ENOUGH in appreciation for my co-author, Eric Asimov. His palate is finely tuned, the depth of his wine knowledge is dazzling (yet he is open to new ideas), and he brings to the table a personal yet sensible point of view when it comes to wine. All of this he has generously shared, over the years, with his readers, with the many participants on our wine panels, and with me, enhancing my own wine expertise.

Then, heading the list of those who helped to make this book possible is Bernard Kirsch, the determined wine gatherer, opener, pourer, and record-keeper for our wine tastings.

The many participants on our wine panels were often invaluable sources of ideas for dishes to accompany what we were tasting, and they were an enormous help and inspiration. My appreciation also goes to the editors and copy editors at the *Times*, whose keen intelligence helped to guarantee that when it came to the recipes, clarity and logic prevailed.

Thanks also to Christopher Steighner of Rizzoli, who helped shape and give a focus to this book and who gently cracked the whip as deadlines loomed. Also to Alex Ward of the *Times*, who supported this project from the start. And finally, a big thank-you to my daughter, Patricia Fabricant, a master of elegant design.

—Florence Fabricant

CONVERSION CHART

ALL CONVERSIONS ARE APPROXIMATE.

Liquid Conversions

U.S.	Metric
1 tsp	5 ml
1 tbs	15 ml
2 tbs	30 ml
3 tbs	45 ml
¼ cup	60 ml
⅓ cup	75 ml
⅓ cup + 1 tbs	90 ml
⅓ cup + 2 tbs	100 ml
½ cup	120 ml
⅔ cup	150 ml
¾ cup	180 ml
¾ cup + 2 tbs	200 ml
1 cup	240 ml
1 cup + 2 tbs	275 ml
1¼ cups	300 ml
1⅓ cups	325 ml
1½ cups	350 ml
1⅔ cups	375 ml
1¾ cups	400 ml
1¾ cups + 2 tbs	450 ml
2 cups (1 pint)	475 ml
2½ cups	600 ml
3 cups	720 ml
4 cups (1 quart)	945 ml
	(1,000 ml is 1 liter)

Weight Conversions

U.S./U.K.	Metric
½ oz	14 g
1 oz	28 g
1½ oz	43 g
2 oz	57 g
2½ oz	71 g
3 oz	85 g
3½ oz	100 g
4 oz	113 g
5 oz	142 g
6 oz	170 g
7 oz	200 g
8 oz	227 g
9 oz	255 g
10 oz	284 g
11 oz	312 g
12 oz	340 g
13 oz	368 g
14 oz	400 g
15 oz	425 g
1 lb	454 g

Oven Temperatures

°F	Gas Mark	°C
250	½	120
275	1	140
300	2	150
325	3	165
350	4	180
375	5	190
400	6	200
425	7	220
450	8	230
475	9	240
500	10	260
550	Broil	290

INDEX

Turbot Poached in Saint-Émilion, 141
Flambée, Tarte, with Caviar, 25
fluke
    with Grapefruit, Nearly Naked, 35
    in Saor, Venetian-Style, 66
foie gras
    with Baked Quince, 29
    Fettuccine with Truffles and, 145
fortified wines
    Madeira, 220–221
    overview, 215
    sherry, 106, 216–218
    storing, 219
    tawny port, 222–225
France
    Alsace, 56, 60, 88, 102
    Bandol, 206
    Beaujolais, 32, 170–173
    Bordeaux, 141, 142
    Burgundy, 70–78, 116–120
    cabernet, 140, 152
    Chablis, 40, 72
    chardonnay, 76
    Châteauneuf-du-Pape, 164
    chenin blanc, 64, 68
    Condrieu, 104
    Cornas, 160
    Côte Chalonnaise, 116–117
    Côte de Beaune, 76
    Côte de Nuits, 118–120
    Côte d'Or, 70
    Côtes du Rhône, 156
    gewürztraminer, 102
    Gigondas, 164
    Graves, 142
    Hermitage, 160
    Irouléguy, 34
    Jura savagnin, 106
    Languedoc-Roussillon, 202–203
    Loire Valley, 40, 64, 68, 82, 138
    Mâconnais, 70
    Médoc, 142
    Muscadet, 82
    Pessac-Léognan, 142
    pinot gris, 88
    Pomerol, 140
    Pouilly-Fuissé, 74
    Pouilly-Fumé, 40
    Provence, 32, 206
    reds from, 116–120, 138–145, 156–167, 202–207
    Rhône, 156, 160, 164
    rieslings, 56, 60

rosés from Provence, 32, 34
Saint-Émilion, 140
Saint-Joseph, 160
Sancerre, 40
Sauternes, 226
Savennières, 68
sparklers, 22
syrahs, 160
Vouvray, 64
Frank, Konstantin, 58
Frittatas, Smoked Trout, 103
Fritters, Squid, 37
Fruit, Flamed, Poached in Tea, 218
fumé blanc. *See* sauvignon blanc

Galette, Goat Cheese and Walnut, 55
gamay grape, 172
garganega grape, 96
garnacha, 34
Genoa bread, 27
German rieslings
    Auslese, 52–53
    dry, 46
    Kabinett, 48
    Spätlese, 50
gewürztraminer, dry, 102–103
Gigondas, 164–167
glassware, 21, 159
Gnocchi, Black Olive, with Tomatoes and Basil, 157
Goat Cheese and Walnut Galette, 55
Gramona, 18
Grapefruit, Nearly Naked Fluke with, 35
grapes. *See also* commonly known grapes
    aglianico, 190
    barbera, 174
    blaufränkisch, 208
    carmenère, 196–197
    chenin blanc, 64, 68, 226
    dolcetto, 182
    gamay, 172
    garganega, 96
    lagrein, 176
    lambrusco, 184
    melon, 82
    montepulciano, 186
    moschofilero, 100
    mourvèdre, 206
    nebbiolo, 128
    nerello, 188
    sangiovese, 114, 186
    savagnin, 106

    syrahs, 160–163
    tempranillo, 198
    verdejo, 98
    viognier, 104
    xinomavro, 210
    zweigelt, 208
grapeseed oil, 79
Graves, 142
Greek wines, 100, 210
Grilled Lamb Kabobs with Rosemary, 207
Grilled Quail with Olives and Polenta, 161
Grilled Ratatouille, 158
Grilled Seafood Salad, 167
grüner veltliner, 94–95
Gutenbrunner, Kurt, 95

ham, as Jambon Persillé, 119
Hermitage, 160
holidays, 218, 228
Horseradish-Mint Pesto, 209
Humbrecht, Zind, 60
Humm, Daniel, 41

III Lustros, 18
Irouléguy, 34
Italy
    aglianico, 190
    barbera, 174
    Barolo and Barbaresco, 128
    Chianti Classico, 110
    Chianti rosé, 34
    dolcetto, 182
    Etna, Mount, 188
    fiano, 84
    lagrein, 176
    lambrusco, 184
    Montalcino, 112–115
    Montepulciano d'Abruzzo, 186–187
    pinot grigio, 88
    prosecco, 16
    reds, 110, 128, 174–191
    Soave, 96
    standards, DOC, 16, 114
    teroldego, 176
    valpolicella, 178
    whites, 84, 88, 96
Izzo, Jean-Claude, 206

Jambon Persillé, 119
Jura savagnin, 106

First published in the United States of America in 2014
by Rizzoli International Publications, Inc.
300 Park Avenue South
New York, NY 10010
www.rizzoliusa.com

Illustrations by Zachary Hewitt
Design by Patricia Fabricant

2014 2015 2016 2017 / 10 9 8 7 6 5 4 3 2 1

Distributed in the U.S. trade by Random House, New York

Printed in China

ISBN-13: 978-0-8478-4221-6

Library of Congress Control Number: 2013952895